Digital
Intelligence

Digital Intelligence

**What Every
Smart Manager
Must Have
for Success
in an Information Age**

Sunil Mithas

Finerplanet

North Potomac

2016

For further information and resources, visit us at http://www.thedigitalintelligence.com and email us at digitalintelligencebook@gmail.com

ISBN for Paperback version: 978-0-9849896-3-8

Digital Intelligence

To Priti

Digital Intelligence

Table of Contents

Digital Intelligence

Acknowledgments

I am indebted to the countless people who have shaped the contents of this book, directly or indirectly, and have allowed me to undertake this effort. There is no way I can name everyone here, so I seek apologies from those whose name does not appear.

I am grateful to my colleagues who have taught information systems and related courses at University of Maryland and other business schools; it is through conversations with them that I realized the need for a book like this. I thank Hank Lucas, Ritu Agarwal, Anand Gopal, Joe Bailey, and Chris Dellarocas for stimulating interactions that shaped some of my thinking articulated in this book. I am also thankful to my other colleagues at the University of Maryland for providing a supportive and encouraging environment for research and teaching, which led to this book. Among them are current and former Deans and colleagues at the Smith School: Alexander Triantis, Anand Anandalingam, Howard Frank, Zhi-Long Chen, Roland Rust, Hugh Courtney, Susan Taylor, and many others. I was inspired by conversations with Dennis Severance, Scott Moore, Tom Schriber, and M.S. Krishnan along with numerous other colleagues in the information systems field with whom I have interacted about teaching- and research-related issues at conferences, teaching workshops or in other settings. I am grateful to Jonathan Whitaker, Gordon Gao, Pankaj Setia, Ali Tafti, Rajiv Kohli, Abhishek Srivastava, Sulin Ba, Vijay Gurbaxani, Omar El-Sawy and Ramanath Subramanyam for encouragement, suggestions and in some cases comments on previous versions to refine the book. The title of the book was inspired by a discussion with Omar El-Sawy for which I am grateful to him.

I thank colleagues and research collaborators with whom I have worked over the years, and I draw on some of that work in writing this book. I would like to acknowledge some of them here, in no particular order: Ritu Agarwal, Lerzan Aksoy, Daniel Almirall,

Indranil Bardhan, Hugh Courtney, Claes Fornell, Jie Mein Goh, Kunsoo Han, Violet Ho, Peng Huang, Tomas Hult, Joni Jones, Tim Keiningham, Chris Kemerer, Jiban Khuntia, Keongtae Kim, Michael Kimbrough, M.S. Krishnan, Bart Lariviere, Dongwon Lee, Hank Lucas, Deepa Mani, Will Mitchell, Forrest Morgeson, Narayan Ramasubbu, Gautam Ray, Roland Rust, Terence Saldanha, Galit Shmueli, V. Sambamurthy, Pratyush Nidhi Sharma, Shirish Srivastava, Ali Tafti, Atakan Yalcin, Ling Xue, and Jonathan Whitaker.

I want to thank friends and executives who have facilitated my research and teaching activities, which form the basis for some of the ideas in this book. I could not have conducted my research without significant help from Bob Evans, Brian Gillooly, Rusty Weston, Stephanie Stahl, and Lisa Smith at *InformationWeek*. I thank Claes Fornell, Forrest Morgeson, David VanAmburg, and Jaesung Cha of the National Quality Research Center (NQRC) at the Ross School of Business at the University of Michigan for making the American Customer Satisfaction Index (ACSI) data available for my dissertation research. I am grateful to Jamshed J. Irani, B. Muthuraman, Bimlendra Jha, Sunil Sinha, Firdose Vandrevala, Jehangir Ardeshir, Shreekant Mokashi, Chetan Tolia, Shrikant Chandratreya, and Ravi Arora for their help in my past and ongoing work with the Tata Group. I thank Prasanto K. Roy and Ed Nair for their support of my research related to Indian IT and the BPO industry.

Among more direct shapers of this work, I thank the hundreds of students and managers with whom I have shared many of the ideas articulated in this book. You have helped to refine my thinking over the years through your questions and curiosity. I thank Andy Seagram for careful editing and numerous suggestions to improve the presentation of ideas in this book.

Finally, I want to thank my family for support and understanding.

Preface

The motivation for writing this book comes out of a conviction that managing information technology (IT) in an organization requires a competence or skill set, what I call "digital intelligence" or digital IQ. Digital intelligence is a fundamental and prerequisite skill for all managers in today's information economy. It is not something that applies only to IT professionals. It is a competence as essential as numeracy, literacy, or basic familiarity with accounting, finance, supply chain, global business, marketing and other forms of intelligences that all managers need.[1] It is perhaps not an overstatement to say that digital intelligence is becoming a critical skill for anyone aspiring to become a senior leader or CEO. While basic numeracy and literacy will still be necessary for economic success, they alone will not be sufficient and adequate for success in jobs in the information economy.

This book is intended for executives, managers, entrepreneurs, investors and students who want to understand the ingredients of digital intelligence. The book espouses the belief that digital intelligence is an important competence that global leaders need to have in today's economy to become more productive and informed members of the society and to enhance the performance of their organizations. The book lays out the most basic competencies and skill sets for thinking about IT and IT-enabled changes that all managers should have. It draws on related work that articulates some of the dimensions of digital intelligence; yet because of the focus on general managers, it avoids details of technologies and implementation that should ideally be handled by trained IT professionals who may have computer science or engineering backgrounds and related education. It is not necessary for managers and entrepreneurs to have a programming or computer science background to acquire digital intelligence. It may surprise some that even Steve Jobs, one of the most successful technology entrepreneurs and executives, did not have a degree or background in computer science or programming. Steve is not alone; this is also true of many other "digital immigrants" who have made significant contributions to IT. If people without a technology background can be technology pioneers, such success should encourage everyone to embrace digital intelligence and use technology intelligently in business and life.[2]

In summary, this book introduces some of the key issues in managing IT. It provides an overview of IT systems in contemporary firms and how they enable and support a firm's strategic and operational goals. By understanding how IT is shaping industry structure and the competitive environment and how to manage IT-related decision making, managers can craft superior strategies and use IT as a lever to innovate and transform to satisfy their internal and external customers.

Sunil Mithas
College Park, Maryland
August 28, 2016

Introduction

Digital Intelligence: A New Competence for Success in the Information Age

"Using the technology to its full potential means using the man to his full potential."

> —An anonymous worker, quoted in Zuboff (1988, p. 414)

"As a great social leveler, information technology ranks second only to death."

> —Sam Pitroda (Pitroda 1993)

Digital intelligence, the ability to understand and make use of the power of information technology to one's advantage, is becoming a critical skill for survival and success in today's economy. Every manager, organization, and even nation needs to be asked and be able to answer the questions about their digital business strategy and how they strategically manage digital resources.[3]

Why focus on digital intelligence and IT? IT is fundamentally changing our society and the world of business. Some believe that IT is "flattening" the world and may have negative consequences for jobs and salaries in developed economies. Others have a somewhat different perspective, arguing that current geographical patterns in occupations and business activity will likely continue and that those with better skills will do well regardless of their location. Despite these differing perspectives, there is general agreement that the changes unleashed by IT are similar in magnitude to those evident in first and second industrial revolutions.[4] It is difficult to think of any business process or functional area that is unaffected by IT in contemporary firms. From our personal experience and what we witness taking place around us, it is easy to see how IT is changing our lives in many ways, including how we learn, work, play, communicate, fight, and do business.

Increasingly, contemporary firms such as Starbucks, Barnes & Noble and Sears are hiring their CEOs and top executives on the basis of their digital intelligence, or their ability to navigate the digital future their industries face. Barnes & Noble chose to appoint a relatively young 39-year-old executive named William Lynch, who joined Barnes &Noble in 2009 as president of the Barnes&Noble.com online unit, to the position of CEO. The CEO of ICICI, a private bank in India, claims to be its CIO as well. In another example of how a lack of digital intelligence can sink a company, Carl Icahn partly acknowledged the lack of digital savvy of Blockbuster's CEO for its bankruptcy, while a former CEO blamed that on board's digital ignorance and dysfunctional governance. Procter & Gamble (P&G) has reportedly created a "digital skills inventory" of its employees, which includes a baseline assessment of skills such as how to connect to the Internet and use basic collaboration and knowledge-exchange tools for online meetings and mail as well as how to participate in firm's internal social network, P&G Pulse, for news and training.[5] Starbucks is another good example where CEO and other top executives are shaping digital strategies.[6]

Why should all this matter to a business manager? From a strategic perspective, IT can create and sustain competitive advantage, if managed well. While there are some examples of leaders and managers having been able to use IT as a lever to transform their organizations for competitive success, many more have failed to successfully manage IT. Those who have used IT effectively have done well for themselves, for their organizations and sometimes for wider society. Those who have ignored or mismanaged IT have destroyed societal value and have led their organizations toward failure or bankruptcy. All conscientious managers, particularly those who are or aspire to be leaders, have a duty to manage resources, including IT resources, in their organizations in a responsible and thoughtful manner. Regardless of their current functional affiliation or career goals, their future success will critically depend on how they lead and manage IT-enabled strategic changes. They also need to take responsibility for developing and harnessing digital intelligence of their direct reports and colleagues in other business functions. To that end, this book can be of help.

By focusing on digital intelligence, I also confront two misconceptions that I came across in my teaching, research, and consulting experience with hundreds of business students and executives. The first misconception is that managing IT is something that should be delegated to IT employees and that business managers can succeed simply by focusing on conventional skills, such as accounting, finance, or marketing. However, this is often not true; in today's economy, all managers need some fundamental IT competencies to be successful in their jobs. They need these IT competencies to address digital opportunities and threats in their competitive environment and to formulate and execute their business strategies and proposals.

A second misconception is that some people believe that they already know how to manage IT because they can shop online, check e-mails, or engage with social media. This misconception is also not true; being able to work with computers and digital devices alone is not going to ensure personal or professional success in today's information age. Digital intelligence is not the same as computer literacy—it encompasses these basic skills but goes beyond them. It is different from IT fluency, in that it focuses more sharply on competencies for success in organizations from a managerial perspective.

Digital Intelligence

Digital intelligence: A New Competence for the Information Age

There is now significant research evidence that IT and digital resources are critical determinants of an organization's success.[7] However, there is also significant variance in achieving success, and realized performance varies significantly across organizations and within an organization over time. Many organizations are still in a nascent stage of developing a coherent understanding of IT's potential. Very few firms have developed a shared understanding of IT's role in an organization and how that role is influenced by—and influences—the firm's business strategy. The success of IT efforts depends on communicating the firm's strategy and enlisting managers at all levels in making decisions about technology. This area is where many organizations flounder.

However, it is possible to overcome this hurdle by investing in what I refer to herein as Digital intelligence. There is a compelling need for CEOs and CIOs to make necessary investments in digital intelligence for key executives and future leaders of their companies. Digital intelligence is a new phrase and skill set that should be a part of boardroom discussions regarding strategy or selecting business leaders; it is a skill that all successful managers must have in today's information economy. Digital intelligence is more than being able to work with computers or IT; it also involves expert thinking and complex communication skills. Digital divide on account of access to technology may be easier to address, addressing digital divide due to digital intelligence being more tacit and intangible is harder but can also provide more sustainable advantages.

More specifically, Digital intelligence rests on three pillars: It implies a basic understanding of (1) how a firm should synchronize its business strategy with its IT strategy, (2) how the firm should govern IT, and (3) how the firm should manage IT infrastructure and implement IT projects. Next, I consider these in turn.

Synchronize IT and Business Strategies

Synchronizing IT and business strategies requires developing an understanding of how a firm can manage IT to improve its

4

competitive position and how it should manage or shape industry transformations. As Michael Porter, a Harvard Business School professor has argued, there are three principal ways to gain competitive advantage using IT. The first is by changing industry structure, which involves using IT to tilt the balance of supplier power, customer power, competitive rivalry and the threat of entry and of new and substitute products in your favor. A second way is to outperform rivals using IT in terms of costs, differentiation, or the ability to serve a niche segment exceptionally well by providing differentiated, cost-effective products and services. A third way is to create new businesses using IT. In addition, the firm needs to decide its strategic posture with respect to industry transformation and new technologies. New technologies, particularly those that create a trade-off between serving current customers and attending to new or underserved customers, are particularly challenging.

Govern IT Effectively

Synchronizing IT and business strategy can be difficult, and is rarely enough. Managers also need to govern IT effectively to ensure that the digital strategy is made part and parcel of an organization's governance processes. In other words, managers must deal with four issues. First, the manager must decide what the key IT decisions are, who should make them, and how they should be decided upon. The second consideration is how the IT function should be organized—as a cost center or a profit center? Also, whether a firm should have a CIO and who should the CIO report to? Third, the manager must determine how much to spend on IT, what types of projects to fund (i.e., for revenue-growth, cost-reduction projects, or dual purpose projects), and how to justify and prioritize different types of IT projects to arrive at a portfolio that will achieve the firm's key strategic objectives. Finally, they should decide what to keep in-house, what to outsource or rent, and the extent to which the firm will use globally dispersed resources. All these governance decisions have options, only some configurations might be prudent given the organization's strategy, resources and competitive environment.

Manage IT with Discipline

Even with effective governance, there is still the issue of having to manage IT projects toward successful completion, given their high failure rates and chance of greater success with executive involvement and appropriate project and risk management strategies. Success requires managers to develop a vision of how they will deal with the evolution of computing, manage legacy upgrade decisions, manage risks in IT projects, determine what systems development life-cycle approach to use, and help to select, adopt and exploit functional, network and enterprise systems.

Note that synchronization–governance–management decisions are interconnected, even though we discuss them separately for ease of exposition. Governance cannot be viewed in isolation from strategy. Poor governance of IT and information resources can impede strategy formulation and execution by creating multiple and misleading versions of "facts" as companies such as Cisco and HP discovered. Governance processes in firms that emphasize revenue growth should differ from governance processes in firms that emphasize cost reduction or dual focus in their digital business strategy. In turn, governance ultimately influences management of IT resources in terms of what types of projects an organization will implement and how certain trade-offs (standardization versus customization, single vendor versus best of breed) will be made.

Toward Digital Intelligence

Like other competencies, such as leadership and emotional intelligence, digital intelligence is not something that a person is born with. Thankfully, it can be acquired through education and appropriate experiences. Managers must find and create educational opportunities to learn about management of digital resources and to engage with IT projects in their organizations for themselves, their direct reports and counterparts and other stakeholders to ensure success.

Digital Intelligence

In conclusion, senior executives and IT professionals have a responsibility to ensure that all IT and strategic decisions in their firms are approached by individuals who have the requisite digital intelligence and who are exposed to the three pillars of a digital business strategy. Doing so will require investing in the education of key professionals, followed by continuous dialogue between business and IT personnel. Only then will digital business strategies successfully lead to business value and contribute to organizations' success in the marketplace.

Part 1
Synchronize IT and Strategy

Chapter 1: Crafting Digital Business Strategies

"All men can see the tactics whereby I conquer, but what none can see is the strategy out of which victory is evolved."

—Anonymous

"Would you tell me, please, which way I ought to walk from here? That depends a good deal on where you want to get to, said the Cat. I don't much care where, said Alice. Then it doesn't matter which way you walk, said the Cat—so long as I get somewhere, Alice added. Oh, you're sure to do that, said the Cat, if you only walk long enough!"

—Carroll (2004)

What do the words "strategic and transformational IT" mean to you? Why has IT become so important that everyone must know about it? To understand IT and its role, it is first necessary to articulate what "strategy" and "transformation" mean? Only then can the role and contribution of IT in strategy and transformation be more fully understood.

1.1 Why Top Managers Need to Bother with IT

Top managers have a responsibility to help their organizations navigate IT-enabled transformations because it is their acts of commission or omission, not those of lower-level employees, that will ultimately shape the destiny, success, or failure of their organizations.[8] The dramatic changes in IT in last 20 years, certainly since mid-1990s when the Internet and the World Wide Web became more pervasive, have made IT even more important from a strategic perspective.

Why has IT become an imperative for any manager who aspires to be a leader or a CEO? There are at least three reasons: IT influences almost all aspects of human life, the importance and ubiquity of IT in today's economy, and the performance implications of managing IT resources that exhibit duality.[9] I consider each in turn.

First, IT has come to influence almost every aspect of human life from cradle to grave—from the moment a baby is born to who will have access to his or her death, and even beyond in Second Life (see Appendix 1.A).

Second, although Internet economy is currently estimated to be 4-5% of the GDP or overall economy in G-20 countries, it is growing at a very fast rate.[10] Partly, it is due the pervasive digitization of activities and business processes and the concomitant and commensurate investments in IT. As a result, the world of business is experiencing a sea change. It may surprise some to know that the worldwide spending on IT now exceeds $3 trillion every year. To put it in context, this spending represents the approximate GDP of the United States in the early 1980s, in 2009 dollars, and is almost equal to the 2010 U.S. federal budget of $3.6 trillion. Although less than 2% of the U.S. economy is dedicated to producing hardware or software, this percentage rises to approximately 7% of the total value added if a wider definition of "information industries" is adopted (including, for example, publishing, IT services, broadcasting, telecommunication, and so forth).

For further perspective on the extent of IT spending, consider this: The United States spent about $3.6 trillion on World War II, which stretched several years[11]—we spend nearly the same amount on IT each year. Worldwide IT spending in 2009 exceeded the GDP of the fourth largest economy in the world. Compared with about

$3.6 trillion of global spending on IT, global spending on research and development (R&D) was approximately $1.1 trillion, and global advertising spending was closer to $.44 trillion in 2009. This is a remarkable feat for a relatively young and emerging industry that first emerged around the 1950s.

Just as IT consumes a lot of money on a worldwide basis every year, it also consumes significant resources at the firm level. In today's business environment, firms spend more than 50% of their investment in equipment on IT; this figure was closer to 15% in the 1960s.[12] The U.S. government spends about $70 billion on IT every year. Some large firms such as Wal-Mart, FedEx, Hewlett-Packard (HP), and Citibank spend more than a billion dollars on IT alone every year. Wal-Mart reportedly spent more than $10.5 billion dollars in 2015, and Wells Fargo and Bank of America spent upwards of $6 billion dollars.

Figure 1.1 provides a perspective on relative magnitude of IT investments.

Figure 1.1: A Perspective on IT Investments

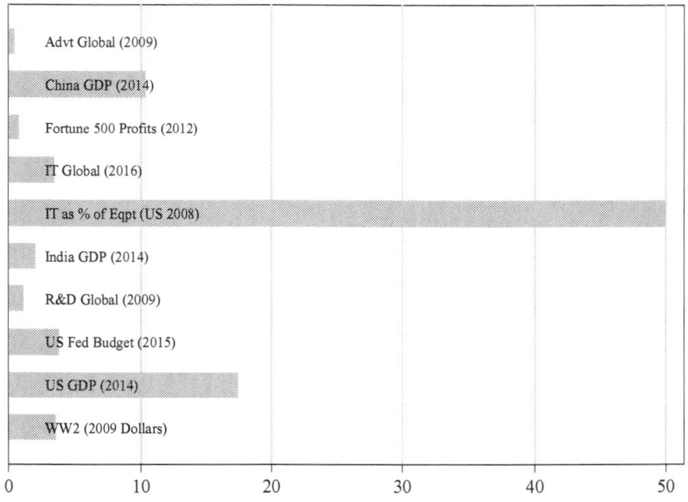

Note: Figures are in trillions of dollars, except for IT as a % of Equipment.

Digital Intelligence

Recent research implies that firms are beginning to allocate their discretionary dollars from R&D and advertising toward IT.[13]

Figure 1.2 shows the trends in IT, R&D, and advertising expenditures for a sample of 452 global firms from 1998 to 2003. The figure shows that average IT expenditures gained a higher share of discretionary expenditures over average R&D and average advertising expenditures, while the relative share of average advertising expenditures declined after 2000.[14]

Figure 1.2: Trends in Discretionary Investments (Adapted from Mithas et al. (2012b))

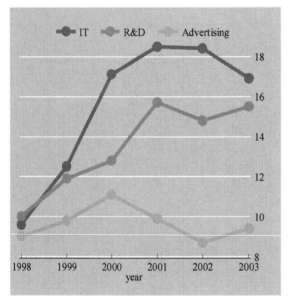

Note: Figure 1.2 shows Annual Investments in Thousands of Dollars per Employee on the y-axis.

IT also appears to have a disproportionately large influence on the overall economic activity if one were to consider some other indicators, such as percentage of venture capital funding devoted to IT production and information industries, the value of nonmarket

12

transactions, and the fraction of time spent on income-generating activities versus that spent on leisure activities.   IT is tightly linked with entrepreneurship. Brynjolfsson and Saunders report that 50%–75% of venture capital funding went to IT production and information industries in the 1995–2007 period. In addition, IT drives many nonmarket transactions that are not fully captured in GDP numbers and tangible products and services. Consider free Google search or the ability to read a free newspaper article on the web, or consider the improvements in automobile quality or health care that are not captured in prices that you pay. [15]

Finally, IT matters for performance, and it has become an extremely critical resource for the competitive success at multiple levels. Being a general-purpose technology like the steam engine, internal combustion engine, electricity, a dynamo, or a laser, IT is extremely powerful in its consequences. It is multifaceted and can have paradoxical effects that reveal its Janus-faced character. For some, IT is flattening the world, but for others, some spikes created by history and geography are too stubborn. Not everything that IT does is favorable: While some of the changes unleashed by IT are good, others are not so good.

Let us begin with some social and societal impacts of IT. Among the dual aspects of IT-induced changes, GPS has made life easier when it comes to driving cars or navigating ships. However, it has also taken some drivers to a cliff and would lead to certain death if they did not know when to disobey the technology. Smartphones have saved lives by locating people and providing them with help. However, they have also raised stress levels and turned some users into phone "addicts"—so much so, some reports suggest, that some people check their smartphones as soon as any new message pops up; they check their phone before they go to sleep, they check it first thing upon waking up, and they keep checking it even while eating breakfast; some people even check it while engaging in more "intimate" human activities. If that is not enough, some people prefer to enjoy Second Life, often at the expense of ignoring their partners or spouses in this (presumably first) life.

Digital Intelligence

IT can make people less productive or more productive, depending on how it is used. Some people worry that the increasing use of computers and IT has affected our ability to think critically and makes us "stupid".[16] Certainly, it has created many new distractions and, if not handled well, can ultimately make us unproductive.

However, evidence suggests that IT has contributed significantly to productivity at the economy level. IT contributed to approximately 80% of the productivity increase from the 1973–1995 period to the 1996–2000 period through an increase in capital deepening and multifactor productivity. Although the share of productivity growth attributable to IT has fallen in the 2000–2006 period, at least some of the multifactor productivity growth among industries that use IT can be attributed to investments in complementary assets and business process redesigns undertaken between 1995 and 2000. I should also note here that some economists argue that reported productivity gains in the U.S. manufacturing sector may be somewhat overstated because price savings realized by U.S. factories from outsourcing and offshoring may have shown up incorrectly as gains in output and productivity. [17]

The relationship between IT and productivity also has implications for jobs, a relevant factor for both individuals and policy makers. Although IT can destroy jobs, it can also create new jobs (e.g., data scientists), change the mix of jobs in the economy, and alter the nature of tasks within jobs. In particular, computers can become a substitute for humans by simplifying the whole job (computerized robots replacing workers on an assembly line), by substituting some tasks within a job that are amenable to rule-based logic (ATMs taking over some of the functions of a human teller), and by supporting outsourcing or offshoring to other countries. At the same time, computers can complement humans in jobs that require pattern recognition or case-based reasoning (e.g., GPS devices helping drivers navigate roads, computer imaging assisting radiological diagnosis). [18]

Although the social, societal, and macroeconomic effects of IT are important, the focus here is on the strategic issues related to

IT: How can managers use IT strategically to create or sustain a competitive advantage? How can they successfully navigate IT-enabled transformations?

There is good reason for firms to invest more in IT. Research on the business value of IT has documented the effect of IT resources on a variety of outcome measures such as:

1. Add to growth prospects of firms through increased revenues,

2. Differentiation: consumer surplus, customer relationships and customer satisfaction, product variety, and product quality improvement

3. Reduced costs: supply chain and inventory costs, non-IT operating costs, cost of debt, productivity

4. Optimizing firm risk

5. Industry structure, innovation output and knowledge contributions, organizational capabilities

6. Transform products, business processes and business models

Although IT shows a positive association with firm performance on average, not all firms are equally good at making use of IT. Just as the successful management of IT can enhance chances of success, poor implementation of IT can be disastrous. It is certainly possible to overspend on IT and mismanage it.

Figure 1.3 shows IT failures across a wide variety of industries over years. IT-related failures come in various forms: waste of scarce organizational resources, poor management of customer trust and loyalty, and failures leading to bankruptcies and even loss of lives. Organizations that have experienced IT-related failures include some of the most reputed and well-known companies. Even organizations that are expected to have particularly smart employees are not immune to IT failures. Some firms have even gone bankrupt while implementing IT projects that were a fraction of the overall revenue of the firm, with adverse consequences for managers, employees, and other stakeholders of these firms. FoxMeyer Drug and Rich-Con Steel are two examples.

Digital Intelligence

Even more serious, many lives have been lost because of the lack of use of proper IT systems or governance (e.g., "9/11 Commission Report," 98,000 preventable deaths in the United States due to wrong medications) or the abuse of IT.

Figure 1.3: IT Hall of Shame

Year	Organization	What happened
2015	Avid Life Media	Hackers post data on 32 million users of the social networking site AshleyMadison.com
2013	Target, Healthcare.gov	Target loses customer data, software glitches create problems for President Obama's signature initiative
2012	Knight Capital	Knight Capital lost more than $400 million in trading due to a software glitch
2011	Sony	About 100 million customer accounts hacked
2010	U.S. Government	WikiLeaks
2009	Citibank	Accounts hacked—front-page story in the *Wall Street Journal* on December 22, 2009.
2008	U.S. Government	Design of U.S. president's helicopter in cyberspace (fiascos in previous years: The Bush White House loses millions of e-mails).
2008	Financial crisis	Some blame lack of IT integration as a contributing reason for the financial crisis; other media reports suggest that CEOs of bankrupt companies did not know how big of a mess they were in and the U.S. government did not track TARP money outflows properly.
2007	TJX	Credit card data stolen—hundreds of millions of dollars of liability.
2005	FBI case file system	Abandoned with $170 million written off.
2001	9/11 tragedy	Loss of human lives, inability of government agencies to share known information.

1996	FoxMeyer Drug	Filed for bankruptcy after a $40 million ERP system went bad.

In summary, all managers need to care about IT and must know about IT for at least three reasons. First, IT has come to pervade almost all aspects of human life. To the extent the world of business is connected with human activities, knowing how IT shapes how we live and work can help managers to make sense of emerging trends in IT and business. Second, the rising share of Internet and information economy due to significant investments in IT is creating new opportunities. IT-induced technological advances affect all industries and functional areas, and managers can navigate these impending changes more successfully by understanding what drives these changes. Finally, smart visionaries and managers can use IT as a lever to enhance their personal and professional competitive advantage. Often, IT is the single largest expenditure in firms. Whether they like it or not, sooner or later, most managers will be involved in an IT project. Given how risky and important these projects are, one must invest the necessary effort to understand how to manage these projects to ensure success. Together, these should be good reasons for managers to invest in their own digital intelligence and that of the people they supervise.

1.2 What is Strategy?

1.2.1 Defining strategy and competitive advantage

Strategy is an amorphous concept and has been defined differently by various authors.[19] Broadly, strategy can be viewed at multiple levels, and it seeks to answer questions such as where to compete (this is related to corporate strategy), and how to compete (this is related to competitive strategy). Sometimes, functional areas, such as operations or marketing, frame strategies at functional levels to support competitive strategy and answer narrower questions, such as whether to compete by attracting new customers or by retaining current customers.

Strategy matters because research suggests that business unit effects account for approximately 37% of variance in return on assets, corporate effects account for approximately 18%, and macroeconomic and industry effects account for approximately 45%. In general, business units and corporate effects are under the control of managers, while this is less often the case for macroeconomic and industry effects.

Fundamentally, strategy is about gaining and sustaining competitive advantage, which is, broadly speaking, the creation of unique added value and the ability to capture some of that value for a firm's stockholders. I must note here that advances in IT are making some question some of the conventional notions of strategy and competitive advantage. Mark Frissora, CEO of Hertz in 2013, notes in an interview with Rik Kirkland:

> "In 34 years, I've never seen a more volatile business environment than the one we are operating in today. Technology and social media have completely changed the concept of competitive advantage. For a long time, companies could test and experiment; they could pilot a new concept or product, but they could keep it confidential. Now, whatever you do and say is almost instantly transferable to your competitors. Pricing strategies, marketing strategies, anything you pilot, even in a small market, immediately gets into your competitors' hands on a global basis. Unless you can patent something, the first-mover advantage—at least the way we learned about it in business school—lasts a very short period of time. What used to be a two-year competitive advantage is two minutes today. This is all due to the exponentially increased use of the Internet, social media, and other technology-based advances."[20]

A practical and tangible way of defining strategy or competitive advantage (CA) is to create and capture economic value (EV). Economic value is the difference between customers' willingness to pay (WTP) and a supplier's opportunity cost (SOC). In mathematical terms, EV or CA = WTP − SOC.[21]

Although willingness to pay and supplier opportunity costs are useful concepts, they are not easily measurable quantities. This is because customers rarely honestly reveal what they are willing to pay. Even if they did, customers vary significantly in their willingness to pay, and it would be very difficult for firms to charge a unique price to each of its customers. A soft drink firm reportedly tried to do this, but it did not succeed.[22] Media reports suggest that Amazon.com also tried such a strategy of first-degree price discrimination sometime in 2000, but very quickly abandoned that. Similarly, suppliers also do not truthfully reveal the lowest amounts they would accept for services and resources to supply specified products and services.

Consider Apple's iPhone 4S as an example. It costs Apple about $188 to buy parts for the 16 GB version of its iPhone 4S, and it sells that phone in the United States for $649. It is difficult to know how much consumers would have been willing to pay for the iPhone and how much less suppliers may have charged just to be part of the growing iPhone ecosystem had Apple negotiated even harder. Even within the United States, consumers pay only about $200 for their iPhone, and telecommunications carriers cover the remaining $450 in exchange for a two-year service plan.

Thus, a practical way to view competitive advantage is simply price of products and services that a firm offers minus their cost. In the case of iPhone 4S, $649 and $188 are much more convenient to work with than more abstract economic concepts and quantities such as willingness to pay and supplier's opportunity cost. In terms of publicly reported financial numbers, competitive advantage or economic value is approximately profit, and it is influenced by a firm's revenues and total costs.

Porter (2001) argues that economic value is reliably measured through sustained profitability. In turn, profitability depends on two fundamental factors: industry structure and sustainable competitive advantage. Industry structure determines the profitability of the average competitor. For example, industry structure of the airline industry can help determine profitability of an average player in that industry. In contrast, sustainable competitive advantage enables a company to outperform the average competitor, and it determines excess profitability relative to an average competitor. For example, Southwest has significantly higher profitability than Delta within the airline industry.

Sustainable competitive advantage depends on operational effectiveness and strategic positioning. Operational effectiveness is doing the same thing your competitors do, but better (e.g., Ford using Internet-based procurement system to reduce costs). Operational effectiveness is necessary but does not provide sustainable advantage in the long run because of two reasons: rapid diffusion of best practices and competitive convergence.[23]

In contrast to operational effectiveness, strategic positioning—doing things differently from competitors in a way that delivers a unique value to customers—is a more sustainable source of competitive advantage. Strategic positions can be based on choice of product or service variety, choice of needs of a specific segment of customers (IKEA serving all needs of its target customers), and access to a particular group of customers (e.g., customers in small rural towns).

While operational effectiveness is about achieving excellence in individual activities, strategy is about combining activities. A sustainable strategic position requires trade-offs and fit. It is fit that drives both competitive advantage and sustainability. Porter mentions three types of fit: simple consistency between each activity and the overall strategy, reinforcing activities, and optimization of effort.

Porter (2001, p. 72) argues for a disciplined approach to strategy with "a strong focus on profitability rather than just growth, an ability to define a unique value proposition, and a willingness to make tough trade-offs in choosing what not to do." He notes,

> "Strategy goes far beyond the pursuit of best practices. It involves the configuration of a tailored value chain—the

series of activities required to produce and deliver a product or service-that enables a company to offer unique value. To be defensible, moreover, the value chain must be highly integrated. When a company's activities fit together as a self-reinforcing system, any competitor wishing to imitate a strategy must replicate the whole system rather than copy just one or two discrete product features or ways of performing particular activities."

Note that creation of value is not enough. Firms should also be able to capture some part of the total value for their stockholders. There are several parties that can stake a claim on the total value: suppliers, customers, employees, complementors, and competitors. The notion of capturing value focuses attention on the unique value added by a firm. The value added here refers to the value that will be lost if this firm were to disappear from the world. Value added is more important than simply the creation of "value". This is a fairly stringent test of competitive advantage because firms are rarely unique; they often have close competitors, and their offering can often be substituted with other products and services. If a firm is not unique, some of the total value that it creates will be competed away.

How is value different from unique value added? Brandenburger and Nalebuff (1995) give a good example of the difference. They ask us to imagine "Adam" and 26 MBA students playing a card game. Adam has 26 black cards, and each other student has a red card. Any red card, when coupled with a black card, gets a prize of $100. Clearly, without Adam, the game has no value, so Adam adds a value of $2,600 to the game. Each student adds a value of $100 each to the game. The total sum of the added values is $5200. However, only $2600 can be divided up among players because of the structure of the game. One way to proceed would be for Adam to share 50% of the $2,600 value; to do so, he should buy each player's card for $50, or he should sell his cards to them at $50. Instead, Adam burns 3 of his cards publicly. The pie is now smaller at $2,300 for Adam, but 3 students will go without a match, so no one particular student is essential to the game. Adam can now demand, say, 90% of the value that he will create for any particular player; that is, he can ask to buy other players' cards for $10. For Adam, 90% of 2300 is better than 50% of 2600. Of course, the success of Adam's strategy depends on whether the students decide to gang up and engage in collective bargaining or not.

Not all firms that create value are also able to appropriate some of that value for themselves. If a firm creates value for customers but is unable to retain any part of that value for itself, that firm is not likely to survive for long. For example, Napster created tremendous value for its customers but could not capture any of it for its own sustainability. In contrast, Apple has demonstrated not only how to create value but also how to capture a huge part of it with great success. Among more recent examples, Skype, Myspace, Twitter, many health information exchanges, and YouTube have reportedly all struggled to capture the value they create.

Xerox is another example of a firm that could not capture value from what it created. Its Palo Alto Research Center (PARC) had many key technologies, such as a graphical user interface and mouse, in the early 1970s that were later responsible for the success of companies such as Apple and Microsoft, but it could not reap the benefit of those technologies for itself.[24]

It took someone like Steve Jobs, a college dropout without any background in computer science or engineering, to realize the significance of those technologies in a visit in 1979 to the PARC lab. He later converted some of those ideas to make Apple the most valuable company in the world in 2011 for a while, even exceeding the market capitalization of Exxon Mobil.

Some argue that Xerox was shortchanged by a lack of business-savvy IT personnel, who could not articulate the business value of new technologies, and a lack of business personnel with IT savvy, or digital intelligence, who failed to pay attention to the potential of technologies likely due to their ignorance. Few managers would like to emulate such behavior.

1.2.2 Strategic significance of IT

The strategic significance of IT arises from several features and capabilities of IT. There are at least three ways to conceptualize strategic significance of IT—these are not mutually exclusive but rather are interrelated. [25]

First, IT transforms value chains and value activities.[26] All firms and business processes are composed of value activities, which have physical and information-processing components. IT can influence these physical and information-processing components and the linkages among activities. IT can also significantly enhance physical processing of activities. For example, IT makes it possible to achieve very close tolerances in machinery manufacturing and in process industries such as steel and chemicals. Examples of IT improving information processing include GPS and OnStar, which couple information with physical products to make those products more useful. A typical car in 2010 contains about 2000 components and 30,000 parts, but close to 10 million lines of code. Some plaintiffs in Toyota's alleged brake failure cases in 2010 are demanding to look at the source code as a potential source of alleged accidents. Apple's iPhone is another example. By unleashing hundreds of thousands of applications, Apple has added a tremendous information component to an otherwise mundane physical device.

IT also improves linkages along the value chain, as evidenced in EDI (electronic data interchange), extranets, and RFID (radio frequency identification). By transforming value chains and value activities, IT allows entrepreneurs to redefine industries, as Jeff Bezos did with Amazon.com in transforming the book-retailing industry and as Apple did in transforming the music-retailing industry. Entry of unfamiliar players in an established industry can be very troublesome for incumbents because these entrants often have no respect for industry rules and might have competencies that the incumbents lack. For example, Kodak was flat-footed in its response to compete with HP and others in the digital-imaging and printing markets.

Second, IT is transforming products. Almost all things that we see or feel are some combination of "atoms" and "bits". We can change that combination to create sources of new value. We can add information to a product to increase its value (e.g., iPhone can help us buy a song or locate itself if lost), or we can unbundle bits from atoms, as has happened in the film, music, and movie industries.

Third, IT allows firms to become ambidextrous; that is, IT makes it possible to go from an "either/or" to an "and" paradigm as advocated in ambidexterity[27] and blue ocean strategy frameworks. For example, IT is helping break away from conventional trade-offs between reach and richness (bandwidth, customization). Such changes have implications for human resources, marketing, and procurement strategy. Technologies such as Cisco's TelePresence are breaking down the barriers of geographical separation, allowing managers not only to supervise and monitor employees but also to coordinate with customers and vendors in far-off corners of the world. The potential of interactive television makes it possible to customize advertising for customers in different parts of the country.

Figure 1.4 illustrates how the evolution of IT and computing power has given rise to new ways of competing and innovations in organizational practices and business processes since 1960.[28] The challenge for managers is to figure out how they can leverage the power of emerging technologies of today (e.g., cloud computing, social media) to improve or "future-proof" their business model. In other words, how can your business avoid becoming Napstered, Amazoned, or Netflixed? Developing a digital business strategy and continuously refining that strategy may be one way to proceed.

1.2.3 How IT creates competitive advantage

Although some leading firms used IT to gain competitive advantage beginning in the 1950s, it took a while for strategy scholars to fully grasp the significance of IT. In an influential book on competitive strategy written in 1980, IT is not even mentioned among the key operating policies in what was depicted as "The Wheel of Competitive Strategy." Michael Porter was among one of the early strategy scholars to eventually recognize the potential of IT. In contrast to his 1980 book, his 1985 book more explicitly recognizes the role and importance of IT because of its pervasiveness in the value chain and its ability to help firms simultaneously achieve both cost leadership and differentiation. Porter also coauthored a 1985 article in *Harvard Business Review* titled "How Information Gives You Competitive Advantage."[29]

Figure 1.4: Computing Trends and How Firms Compete

	Data Processing Era (1960-1980)	Micro era (1980-1995)	Networked era (1995-onwards)	Mobile era (2002-present)
IT Trends	1.Mainframes, minis 2. Bundled software 3. Standalone computing 4. Hierarchical database systems	1. PCs 2. Software unbundled 3. Local area networks 4. Flat file systems, beginning of relational database management system (RDBMS)	1. More computing devices, handhelds 2. Open standards and open source software 3. WANs, Internet, intranets, extranets 4. RDBMS, ERPs	1. Mobile computing becomes pervasive 2. Cloud computing 3. Social networks 4. Big Data and Analytics
How Firms Compete	1. Multidivisional (M-form) functional hierarchy 2. Annual budgeting at the divisional level 3. Computers to "automate" tasks	1. Beginning of process orientation 2. Budgeting moves to lower levels 3. From "automate" to "informate"	1. Matrix structure 2. Real-time computing Profitability at even lower levels (e.g., customer) 3. From "informate" to "transform"	1. More transformation of businesses 2. Sharing economy?

In terms of the definition of competitive advantage introduced earlier, IT can influence competitive advantage through its impact on price and cost or revenues and total costs. IT can affect revenues by enhancing the sales through existing products, customers, and channels; by creating new products and channels and targeting new customers; and by reducing prices through cost reduction or cost avoidance.

Viewing strategy as the creation or capture of economic value, firms can increase added value in several ways: They can (1) either increase price or willingness to pay without affecting costs, (2) decrease costs without affecting price or willingness to pay, or (3) increase the difference between price and cost by changing both at the same time, but in such a way that a price increase is more than a cost increase or a cost decrease is more than a price decrease. IT can help in all these choices.

How can IT help capture value? There are at least three ways to do this: by shaping industry structure, by strengthening resource endowments, and by allowing firms to capture fleeting opportunities through alliances, outsourcing, and agility. Which of these ways of capturing value is most preferable? It depends on how managers perceive the role of IT and how dynamic the industry environment is.[30] In relatively stable environments, firms should try to improve power and market position by shaping industry structure in their favor. In the longer run, the goal should be to leverage resources, relationships, and other assets.

For some, good strategy is all about "capturing fleeting opportunities." They argue that deliberating over strategy is a waste of time, and no worthwhile CEO will take more than ten minutes to rewrite a strategy statement if he or she sees a better way of making more money. That may be true of dynamic environments such as that of firms in high-technology or high-information-intensity industries. However, even in such dynamic and "high-clock-speed" environments, IT can provide the capability to act proactively or reactively with greater agility.

Figure 1.5 shows an easy way to understand the role of IT in creating competitive advantage by remembering the acronym ADROIT. This acronym helps to parse the value created by IT into six components: adding volume or growth, differentiating or increasing willingness-to-pay, reducing costs, optimizing risks, improving industry attractiveness or innovating by generating and deploying knowledge and other resources and capabilities, and transforming business models and business processes. The acronym captures the role of IT in creating competitive advantage through five key drivers of sustainable economic value: volume, margins (through differentiating, reducing costs or improving industry attractiveness), optimizing uncertainty or risks in competitive environment, improving resources and capabilities of an organization, and continuous transformation to shape and respond to changing competitive landscape.

In other words, the ADROIT framework aligns closely with what can be called the fundamental equation for Economic Value (EV) as follows:

EV= Volume (A) X Margin (Differentiate, Reduce Costs)

+ Optimize Risk + Innovate/ Improve industry structure

+ Transform

Figure 1.5: ADROIT Framework to Assess True Economic Value of Information Technology and Innovations

A	Add volume or growth through existing or new products, customers, and channels
D	Differentiate or increase willingness-to-pay (WTP)
R	Reduce costs (operating costs, post-merger integration costs, capital costs, etc.)
O	Optimize risk (systematic, idiosyncratic, downside): reduction in volatility of cash flows and reduction in competitive risk
I	Innovate by generating knowledge and other resources and capabilities and Improve industry attractiveness
T	Transform industry, products, services, or business models

Digital Intelligence

Let us discuss how IT can be used to influence various dimensions of ADROIT framework. First, IT can help to add volume or growth through inorganic (e.g., by acquiring other companies) or organic means that may involve increasing sales to existing or new customers through existing or new channels by selling existing or new products. Growth can also be driven by ability to price or produce more competitively and dynamically and by targeting unserved or underserved markets through IT.

Second, IT can help to differentiate or increasing willingness-to-pay by competing on non-price attributes such as perceived quality or convenience that often reflects in customer satisfaction. For example, IT can help to increase WTP by complementing atoms with bits (as Apple did). Perceived quality is often a stronger driver of customer satisfaction and WTP than perceived value and firms can use CRM systems to improve customer knowledge and perceived quality for improved customer satisfaction.

Third, IT can help to reduce overall costs of the company through outsourcing while also investing in internal capabilities. For example, firms can reduce wasteful costs such as unnecessary post-merger integration costs, or costs of poor quality that reflect in returns of goods sold or customer defection. Note that benchmarking on IT costs alone can be counterproductive if IT investments can help to reduce non-IT costs substantially.

Fourth, IT can help to optimize risks (not necessarily reduce risks). Managers must try to reduce downside risk due to not investing in IT by engaging in counterfactual reasoning. They should also consider the effect of IT investments on intangibles such as customer satisfaction that can in turn help to reduce downside or idiosyncratic risk. One way to reduce downside risk is by splitting IT projects into must-do and may-do components and managing IT projects as real options.

Fifth, IT can help to improve industry attractiveness by changing the balance of Porter's five forces in favor of the firm (e.g., Apple, Cemex). IT can also help firms to pursue IT-embodied or IT-enabled innovations by making R&D more effective and scalable, and by using innovation from outside the firm as P&G (through Connect and Develop or "C&D") and SAP have tried to do. IT can also help to innovate by generating and deploying knowledge and other resources and capabilities.

Finally, IT can help to transform business models and business processes by replacing atoms with bits or complementing atoms with bits. Dealing with transformations requires that managers (1) calibrate their response to the triggers that are causing transformation, (2) protect their current revenue streams to the extent possible while finding ways to develop or grow new revenue streams, and (3) develop capabilities for dealing with change and transformation without being blinded by the rush to outsource key capabilities that may be necessary for future competitive advantage.

At this point, one may ask: Why do IT investments help to create or sustain competitive advantage when many of the IT components are easily available and readily deployable by almost any firm? Academic research suggests at least three arguments: virtuous cycle, learning, and strategic posture of differentiating through revenue growth rather than through cost reduction.[31] First, an explanation based on virtuous cycle argument suggests that firms that invest in IT in period 1 reap benefits and then invest more in IT in period 2. Over time, these effects become magnified, leading some firms to continue investing more in IT compared with their historical investment and that of their competitors and maintain a more proactive digital strategic posture. Because of their higher investments in IT and greater opportunities to learn from occasional failures in their overall IT portfolio, the firms undergoing the virtuous cycle are also likely to become better at managing IT.

A second, learning-based explanation suggests that years of continued investments in IT and experience in managing these systems may have improved the capability of firms to leverage information and strengthen other organizational capabilities. In support of this explanation, several empirical studies show that firms have learned how to make use of IT to improve customer satisfaction, at the same time boosting profitability through the positive effects of customer loyalty, cross-selling, and reduced marketing and selling costs.

A third explanation is that because of a long history of firms viewing IT mainly as an automation-related investment, with a focus on cost reduction rather than revenue generation, firms may have exhausted efficiency gains from IT. To the extent that RBV's logic focuses on differential firm performance; if revenue growth has become a primary driver for differentiation because of exhaustion of cost-based differentiation, tracing the effect of IT on profitability through revenue growth may be more promising.

The preceding three explanations (virtuous cycle, learning, and strategic posture of differentiating through revenue growth rather than through cost reduction) relate to the key tenets of resource-based view in strategy, which uses the notions of social complexity, erosion barriers, path dependence, and organizational learning to explain why resources create and sustain a competitive advantage. IT initiatives often require subtle changes in interlinkages among business processes involving multiple stakeholders, which involves high levels of social complexity. Such IT-enabled opportunities are characterized by organizational learning and path dependence, which create significant barriers to the erosion of competitive advantage. For example, Dell makes extensive use of IT (e.g., social media) to help engage its employees and customers. Investments into online conversational spaces, such as IdeaStorm and EmployeeStorm, forge interlinkages between customers and business units. In turn, these tools help Dell embed feedback into business processes and improve its customer resource life-cycle management. Similarly, Southwest Airlines created an integrated system to form extensive links among customers, employees, and other airlines. Both Dell and Southwest show how IT investments contribute to an ambidextrous capability: IT infrastructure facilitates complex operational tasks on the back end while presenting a friendly interface to consumers. Furthermore, the operational and customer-facing facets of IT capability are integrated and interdependent with built-in feedback mechanisms, allowing for continual process improvements and organizational learning. These examples illustrate how IT investments can help firms build IT resources and develop capabilities.

Likewise, IT-enabled opportunities for cost reduction and cost avoidance can also be socially complex (because of the inherent complexity involved in integrating multiple systems) and may require significant organizational learning to replicate cost-saving routines across the organization. For example, Wal-Mart uses IT to forge links with vendors and employees in a socially complex way. Investing in the RetailLink system enables Wal-Mart to be tightly linked with its vendors, providing them with frequent, timely, and store-specific sales information. This information system led to quick turnaround times for Wal-Mart and has driven labor and inventory costs down. Wal-Mart's earlier investments in a satellite network created a foundation for its later investments. The company heavily invested in RFID, building on top of its existing satellite network to increase efficiency and reduce costs, illustrating how IT investment can enable the reduction of operating costs through greater social complexity, path dependence, and organizational learning.

While both revenue growth and cost savings are likely to mediate the impact of IT investments on firm profitability, IT-enabled revenue growth is a stronger driver of profitability than IT-enabled cost savings because revenue-enhancing IT projects are likely to have greater social complexity, path dependence, organizational learning and higher barriers to erosion than cost-saving IT projects. The social complexity of revenue-enhancing IT projects stems from interlinkages of such IT projects with customer-facing business processes and customer life-cycle management, making successful implementation of these projects more sustainable and making it difficult for competitors to replicate successes. In contrast, IT projects focused mainly on cost savings may be easier to deploy because they may be based on transaction automation or information sharing rather than on reconfiguration of business processes that are more often associated with revenue-enhancing IT projects. In addition, because it is difficult to attribute the advantages of revenue-enhancing IT projects to publicly available information, competitors are unlikely to grasp the real sources of competitive advantage and revenue creation potential of these projects. Furthermore, because revenue-enhancing projects are often enmeshed in existing business processes, they have inherent path dependence, involve significant organizational learning, and may require substantial complementary resources for successful implementation. Therefore, revenue-enhancing IT projects are more difficult for competitors to replicate than IT projects that involve cost reduction.

Note also that many cost reduction innovations in IT are not firm specific, particularly considering that they often involve automation tools that are purchased from vendors. Although there are exceptions, many cost-reducing IT tools can be purchased or developed through contracts with specialized IT vendors or consulting firms. Because there is greater industry concentration (fewer firms) upstream in a supply chain, the cost side of firm operations is likely to be less differentiated than the customer-facing revenue side of firm operations. Revenue-generating projects are more firm specific because they align with the downstream or customer-facing side of the business, which thrives on unique customer profiles, niche markets, and heterogeneity in products and services. For this reason, revenue-generating projects are less likely to be replicable, and firms are more likely to differentiate themselves and find a niche based on revenue-generating capabilities than on cost reduction capabilities.

Together, greater social complexity, path dependence, and organizational learning and higher barriers to erosion of revenue-enhancing IT projects can provide effective *ex post* limits to competition and can protect a firm against resource imitation, transfer, and substitution, thereby improving the profit-generating potential of revenue-enhancing IT projects more than that of cost-saving IT projects.

One should remember, however, that IT is just one of the discretionary investments that a firm has to make. CEOs often struggle as they allocate their company's discretionary dollars among various categories of investments. Should they invest more in IT than, say in advertising or R&D? Furthermore, when they invest in

IT, what kinds of projects should they focus on? Information technology can be used to reduce costs by creating more efficient operations, or it can be used to support sales growth through, say, customer satisfaction and customer retention strategies.

An academic study, using data from more than 400 global companies from 1998 to 2003, offers some insight on such questions.[32] Unlike other studies that failed to detect a significant effect of IT investments on profitability, it found that information technologies deployed since 1995 had a significant positive impact on firm profitability. What's more, investment in IT had more of an impact on a company's profits and sales than comparable spending on either advertising or research and development.[33]

A significant portion of IT's impact on firm profitability is accounted for by IT-enabled revenue growth, but there is no evidence for the effect of IT on profitability through operating cost reduction. These findings suggest that firms have had greater success in achieving higher profitability through IT-enabled revenue growth than through IT-enabled cost reduction. In fact, IT investments had a marked positive effect on revenue growth; for example, a $1 increase in IT expenditures per employee was associated with a $12.22 increase in sales per employee. However, the effect of an increase in IT expenditures on reducing overall operating expenses was negligible.[34] One key takeaway from this research seemed to be that, all other things being equal, executives should accord higher priority to IT projects that have revenue growth potential over those that focus mainly on cost savings.

These findings have important implications. First, the positive linkage between IT investments and profitability underscores the strategic importance of managing overall levels of IT investments as a critical intangible firm resource. Although prior work argued for the superiority of proprietary in-house built systems of the 1970s and 1980s that fostered switching costs and price premiums, these features of old IT systems were expected to be difficult to sustain in an environment of open architectures, reverse engineering, and hypercompetition. While such open networks are wringing cost efficiencies out of supply chains through higher process visibility, this does not mean that IT is totally commoditized as some have argued. It is likely that newer technologies and Internet-enabled IT systems may have created further opportunities for value creation and value capture to establish distinctive strategic positioning and that firms may have learned to make better use of IT to their advantage, in general, over time.[35]

Second, the findings provide implications for how the resource-based view works when it comes to IT investments. To the extent that resource-based view logic focuses on the role of resources in terms of their impact on differential firm performance, it appears that IT-enabled revenue growth opportunities may be more promising than IT-enabled cost reduction opportunities to create sustainable competitive advantage. This may be because there may not be enough variation across firms in using IT for cost reduction. If Firm A can use an enterprise resource planning or supply chain management solution to reduce its costs, nothing prevents the vendor from selling the same solution to other firms and thereby eroding that cost-based competitive advantage of Firm A. In addition, IT-enabled revenue growth may have stronger virtuous cycles and learning-based advantages, leading to stronger path dependence and relatively less replicability of such advantages, thus causing a more sustainable differential advantage in profitability. An indirect implication of the findings is that IT-enabled revenue growth projects are more rewarding from a profitability perspective than IT-enabled cost reduction projects and should help managers allocate resources among IT projects that differ with respect to these two objectives.[36]

Third, the substantial returns to IT investment in terms of both revenue growth and profitability compared with other discretionary expenditures, such as advertising and R&D provides an explanation for high shareholder valuations of IT investments. Even after one allows for the difficulty in accounting for all of the other complementary investments or the higher risk or uncertainty associated with IT investments, substantial returns on IT compared with returns on similarly risky expenditures, such as advertising and R&D, make IT investments attractive from a profitability perspective. They also provide an explanation for observed patterns in relative allocations among discretionary expenditures over the 1998–2003 period.

Finally, from a top management or board perspective, IT investments should receive significant attention in governance and resource allocation processes because they appear to be more important than R&D and advertising in terms of profitability. Chief information officers can use the findings to develop a business case and justification for continued investments in IT. Insofar as IT investments may be more profitable than R&D and advertising investments, investors should consider this when determining the market valuations of firms based on their relative allocations to such discretionary investments. Financial analysts should pay attention to the shifts in relative allocations among IT, advertising, and R&D dollars because these shifts can provide early signals about subsequent sales growth or firm profitability.

1.3 Synchronize IT and Strategy

As noted previously, strategy can be viewed at multiple levels: corporate strategy, competitive strategy, and functional strategy. Synchronizing IT with strategy implies that managers should try to achieve IT–strategy synchronization at all the three levels.

1.3.1 Synchronize Corporate Strategy and IT Strategy

A corporate strategy of diversification will have very different implications for approaching IT strategy, than what a corporate strategy of focusing on core competence might entail. Jaguar Land Rover (JLR) is a good example of how the role of IT systems can influence and shape strategies and performance of companies. Tata Motors got an opportunity to buy JLR when Ford was trying to restructure following a $12.6 billion loss in 2006. After months of negotiations beginning in early 2007 and a nine-month-long period of due diligence, Tata Motors acquired JLR from Ford in 2008 for $2.3 billion. According to Richard Shore, Director of the Business Transformation Office in July 2014, Jaguar Land Rover's transformational journey could only begin after Jaguar Land Rover achieved independence from Ford's IT systems in September 2010. Up to that point, Jaguar Land Rover was reliant on Ford's legacy systems, and many of them were not interoperable.[37]

The role of IT in corporate strategy can be illustrated in how firms form strategic alliances as they configure their portfolio of different businesses. Although IT can serve as an enabler of strategic alliances, it can also create obstacles in forming partnerships, particularly when IT systems are inflexible. Indeed, research shows that flexible IT systems can serve as an enabler to successful partnerships.[38]

When IT systems are inflexible, they can create serious obstacles to beneficial partnerships. For example, several years ago, Amtrak intended to make online reservations and tickets available to third-party travel sites, but setting up connections to its old mainframe systems proved to be too difficult for its partners. Eventually, Amtrak modernized its systems with a service-oriented architecture (SOA), which can be accessed through open communication protocols over the Internet. More recently, Santander Bank of Spain cancelled its deal to buy 316 retail-banking branches from the Royal Bank of Scotland (RBS), in part because of incompatibilities between their IT systems. The lesson: Major deals can fall apart when IT systems are inflexible. One key to making IT infrastructures more flexible -- as Amtrak found out -- is SOA adoption. And Amtrak is not the only example. Lufthansa, for its part, leveraged SOA to create a common platform with Star Alliance partners; this would have been impossible with Lufthansa's old legacy systems. Mohawk Fine Papers (MFP) used SOA to quickly form hundreds of digital business-to-business (B2B) partnerships; the SOA adoption allowed pricing information from multiple suppliers to appear instantly whenever MFP clients wish to place an order.

It is possible to identify at least three dimensions of IT flexibility, which can foster a wide array of strategic alliances: open communication standards, cross-functional transparency, and modularity.[39] First, open communication standards such as Extensible Markup Language (XML), which are based upon common understanding of the format and structure of information to be exchanged among business partners. Second, cross-functional transparency, which ensures that capabilities are widely deployable, visible, and accessible across different functions of the organization. Finally, modularity, which enables the company to define atomic, fine-grained units of functionality, which can be easily disaggregated and recombined into new combinations of services or business processes. If potential partners can seamlessly mesh one or multiple parts of your IT infrastructure into their systems, then your system possesses modularity.

A comparison of the effects of IT flexibility on several types of alliances (arm's-length, collaborative, and joint-venture alliances) and firm performance (measured as the ratio of market value over book value, also known as Tobin's q) revealed the following:

1. Adoption of open-communication standards helps with the formation of Arm's Length alliances (typically such alliances involve an agreement to provide, sell, or exchange a service; arm's-length partners share information or license rights to a product, but do not jointly develop, integrate or recombine their processes or capabilities). Moreover, open-communication standards have a positive effect on the value that companies derive from arm's-length alliances. This is because open standards reduce the need for investing in information systems that tie alliance partners down into long-term investments, freeing them to form new alliances with the knowledge that an alliance can be disbanded quickly when it has run its course.

2. Cross-functional transparency has a positive effect on the value that companies derive from collaborative alliances. Collaborative alliances involve sharing of company-specific or tacit knowledge, such as in joint design or development, recombining products and services, or heavy coupling of inter-organizational processes, making collaborative alliances more difficult to form than arm's-length alliances. They also present a greater challenge in detecting new opportunities for value-creation, which is where cross-functional transparency can be particularly helpful.

3. Modularity helps with the formation of joint ventures. Joint-ventures share features of both arm's-length and collaborative alliances; they resemble collaborative alliances in that they involve bilateral investments in capital, technology, and company-specific assets, however, they are distinguished by their basis in joint equity or joint ownership in the formation of a new business entity. Modularity reduces the cost of reconfiguring business processes, which is important in joint ventures since they require substantial integration and reconfiguration of processes in the creation of new business entities.

One surprising finding was that flexible IT shows a greater role in deriving collaborative alliance value than in arm's-length alliances. In terms of the effects of overall IT-enabled flexibility (as a combination of open standards, cross-functional transparency and modularity), it leads to greater value derived from all three types of alliances: arm's-length, collaborative, and joint-venture alliances. In summary, research suggests that IT-enabled flexibility is a critical capability in navigating a wide range of partnerships.

Turning now to competitive strategy, a competitive strategy of differentiation will have different implications for IT strategy than that for a competitive strategy of cost leadership. Focusing on differentiation may require emphasizing revenue growth in IT strategy and investments in CRM or personalization systems. In contrast, focusing on cost leadership may involve deployment of robust IT systems that provide end-to-end visibility of costs and promote efficient execution of business processes.

1.3.2 Synchronize Competitive Strategy and IT Strategy: Revenue Growth, Cost Reduction, or Both?

How should managers determine the choice of their IT strategy? Given that profit is equal to revenue minus cost, it is clear that there are three strategic paths from IT to firm performance: IT can be used to (1) *reduce costs* by improving productivity and efficiency; (2) *increase revenues* by fully exploiting opportunities through existing customers, channels, and products/services and by finding or creating new customers, channels, and products/services; or (3) *reduce costs and increase revenues* simultaneously. [40] The question for managers is which pathway is more profitable when it comes to gaining competitive advantage through IT: revenue growth as FedEx does, cost reduction as Wal-Mart does, or doing both at the same time as GE and P&G seem to do? The answer may depend on both a firm's strategy and how much it wants to invest in IT.

Although IT, being a general-purpose technology, can be viewed as being capable of both increasing revenues and reducing costs, does this mean that firms no longer have to choose a strategic emphasis? Choosing a particular strategy implies making some trade-offs—that is, choosing some goals and functionalities while forsaking others in the hope that the overall combination of choices will ensure a better fit for organizational activities in the value chain and will make that fit less replicable for competitors. Accordingly, firms often choose between revenue expansion or cost reduction in their strategic IT emphasis. For example, the CIO of FedEx, Robert Carter, contrasts FedEx's approach to IT with that of UPS in the following way:

> "We tend to focus slightly less on operational technology. We focus a little more on revenue-generating, customer-satisfaction-generating, strategic-advantage technology. The key focus of my job is driving technology that increases the top line."[41]

In other words, in Carter's view, FedEx has a revenue emphasis while UPS has a cost emphasis. Likewise, firms, such as Johnson & Johnson and Coca-Cola, have tried to emphasize revenue growth in their IT strategy. As we have noted, FedEx and UPS do not have to restrict themselves to either revenue growth or cost reduction; alternatively, they can adopt a dual emphasis.

Consider some examples. While customer relationship management (CRM) systems can enable some cost savings if they help reduce the costs of maintaining customer relationships, the primary reason for deploying these systems is often to increase revenues by either attracting new customers or enabling cross-selling, upselling, or repeat sales from existing customers. If firms use CRM systems to help with revenue growth and cost reduction in equal measure, then such an approach could be characterized as a dual-focus investment. Likewise, in an academic setting, systems used to maintain alumni development and relationships may be characterized primarily as revenue enhancing, while systems related to the automation of class scheduling or course bidding systems (as opposed to manual processes) can be viewed as cost reducing.

Among cost-focused applications, firms often use reverse auctions and many other supply chain management applications primarily to reduce their procurement costs. As another example of a cost-focused project, UPS linked bar-code data on its packages (called Package Level Detail) but retained the capability to provide seamless tracking information to its customers while outsourcing some rural deliveries to USPS to lower its overall costs. A similar opportunity for cost reduction was provided by UPS's Geographical Information Systems, which enabled the firm to get its customers to do some data entry themselves, further reducing UPS's costs. UPS also used its integrated supply chain assets to do customers' work for them, which helped realize revenue opportunities; in this case, we could characterize the investment as being revenue-focused. It is also likely that some systems can initially be deployed for their cost-saving potential or to streamline internal processes, but later they may provide revenue benefits.[42]

In the end, it is not so much which applications firms use but rather what their strategic objectives are for deploying those applications, in that managerial beliefs and strategic posture shape an organization's IT governance and management of IT projects to create business value. This logic applies to IT assets, which are mostly general in nature and, with some customization and appropriate changes in business processes, training, and incentive structures, can be targeted to achieve strategic objectives defined by managers. These changes in business processes and reengineering efforts are often shaped by the firm's overarching IT strategic objectives. In other words, while any individual IT system presents potential opportunities to reduce costs or to enhance revenue, or both, we argue that it is perhaps more useful to think of the portfolio of IT applications that firms want to create to operationalize their strategic emphasis by instantiating necessary configurations of individual IT applications.

Although some argue that the pursuit of both revenue growth and cost reduction objectives simultaneously may hurt firm performance because of the natural tensions between these polar strategic management approaches, [43] there are reasons to believe that IT may allow firms to pursue dual strategies more effectively. While academic research suggests that firms may have greater success in achieving higher profitability through IT-enabled revenue growth than through IT-enabled cost reduction, it also acknowledges that IT investments can enable firms to achieve both revenue growth and cost reduction objectives. Firms such as GE, P&G and Chevron seem to use IT to achieve multiple objectives.[44]

To understand how IT strategic emphasis and IT investments jointly influence profitability and market value, let us first understand why a firm's IT strategic emphasis will affect firm performance at typical levels of IT investments. A firm's strategic emphasis affects the firm's choices with respect to the types of technologies and applications it acquires and the types of governance processes and firm performance metrics it uses.

Ultimately, any strategy needs to be instantiated through appropriate combinations of IT systems to result in firm performance. In other words, strategy execution can be viewed as the actualization of a specific configuration of systems. A dual emphasis in IT strategy may lead to better firm performance than a single emphasis in IT strategy, despite some risks in executing a dual-emphasis strategy (see Figure 1.6).[45]

41

Figure 1.6: Rewards and Risks of Dual IT Strategies

Key Mechanisms	Rewards of a Dual IT Strategic Emphasis	Risks of a Dual IT Strategic Emphasis
1. Resource-based view		
Social Complexity	Much higher social complexity of IT because of its role in enhancing the breadth and depth of relationships. For example, firms will need to work on both the front end with customers to create one-to-one customer relationships through CRM and on the back end with suppliers to create highly responsive yet low-cost delivery mechanisms.	Firms may not be able to realize complex interrelationships among IT systems.
Barriers to the Erosion of Competitive Advantage	The scope of activities spanning business processes that touch customers and suppliers create higher barriers to erosion along several dimensions simultaneously due to the cross-functional nature of IT initiatives	Cross-functional IT projects are more prone to coordination problems.
Path Dependence and/or Asset Stock Accumulation	Much greater path dependence and/or asset stock accumulation because IT capabilities that evolve gradually through integration with many business processes are likely to be more tacit and sustainable over a longer time.	Firms may get locked into poor and incompatible systems due to inertia.
Organizational Learning	Higher levels of organizational learning because learning spans many more interrelated business processes, routines, and IT systems that are more tacit, complex, and novel than that for a single-emphasis strategy.	The organization may suffer from information overload, leading to reduced learning.
2. Reduced Diminishing Returns in Opportunity Space	Plentiful "low-hanging fruit" to increase revenues and reduce costs.	Firms may lose the ability to spot fundamental transformations or avoid reaching for "higher-hanging fruit" that may be rewarding in the long run.
3. Stretch Targets	Stretch targets can motivate managers toward high performance.	Too much stretch can be debilitating.

Why will dual emphasis in IT lead to better firm performance? First, following resource-based view of strategy, a dual-emphasis IT strategy (compared with either a revenue- or a cost-emphasis IT strategy) is likely to lead to potentially superior firm performance due to (a) greater social complexity, (b) greater causal ambiguity, (c) greater path dependence, and (d) organizational learning. Let us consider these four mechanisms (social complexity, causal ambiguity, path dependence, and organizational learning) in turn.

(a) Social Complexity: The social complexity of a dual-emphasis strategy comes from its relatively ambitious scope of trying to achieve two goals at the same time. Because of the complexity and breadth of applications that a dual-emphasis strategy requires, it is much more difficult for competitors to replicate the successful execution of such a strategy than it is to replicate a revenue- or a cost-emphasis strategy. Prior research in the quality management literature suggests that "simultaneous pursuit" of several competitive advantages can lead to a stronger performance because competing on "several fronts simultaneously" makes it more difficult for competitors to replicate such configurations. In addition to the breadth and variety of IT applications needed in a dual-emphasis IT strategy, it also requires much more reconfiguration or restructuring of business processes, thus contributing to the greater social complexity inherent in such an emphasis.

(b) Causal Ambiguity: It may be more difficult to disentangle and attribute the advantages resulting from a dual-emphasis IT strategy from publicly available information because firms following a dual-emphasis strategy defy conventional logic and their initiatives and resulting competitive advantages are harder to classify or are more ambiguous to decipher for competitors.

(c) Path Dependence: A dual strategic emphasis may have an inherent path dependence that is relatively more difficult to replicate compared with that in either a revenue or a cost emphasis. For example, for a firm employing a dual strategic emphasis, cost-reduction efforts may provide opportunities to target new market segments, such as the bottom of the pyramid, which in turn could enable the firm to realize higher revenue growth than if it were to focus only on cost reduction without a link to its revenue growth strategy or only on revenue growth by focusing on premium market segments. Tighter coupling between strategic options, such as revenue growth and cost reduction, is much less replicable by competitors than only one such option. Likewise, firms with a dual strategic emphasis can use outsourcing and offshoring for both cost reduction (through arbitrage) and revenue expansion (through sales in foreign markets by adapting offerings in those markets).

(d) Organizational Learning: Dual emphasis firms may have higher levels of organizational learning because learning spans many more interrelated business processes, routines, and IT systems that are more tacit, complex, and novel than that for a single-emphasis strategy. Together, the greater social complexity, causal ambiguity, path dependence and organizational learning of a dual-emphasis IT strategy can provide effective *ex post* limits to competition and can protect a firm against resource imitation, transfer, and substitution, thereby making firms with a dual strategic emphasis more profitable and more valuable.

Second, a dual emphasis opens up many more "low-hanging" positive-return investment opportunities than either single emphasis would, thereby creating more options for profitable growth. Firms with a dual emphasis are likely to have lower cycle times in product development, supply chain management, and customer relationship management processes for realizing their revenue and cost targets and thereby have accelerated cash flows. Dual-emphasis firms may have less variability in cash flows because their IT-enabled cash flows have two sources (both revenue growth and cost reduction), while firms with a primary emphasis on either revenue growth or cost reduction have only one source of IT-enabled cash flow.

Third, a dual strategic emphasis, being more ambitious in its scope, might provide stretch targets to employees and implementation partners for higher revenues and lower costs, thereby improving the chances of getting more from the same levels of investments. In turn, that will lead to higher levels of cash flows, profits and market value.

There are, however, potential risks inherent to a dual strategic emphasis, and despite the potential of IT to enable firms to achieve both revenue growth and cost reduction goals, there are reasons firms may be better off focusing on only one of these overarching goals. Compared with revenue expansion or cost reduction strategic emphases, it may be more difficult for firms to follow a dual strategic emphasis because the latter entails greater complexity and risk in ensuring fit between all the IT-related decisions the firm must make. First, focusing on two goals simultaneously can be confusing in terms of target setting and performance metrics that managers across business units pursue. Second, dual-emphasis firms may end up having a portfolio of IT systems that do not allow seamless integration of data and information flow. One example of this comes from the financial services industry: Some observers argue that one reason for the credit crisis may be that while firms were pursuing revenue growth from a business perspective as reflected in their quest for additional revenues, even with some disregard for prudent risk management, they were emphasizing cost reduction in the IT function. Finally, focusing on two goals simultaneously can make it difficult for managers to agree on prioritizing IT projects.

Ultimately, whether the advantages of a dual strategic emphasis outweigh the disadvantages and risks is largely an empirical question; it is also hard to make a specific prediction at typical levels of IT investments because a more complete understanding of the effect of IT strategic emphasis requires taking into consideration how a dual strategic emphasis moderates the relationship between IT investments and firm performance.

Consider profitability first. Why will a firm's strategic emphasis affect the relationship between IT investments and firm profitability? A firm's strategic emphasis affects its choices with respect to the types of technologies and applications it acquires, its IT governance mechanisms, and its metrics for firm performance. Firms with a dual emphasis may have more diverse IT resources for revenue growth as well as cost reduction. Managing these diverse resources requires hiring a larger number of IT employees and having greater managerial expertise in managing diverse projects, which in turn may require using a more diverse network of external IT implementation partners. Together, managing diverse IT infrastructure elements and IT human resources in dual-emphasis firms will require a higher degree of management attention, bandwidth, and focus than if the firm were to focus on only revenue growth or cost reduction. However, despite these challenges and risks, firms are likely to benefit more from IT spending if they adopt a dual strategic emphasis (than if they adopt only a revenue growth or a cost reduction emphasis) because of differences in expectations and targets that managers set for their IT implementations.

Next, consider the moderating effect of a firm's strategic emphasis on the relationship between IT investments and market value (measured by Tobin's Q). The strategic emphasis of a firm can moderate the influence of IT investments on market value because of the types of technologies and risks associated with each strategic emphasis. Arguably, firms with a dual emphasis are likely to have lower cycle times in product development, supply chain management, and customer relationship management processes for realizing their revenue and cost targets and thereby have accelerated cash flows. Dual-emphasis firms may also have higher levels of cash flows because of simultaneous targets for higher revenues and lower costs. Finally, dual-emphasis firms may have less variability in cash flows because their IT-enabled cash flows have two sources (both revenue growth and cost reduction), while firms with a primary emphasis on either revenue growth or cost reduction have only one source of IT-enabled cash flow. Due to the diversification of sources of cash flows, the overall variability of cash flows is likely to be lower for dual-emphasis firms.

The foregoing discussion suggests that (1) IT investments will have a stronger positive association with profitability for firms with a dual strategic emphasis than for firms with a single strategic emphasis, and (2) IT investments will have a stronger positive association with Tobin's Q for firms with a dual strategic emphasis than for firms with a single strategic emphasis.

Digital Intelligence

Indeed, recent research finds that IT investments can allow firms to make higher profits and enjoy greater market value by focusing on revenues and costs in their IT strategy at the same time. Doing so requires more IT resources and IT investments.

Figure 1.7 shows that at the mean value of IT investments, shown by a vertical line, revenue-emphasis firms and dual-emphasis firms have approximately the same profitability as cost-emphasis firms. Again, although profitability may be approximately the same at the mean value of IT investments, the differences can be much larger at higher levels of IT investment. In particular, at higher levels of IT investments, dual-emphasis firms can significantly outperform revenue- and cost-emphasis firms.

Figure 1.7: IT–Profitability Relationship by Dual, Revenue and Cost IT Strategic Emphasis

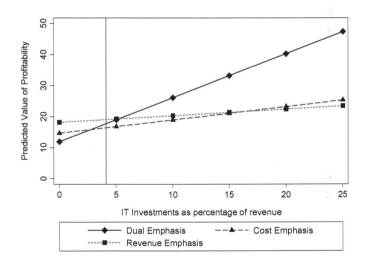

Figure 1.8 shows that at the mean value of IT investments, shown by a vertical line, revenue-emphasis firms and dual-emphasis firms have a higher market value than cost-emphasis firms. From this figure, it appears that the market has a generally favorable

47

assessment of dual- and revenue-emphasis firms over a significantly large range of IT investments.

Figure 1.8: IT–Tobin's Q Relationship by Dual, Revenue and Cost IT Strategic Emphasis

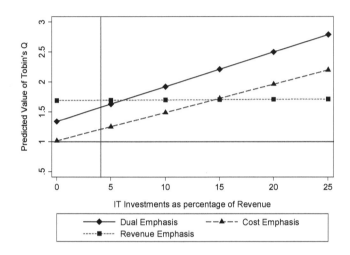

1.3.3 Synchronize Functional Strategies and IT Strategy

Finally, a functional human resources or knowledge management strategy of "people to people" will have different implications for IT strategy than that for a knowledge management strategy of "people to documents." Likewise, a quality strategy that focuses on revenue growth will have different implications for IT strategy than that for a quality management strategy of "cost reduction." [46]

1.3.4 Toward Synchronization

Note that the word "synchronization" is used here, not "alignment." How is synchronization different from alignment? Alignment implies that either IT or strategy is preordained and that the other element is then brought in alignment with the primary element. In contrast, synchronization implies a continuous two-way exchange or interaction between IT and strategy: IT can influence strategy, and strategy can influence how a firm approaches IT—one need not precede or trump the other. Synchronization requires a mind-set that is open to new possibilities enabled by technology, at the same time ensuring that use of IT is consistent with business needs and business processes. More recently, some leading researchers and practitioners have begun using terms such as "convergence" or "fusion" as the desired state of a digital business strategy in which IT and business strategy are one and the same[47] or are "forged together." However, many firms are nowhere close to achieving synchronization between IT and strategy. According to a McKinsey survey, approximately 67% of respondents desire a tight integration between IT and business strategies. However, only 22% report that this is actually happening in their organizations.[48]

Recent research suggests that firms with IT change-business change alignment and IT delivery-business priority alignment have higher revenue at higher levels of IT investment than firms that display IT investment-business strategy alignment. Also, at high levels of software and service investments, firms with IT change-business change alignment outperform firms that show alignment in other dimensions of IT-business alignment. These findings highlight the importance of aligning IT delivery with business priorities and aligning IT change with business change.[49]

How should firms begin to move toward synchronization? An increasing involvement of IT professionals in strategy formulation and a greater involvement of business executives in IT governance and managing IT projects are both key to achieving IT–strategy synchronization. Fortunately, some leading companies are beginning to move in that direction, giving their CIOs responsibility for managing line businesses.[50] Some other firms are providing exposure to IT projects and the IT function to their promising executives as part of their grooming for top management positions or picking those who have managed the IT function as their CEO.[51] In some cases, CEOs are going as far as to assume the role of CIO in their firm.[52]

1.4 Toward Digital Business Strategy

Given the importance of IT in contemporary firms, some even argue that all companies must have a digital business strategy. We consider here how a digital business strategy can help companies leverage IT by recognizing the duality of IT.[53]

This duality of IT creates dilemmas for business leaders; it manifests in the following five forms. First, IT enables both sustaining and what are sometimes characterized as "disruptive" innovations, despite controversy on definition and basis of the underlying research on so called "disruptive innovations". Thus, a key strategic issue for digital business strategists involves discerning whether an IT innovation is sustaining, disruptive, or potentially both. To the extent that managers' perceptions can become self-fulfilling prophecies, viewing every technology-enabled change as potentially disruptive can be as damaging as being completely oblivious to not recognizing the sustaining potential of technology. Second, IT often creates new opportunities to reshape markets while at the same time enabling faster adaptation. Thus, a key strategic issue for digital business strategists is deciding whether to leverage IT to attempt to shape their environment, or to use IT to adapt to the environment instead.

Third, IT offers firms new sources of competitive advantage while concurrently offering more transparency in the sources of those advantages, allowing rivals to quickly imitate. Thus, a key strategic issue is whether to make the first move or to be a fast follower to free ride on the pioneering costs and risks borne by the first mover. Fourth, IT has tended to drive both disaggregation (especially throughout the vertical value chain) and aggregation (especially horizontally) at the same time. The choice facing digital business strategists then is how best to exploit IT capabilities to both "aggregate" and "disaggregate" the firm. Finally, the rapid pace of IT-enabled change overall creates immense uncertainty for business strategists while providing powerful new tools and data sources to better understand that uncertainty and the range and relative likelihood of alternative outcomes. A coherent digital business strategy should address and manage these five elements of duality, and digital uncertainty.

How does digital business strategy differ from conventional business strategies? We consider at least three dimensions. First, digital business strategy is about thriving on digital uncertainty. With a conventional business strategy, firms often react to or accept competitive uncertainty as given. A digital business strategy is about using digital uncertainty to your advantage; firms can use IT to proactively shape the environment in their favor, as manifest in the actions of Amazon.com and Netflix. Firms that exploit IT can use it as a lever to create digital "eddies" or "turbulence" in their competitive environment, thereby benefiting from that turbulence by throwing their competitors in disarray.

Second, while the conventional business strategy is to effectively play the current game in a "red ocean" of known markets, the digital business strategy is about creating a new game or "a blue ocean." It's about anticipating and creating the future and imagining new competitive moves, while conventional strategy tools tend to focus more on competitive positions in existing industry spaces, or based on current products and offerings. Amazon.com, which started as a pure online book retailer in 1994, has continually morphed its business model, making forays into a variety of businesses. A digital business strategy uses information-based advantages, and turns conventional sources of competitive advantage into liability for competitors. Amazon.com and Netflix made the physical assets of retailers—such as large stores and ownership of an impressive physical inventory—strategically irrelevant and even a liability by substituting information for inventories.

Fourth, whereas conventional strategy makes relatively rigid commitments to a few big bets that are revisited infrequently, digital business strategy is about developing ambidextrous dynamic capabilities in real time, often through multiple simultaneous IT-enabled experiments. A digital business strategy focuses on the development of operational, improvisational, and dynamic capabilities such as customer-, process-, and performance-management capabilities. Often these capabilities require significant investments in IT infrastructure to pursue ambidextrous strategies that allow firms to focus on seemingly conflicting goals at the same time such as revenue growth versus cost reduction.

How should managers and boards approach digital strategy given the above discussion? First, managers must understand the duality inherent in IT, and question their conventional-strategy concepts, which focus on tradeoffs without recognizing that IT can, at times, help overcome the tradeoffs altogether. For example, IT can help firms pursue both revenue growth and cost reduction, or higher quality and lower costs—things that a purist approach to conventional strategy might not consider.

Second, the notion of a digital business strategy also has implications for the role of corporate boards in discharging their responsibility—not only as a steward to ensure that the firm is held accountable to its acts of commission, but also to hold a firm accountable for acts of omission, such as moving too late in the digital space, as Blockbuster might have done. In some cases, the boards might be faulted for not demanding the information necessary to properly understand the companies' risks arising out of digital strategies of competitors, make key hiring decisions, and fully perform their fiduciary duties.

Third, companies also need to incorporate a bottom-up perspective in strategy formulation by using more sophisticated tools, such as prediction markets. Such tools might help guard against the temptation to rely too much on executive judgment, which can sometimes be limited in breadth or simply off the mark. Consider Jeff Bezos, who is often credited for many astute digital strategic moves, yet remarked in a 2006 interview, "I guarantee that five years from now, no one will want to be a social-networking company."

1.5 What Academic Research Informs on Digital Business Strategy

Many companies have failed because of poor planning and execution of their digital business strategy.[54] John Chambers, the

CEO of Cisco, noted in a 2012 interview that since his becoming the CEO in 1995, more than 50% of the companies in the Fortune 500 are no longer on that list.[55] Often, managers have a poor understanding of why digital initiatives fail and what their strategic posture should be in managing digital initiatives. They sometimes blame their IT departments when things go wrong, not recognizing that many digital business initiatives fail because executives do not adjust their strategies appropriately with respect to their competitors and their competitive environment.

Consider the contrast in digital strategies of Amazon and the Borders Group. While Amazon pursued a digital strategy involving heavy investments in IT and online infrastructure in the book retailing industry, Borders pursued a very different strategy of investing in offline assets with little attention to online sales. While Amazon started with a digital strategic posture that reflected investments in IT assets higher than the industry norm, Borders started with a digital strategic posture that reflected investments in IT assets lower than what was the competitive norm for the industry. Over time, Amazon and Borders further diverged from each other: While Amazon kept increasing the scale of its digital assets, Borders focused more on offline sources of growth.

The digital strategic moves of Amazon and Borders also reflect how they approached digital strategy and how they viewed what they should do in-house versus what they should outsource. Amazon kept much of its website development in-house, while Borders outsourced that to its competitor Amazon in 2001. Borders defended that strategic choice as a "focus on building more [offline] stores," which it believed was a core competency. That ultimately turned out to be its core rigidity.

Another industry player Barnes & Noble tried to imitate Amazon by investing in IT assets and an online presence through BN.com. However, neither Borders nor Barnes & Noble could match Amazon's lead in capturing value from its digital assets. Eventually, Borders reversed course; it terminated the outsourcing deal with Amazon, sold off some of its offline international bookstores, and closed half of its Waldenbooks outlets in the U.S. Sadly, these actions came too late.

These examples illustrate how strategic postures and moves can influence firms' subsequent performance: while Borders' became bankrupt and Barnes & Noble continues to struggle, Amazon continued to thrive. Indeed, research offers some insights on what went wrong for Borders' digital strategic posture and moves. Digital business strategy (how much to spend on IT and the extent to which a company should use outsourcing) is not solely a matter of optimizing firm operations internally or of responding to one or two focal competitors, but it should also be responsive to the digital business competitive environment. Firms are better off diverging from their industry peers under higher industry turbulence, while they should converge under higher industry concentration and higher industry growth.

Relating back to the example of Borders', Borders' ultimate failure was partly due to its inability to respond more aggressively to Amazon's digital business initiatives by developing similar capabilities. A competitive response of convergence, to catch up in its IT capabilities to its main competitor may have served Borders better than the differentiating response that it chose in this particular case.

Borders would have been better off following a behavior characterized as the "red queen effect" in which firms try to match or exceed rivals' actions. The red queen effect from a conversation between the Red Queen and Alice in a famous children's story by Lewis Carroll's "Through the Looking Glass" provides a useful metaphor to understand today's competitive markets. The Red Queen's remark to Alice that "...it takes all the running you can do, to keep in the same place...if you want to get somewhere else, you must run at least twice as fast as that" is particularly instructive. The "red queen" idea is an appropriate metaphor for the notion of hypercompetition; a phenomenon characterized by high industry clock-speeds or churns rates, and low durations of market leadership. As the overall economy becomes more information-intensive, this affects other than just the technology-intensive industries.

For example, Target is now trying to play catch-up with Amazon and spending about as much of its $2.3 billion capital budget on IT, apps and supply chain management as it is spending on offline assets such as opening or remodeling stores (interestingly, Target was outsourcing its website to Amazon at one point).[56] Likewise, Wal-Mart is playing a catch-up with Amazon in online sales that are only about 2% of Wal-Mart's revenues in 2013.[57]

Applying the red queen idea to the context of IT, many IT investments are externally observable—especially when manifested as products, services, or consumer-facing channels (ATMs, web sites, etc.) that are highly publicized. In addition, technological advances in IT, as well as broadly administered surveys that measure annual firm IT investment (aggregated at industry levels), are published in trade magazines. Hence, it is possible for firms to observe the industry norm in IT investments and formulate appropriate strategies in terms of differentiating from or imitating the industry norm.

Because IT investments can help firms to create a competitive advantage or render old advantages obsolete, firms should take appropriate IT investment decisions to shield themselves against the erosion of competitive advantage. Notably, while the strategic posture of a firm influences IT investments, it does not by itself affect firm performance. Results suggest that IT strategic posture and outsourcing strategic posture influence financial performance through their influence on IT investments. Outsourcing strategies of firms matter because firms that allocated less to IT outsourcing compared to their peers in the prior period have higher IT investments in the next period. The effect of IT investment on firm performance is attenuated in more dynamic industries but amplified in high-growth industries. This finding underscores the importance of IT investments as a strategic lever that more directly influences firm performance. Therefore, firms need to be aware of the role of the industry environment in influencing IT investment levels, and consider whether their IT investment levels are driven by a coherent strategy or by a tendency to simply react piecemeal to the industry environment. All other things being equal, it is important for executives to avoid path dependence and "focus on knitting" when their historical strategies do not synchronize with the competitive environment.

1.6 Chapter Summary

Managers are in the business of making profits. In turn, profits are a function of superior judgment and insight. Realizing that IT can be used as a powerful lever for change and improved profitability can provide a competitive advantage to the firm. As such, the notion of IT as a more novel and potentially differentiating resource is gaining considerable importance compared with more traditional resources such as advertising or R&D.

The ADROIT acronym provides an easy way to understand the broader role of IT in creating and sustaining competitive advantage by parsing the value created by IT into six components: adding volume or growth, differentiating or increasing willingness-to-pay, reducing costs, optimizing risks, improving industry attractiveness or innovating by generating and deploying knowledge and other resources and capabilities, and transforming business models and business processes. IT is changing strategic thinking in fundamental ways and now allows the unbundling of businesses that have traditionally been organized together. This change is evident in many industries such as credit cards and newspapers. IT can provide competitive advantage even in industries that have nothing to do with IT or are classified as non–IT intensive, such as cement and paper.

Given IT's potential to affect performance favorably if managed well, or to bankrupt a firm if managed poorly, business leaders must formulate and execute their strategies using IT. They must proactively engage with IT-related decision making and not leave it only to the IT department. At the same time, they should involve IT professionals in strategy discussions much sooner than they currently do so that IT can shape strategy just as it is shaped by strategy.

Chapter 2: Digital Strategies for Digital Businesses and Markets

"Scale now trumps differentiation."

—Van Alstyne, Parker and Choudary (2016)

This chapter focuses on digital strategies for digital businesses and markets that are becoming increasingly pervasive in today's economy. We will discuss why digital businesses (firms that sell digital or information goods or connect users using digital networks or platforms) are different from conventional businesses. How should one approach pricing for digital goods? How should one approach strategy for competing in platform and networked markets during entry and mature phases?

2.1 Digital Goods and Digital Businesses

How do digital goods and digital businesses differ from conventional goods and businesses? Do we need new approaches for regulation and technology management for digital goods and digital businesses?

To make sense of these questions, we begin with some definitions and concepts. Almost all goods that we experience are some combinations of atoms (A) and bits (B), and can be described by a combination represented by A, B and P where P represents Price. As discussed in chapter 1, increasing digitization of the economy means bits replacing atoms or complementing atoms.

Broadly speaking, digital or information goods are those that *can be* described by strings of 1s and 0s (or bits). They are a collection of symbols and their utility depends on the arrangement of symbols, instead of physical containers that sometimes envelope or represent these symbols. For example, music or movies are information goods, even though the physical form (e.g., cassettes, CDs or DVDs) they were earlier associated with have now almost lost relevance and as consumers we can simply download symbols in the form of bits or bytes over the Internet.

In terms of their economic properties, digital goods are different from atom-centric businesses in that they exhibit high first copy costs and economies of scale, are experience goods and can be considered public goods from a policy perspective. We consider these in turn.

2.1.1 High fixed costs, economies of scale and increasing returns on scale

First, let us consider the property of high fixed costs, economies of scale, and increasing returns on scale. Many information goods have very high fixed costs (or first copy costs) and very low or almost zero marginal or replication costs. In other words, they do not suffer from the curse of diseconomies of scale that characterizes conventional businesses. For example, steel and cement plants have a minimum efficient scale, below which or beyond which, the average cost of producing a ton of steel or cement is higher than it would be if the plant had the minimum efficient scale. The cost curves for steel or cement plants first show economies of scale and beyond a point show diseconomies of scale.

In contrast, because of almost zero marginal costs and presence of network effects (or network externalities that arise because of positive feedback), digital goods can serve almost the 100% of the world-wide demand with their economies of scale. This begins to explain why we often see only one dominant firm in digital businesses, while multiple firms co-exist in conventional businesses. One implication of this property is that it may be possible for a company to have almost 100% market share without hurting consumer interests, if the company is not misusing its monopoly power to squeeze suppliers or for "tying" products.

Another implication of this economic property for digital goods businesses is that in the event of perfect competition for digital goods, market prices will be driven to near zero marginal costs making it difficult to recoup very high fixed costs. This may explain why digital businesses often become bankrupt or fail at very high rates if they cannot find a way to monetize their content and services in the face of competition with free "substitutes". Indeed, many newspapers and magazines have shut down or downscaled their operations in the face of competition with "free" or "inferior" content. In some cases, serious journalism has also been a casualty. Therefore, firms use value-based pricing or differential pricing by either finding identifiable markets or by versioning.

2.1.2 Experience Goods

Second, digital goods are experience goods, in that their quality or value is harder to describe or evaluate before consuming them (Shapiro and Varian argue that "information is an experience good every time it's consumed", example: consuming a story in *Wall Street Journal*). Contrast this with search goods whose quality or value can be described or evaluated before consuming them (think of stock price), and credence goods whose quality or value cannot be described or evaluated even after consuming them (think of complex brain or liver surgery).

An implication of this property is that valuations or willingness-top-pay (WTP) for digital goods vary significantly because of quality uncertainty. Therefore, digital businesses have to find a way to provide credible signals about quality through branding, reputation and differentiation efforts. Firms often use free samples, promotional pricing, and testimonials to signal quality and entice buyers to try their quality before buying.

2.1.3 Like Public Goods

A third property of digital goods is that they are like public goods in that their consumption is largely nonrival (my value from reading a Kindle book does not diminish your value of owning or reading it) and largely nonexcludable (it may be costly to prevent others from using say WiFi, just like preventing others from using Lighthouse, National defense, or radio broadcast like NPR).

It is because of this public goods nature of digital goods that information goods need some protection for their intellectual property to recoup their costs and digital goods industries often end up in court fights with regulators or competitors. Is that enough to suggest that conventional tools for intellectual property (IP) protection such as patents (granted for novelty and usefulness), trademarks (distinctive symbols), copyright (granted for original work of authorship) and trade secrets are not suitable for digital goods? Do we need new ways of thinking about balancing public and private interests?

2.2 Digital Businesses

Turning now to digital businesses, we can define digital businesses as those that sell digital goods (as opposed to physical goods) or that connect users using digital markets or platforms. For example, Google, Match and Facebook connect or match users searching for information or relationships with advertisers or content providers.

Digital businesses are different from conventional businesses in several ways in terms of industry structures, evolutionary paths and valuations. First, digital businesses exhibit very different and highly concentrated industry structures. In contrast to many conventional industries which follow 3 plus or minus 1 rule (think of Big 3 auto players in the US such as GM, Ford and Chrysler; and Coke/Pepsi as being dominant in soda drinks), digital businesses are characterized by winner-take-all (WTA) markets. They seem to have room for only one dominant player, as exemplified by dominance of

Microsoft, Google and Apple when it comes to computer operating system, search, and retail music, respectively.

Second, digital businesses follow unusual evolutionary paths and are sometimes characterized by economies of scope, in contrast to relatively more focused conventional businesses. Consider the evolution of Amazon.com from selling books to now selling almost everything that one can think of, and becoming a dominant platform for connecting consumers with many small retailers. Likewise, Google has diversified into many areas beyond its initial search offering; it changed its name to Alphabet to reflect its conglomerate nature.

Third, digital businesses and platforms enjoy very high valuations, coupled with very high variations in valuations. Often firms with zero revenues or profits are valued in billions of dollars. The variation in values is partly because of large variations in WTP of users.

Because of these differences between conventional and digital businesses, it is important to understand how firms or entrepreneurs must adapt their strategies for digital businesses. They have to grapple with at least three sets of issues: how to price information goods, understanding the economics of platforms and networks, and how to craft based strategies for platforms and networks. I consider each in turn.

2.3 Pricing Information Goods

We discussed earlier that in a competitive market, prices of perfect substitutes will be driven to marginal cost, implying that firms will be unable to recover their fixed costs. Clearly, firms would like to avoid this situation and differentiate themselves by developing some form of monopoly power through lock-in, personalized pricing, versioning, bundling and network effects. We consider these in turn.

Firms often use lock-in strategies such as use of long-term contracts (recall Verizon or AT&T contracts), loyalty programs (frequent flier programs), proprietary data formats (.xls or .doc extensions), reputation mechanisms (e.g., ratings by consumers or readers), personalization (Amazon.com), and community features (e.g., Facebook). The key idea is to create loyalty among customers so that they become less price sensitive or do not switch to competitors. In contrast to physical goods which exhibit declining lock-in over time, information goods often show stronger lock-in effects over time due to network effects or because of relationships with other users.

Just as incumbents try to create lock-in, competitors try to find ways of overcoming lock-in. This can be done by developing closer substitutes, while taking care to avoid direct price competition and churn. Companies often lure customers away by giving them incentives to switch, and facilitate switching by developing converters or adapters, and encouraging open standards. When none of these strategies work or in combination with other strategies, competitors also use law-suits to take on incumbents.

When it comes to pricing, firms have options. They can use personalized pricing (known as first-degree price discrimination), and charge each customers what he or she is willing to pay. This can be a good policy but needs care because it can backfire and may result in bad public relations as Amazon.com discovered when some alleged the company to be testing this pricing strategy.

Alternatively, they can use versioning (second-degree price discrimination) by offering multiple products and let customers self-select the version that helps to maximize surplus. This strategy requires use of some form of quality differentiation. It involves developing different versions based on capability, speed, convenience, annoyance (banner ads, pop-ups), quality, customer support, flexibility (number of machines on which you can install software), and interface (e.g., different versions of Stata for statistical analyses, hardcover versus paperback or Kindle version) or timeliness of news or information (e.g., stock quotes). How many versions are right? The answer depends but in most cases using three versions works, following the Golden mean or Goldilocks pricing (aversion to extremes). The key is to ensure that premium customers are not able to reverse engineer from the lower-end version.

Sometimes companies offer a free version to build awareness and once customers become familiar or dependent, charge them for upgrades after a free trial period or for upgrade to a better product. An alternative way to make money from free is to create network and make money from complements or the other side of the market (e.g., Adobe). Sometimes companies offer free products to limit competitive entry or to signal a threat (Microsoft gave away Internet Explorer to counter Netscape, Sun offering Java to limit Microsoft's influence on operating system, Google Docs to compete with Microsoft Office).

Although versioning is a general idea, it is particularly suitable for software goods because it is so much easier to create multiple versions and added value of versioning becomes higher because of potentially heterogeneous customer base. When versioning, it may help to design for the high-end and subtract for other segments, accentuate differences across segments and price accordingly, recognize complementarities and upsell possibilities, avoid cannibalization to protect high-end, and follow Goldilocks principle.

Finally, bundling strategy may be an attractive solution when high and low valuations for individual goods in a bundle average out and the bundle has more consumers with "moderate" valuations. This follows from the Law of Large Numbers in statistics. Often, it may be easier for sellers to predict consumers' willingness-to-pay for the bundle than for the individual components within the bundle. However, bundling can be costly and massive bundling may work when components are nearly costless. In a way, bundling allows aggregation which can be done on multiple dimensions: site licensing (aggregation across users), subscriptions (aggregation across time), and combinations of different aggregation dimensions (library subscription for a database for all students of a University for a year).

2.4 Platforms and Networks

Contemporary economy is characterized by prevalence of networks that connect distinct groups of users.[58] Some call the products and services that connect users in two-sided networks as platforms, each side in such networks can incurs costs and provide revenues (unlike traditional value chains where one side incurs costs and the other side provides revenues). Platforms can be classified in terms of their structure (e.g., proprietary [Apple Macintosh], shared [Visa], joint venture [Hulu], licensor [American licensing MBNA for issuing cards]) or primary function in terms of whether they provide connectivity (email network), variety (ATMs), matching (real estate brokerage firms, dating sites), or price setting (securities exchanges).

Conceptually, one-sided networks are those where transaction partners alternate roles such as buying or selling as in trading, or sending or receiving emails as in an email network. However, in two-sided networks, users are typically "permanent" members of one distinct group on one side of the network. For example, once can think of cardholders and merchants in credit-card network, job seekers and employers in a LinkedIn network and software developers and users in an operating system or app platform context. Likewise, one can think of newspaper subscribers and advertisers as forming two distinct sides of a network for say Wall Street Journal or Times of India. Three-sided will have three distinct users, for example, content providers, advertisers and consumers in the YouTube platform.

Note that a two-sided network has four network effects: two same-side effects and two cross-side effects and each of these effects can be positive or negative (many economists refer to the same- and cross-side network effects as "direct" and "indirect" network effects). Because of network effects, the phenomenon that one group attracts the other (e.g., presence of buyers attracting sellers), successful platforms often exhibit returns to scale. Direct network effects can arise in settings where value of a network depends on communication among users (fax machine), sharing of information among users (e.g. Word, Excel), volume of user-generated content, and number of exchange partners as in trading exchanges. Indirect network effects arise when value depends on quality and variety of complementary services. For example, a larger number of Windows users attracts a larger number of developers for Windows-based applications.[59]

Note that network effects are typically demand-related scale economies where average revenue or demand increases with scale because they influence revenue side through user adoption and willingness to pay of users. They are conceptually distinct from supply-related scale economies where average costs decrease with scale as a result of spreading fixed costs over larger sales volume or due to learning by doing.

Markets with network effects exhibit multiple equilibria such that willingness to pay peaks at a certain network size with a "critical mass": product becomes successful beyond this network size due to positive feedback effects, and product never takes off if network size never reaches a critical mass of adoption.

2.5 Strategies for Platforms and Networks

Designing strategies for two-sided networks when products exhibit network effects requires a consideration of at least three factors: pricing, consideration of winner-take-all (WTA) competition, and envelopment. Consider pricing first. Typically, two-sided networks have a "subsidy" side and a "money" side and the challenge for managers is to decide how much to subsidize one side to attract users on the money side by creating strong cross-side network effects.

These considerations should take into account "same-side" network effects which can be positive (my buying a fax machine or a phone makes your fax machine or phone more valuable) or negative (more suppliers may mean more competition). To get pricing right, managers should think about issues related to capturing cross-side network effects, users' price sensitivity, users' quality sensitivity, output costs, same side network effects, and users' brand value ("marquee" users).

Digital Intelligence

The second issue is WTA dynamics which requires understanding whether market will be served by a single platform or not; and then determining whether to fight for dominance or share the platform. Single platforms become likely when multi-homing is costly for at least one user side, network effects are strong and positive at least for the users on the side with multi-homing costs, and neither side has a strong preference for special features. Commitment to winning the WTA battle requires at least four factors: differentiation or cost advantage, pre-existing relationships with users, prior reputation for success (e.g., Microsoft), and deep pockets.

Note that homing costs are different from switching costs, even though these costs often move together (some exceptions are eBook Readers or email where multi-homing costs may be low but switching may be costly because you may have to notify all your contacts or change your library of books). One should focus on multi-homing costs to answer whether a new market will be served by a single platform, and focus on switching costs when deciding whether to race to acquire network users, and focus on both multi-homing and switching costs to predict whether an established platform is vulnerable to displacement by another platform.

Sharing the platform may be a sensible decision if a firm is not sure of its superiority and resources to prevail, doing so may also be less risky in terms of savings in marketing costs and potentially larger market due to presence of a shared platform that may create faster user adoption by removing uncertainty due to standards war.

The third important factor is threat due to envelopment from "adjacent" platform providers, particularly those that have a multiplatform bundle. This threat is particularly strong when technologies change rapidly leading to convergence and blurring of boundaries between products and industries. However, focused firms have a chance to survive by changing business models (change the money side or to become a systems integrator), partner with a "bigger" brother, and sue competitors.

Network effects (or demand-related scale economies) are sometimes measured by Metcalfe's law, which suggests that the value of a one-to-one or transactional network is roughly equal to the square of the number of nodes or users in a network (in its precise form, value is proportional to [N X (N-1)] which approaches N squared when N is very large). Sometimes, this law is used to explain very high valuations of networked businesses. Some invoke Reed's law to justify even higher valuations for many-to-many networks whose value is proportional to 2 to the power N when N is very large.[60]

However, in real world, diminishing returns are likely to set in and the value of a network is likely to increase with network size but at a decreasing rate due to factors such as constraints on budget and attention, and the increase in size may come with inferior quality of users or nodes. Together, these factors imply that WTP per capita may not be same across all users and transaction volumes per capita may not increase as the network size grows. Therefore, caution is necessary when applying Metcalfe's Law or Reed's Law to assess value of a network. Indeed, many B2B exchanges and even AOL did not come to enjoy the high valuations that a literal application of Reed's Law may have promised (Reed himself used these examples in his Harvard Business Review article in 2001).

Expectations about projected size of the network and homing costs (initial, recurring and termination expenses to affiliate with a platform) also play a role in determining whether a network will take off or not. Uncertainty about technology, consumer demand, business models and fragmentation of demand with heterogeneous users can lead users to defer their purchase or joining leading to the "excess inertia" or "Penguin problem" where "no one moves unless everyone moves, so no one moves."

One of the reasons for such excess inertia is network externalities, where externality is defined as a benefit or a harm experienced by a party due to the actions (or inaction) or another party, with no compensating payment between the parties. Positive externalities arise when I benefit from your actions even though I do not pay you anything for such benefits (e.g., everyone gets vaccinated), and negative externalities arise when I am hurt by your actions even though you don't compensate me for such harm (e.g., secondary smoking).

To overcome penguin problem, firms can internalize externalities by providing temporary or permanent subsidies or side payments to some users, create exclusive relationships with some marquee users, vertically integrate or morph into a platform to avoid chicken and egg problem, and race to acquire early adopters or users offering below cost penetration pricing or through significant marketing expenditures by burning cash. Note that penetration pricing works in both 1-sided and 2-sided networks, while permanent subsidies only apply to 2-sided networks.

One key decision is whether to fight for dominating a market or whether to share? Fighting for market dominance for a WTA market depends on estimation of market size, market share and margins. Competing for the market versus competing in the market depends on expectations about WTA outcome, how much investments may be needed to achieve WTA outcome in one's favor and edge over competition vis-a-vis the split of benefits in a shared platform accounting for any costs and free-rider problems. Managing consumer expectation is an important consideration in the fight to achieve a critical mass or in competing to become the standard, and firms use competitive "pre-announcements" and other tactics to manage expectations and stifle competition.

Firms frequently share platforms when they worry about penguin effect, WTA outcome, balkanization, and outside threats. However, they are pulled apart by countervailing factors that affect appropriability of platform rent; these include concerns about too many rivals, desire to incorporate own technology in the standard or to differentiate a standardized product, friction between intellectual property owners and free riders, and propensity to form coalitions to exclude close rivals.

The life of a strategist is not easy. Even in matured markets one has to worry about threat of envelopment, or entry by another platform that combines target's functionality in a multi-platform bundle leveraging common components and/or shared user relationships. This can be viewed as another form of bundling mainly to deter or compete with stand-alone competitors, in contrast to bundling as a price discrimination mechanism.

Bundling can be a very effective strategy because it may confer both pricing advantage and cost efficiencies (think of Microsoft Office bundle that includes Word, Excel, Powerpoint and Access). To some extent, bundling can allow an aggregator with mediocre component technologies to win over stand-alone suppliers of superior component technologies posing a challenge for innovation policy. On the other hand, because larger bundles benefit more from adding more components and services, that may prompt larger bundlers to spend more on in-house development or to bid more for new goods created by third parties. Bundling can also be used to deny rivals access to strong complementary technologies, to neutralize emerging threats before they become serious.

If the life of a strategist is difficult, so is the life of a regulator that tries to protect consumer interests, provide a level-playing field for entrepreneurs to compete and to ensure sufficient incentives for innovation. In the past, regulators have focused on prohibiting practices that can restrict trade or competition through cartels, predatory pricing, tying, price gouging, refusing to deal on fair terms and by merging with large competitors to reduce competition and consumer welfare.

Some of the underlying ideas made sense for atom-centric businesses where monopolies often resulted in higher prices and lower market coverage given the existence of minimum efficient scale. However, how should regulators approach market concentration when that dominance is due to consumer-driven network effects? The debate on this issue is far from settled.

2.6 Chapter Summary

This chapter explained why digital or information goods differ from conventional or physical goods in terms of their economic properties such as high fixed costs but almost zero marginal costs, increasing returns on scale, and their experience and public good nature. Because of some of these differences, digital businesses exhibit have unusually different industry structure and such industries have high market concentration, very high but uncertain valuations, and unusual evolutionary paths.

In turn, these factors make it imperative to approach strategy differently in such markets. In particular, managers need to understand how to price information goods, and how to craft strategies for platforms and networks.

First, pricing decisions should not be based only on marginal costs; firms should differentiate from competition by creating lock-in, and using personalized pricing, versioning, bundling and charging the "money" side considering network effects.

Second, designing strategies when products exhibit network effects requires a consideration of winner-take-all (WTA) competition, and envelopment. While firms should try to get-big-fast if they have inherent competitive advantage and anticipate winner-take-all outcomes that are likely when multi-homing is costly for at least one user side, network effects are strong and positive at least for the users on the side with multi-homing costs, and neither side has a strong preference for special features. However, a strategy of sharing the platform may be wiser if it promises potentially larger market due to presence of a shared platform that may create faster user adoption by removing uncertainty due to standards war and doing so may also be less risky in terms of savings in marketing costs.

The discussion in this chapter also suggests that regulating digital goods industries is by no means easy; such industries present thorny issues for regulators in striking a balance between providing incentives to entrepreneurs for innovation, while ensuring a level-playing field for competitors, and ensuring that consumers are not hurt.

Chapter 3: Navigating Digital Innovations and Transformations

"The further backward you look, the further forward you can see"

> —Winston Churchill, quoted in Kurzweil (2006, beginning of Chapter 2)

"Everything under heavens is in utter chaos; the situation is excellent"

> —Chairman Mao (quoted in Clissold 2006)

Thus far, I have discussed the importance of synchronizing IT with strategy, and how managers should approach strategies for digital goods and businesses. But the world of technology is forever changing. Just as the launch of Sputnik in 1957 unleashed significant activity and upheaval in space exploration, advances in IT that began around the same time are continuing to transform industries. Steve Jobs alone is credited with transforming at least six industries (personal computers, animated movies, music, phones, tablet computing, and digital publishing) from 1976 to 2011.[61] There are always new technologies on the horizon, and some of them have significant implications for innovation, industry transformation, and firm survival. How can one make sense of these emerging technologies and innovations? How should one think about transformations and manage them?

71

3.1 Transformations: Definition and Quickening Pace

What is your definition of transformation? How does it reflect a departure from a more evolutionary change? Most transformations involve the displacement of old players or their relative position. An example of transformation in the retail industry is the replacement of Sears by Wal-Mart. Likewise, transformation of book retailing are evident in the displacement of Barnes & Noble and Borders by Amazon.com. Transformation of music distribution is evident in the displacement of Tower Records by Apple's iTunes store.

Transformations also involve the redefinition of industries or sometimes the creation of new industry spaces, such as online markets. Wal-Mart and Amazon.com redefined industry boundaries and industry spaces. Apple dropped the word "Computer" from its name in the early 2000s when it realized that its offerings were far broader than the computer industry.[62]

Almost every generation complains that the pace of transformation is quickening, and every generation has witnessed greater transformation than previous generations did. But is there truth to such perceptions? There is some evidence that the pace of transformation has accelerated over the years. It took 4000 years from the invention of writing to Roman-era codex of bound pages to replace scrolls, 1000 years from codex to movable-type printed books, 500 years from the printed press to the Internet, and only 15 years from widespread adoption of Internet in 1995 to the launch of the iPad in 2010.[63] As another example, monopoly time for new products has become shorter since the last century. Duration of complete first-mover monopoly decreased from 33 years (for products introduced between 1887 and 1906) to 3.4 years (for products introduced between 1967 and 86).[64]

3.2 Technology and Transformations

Technology and transformations go hand-in-hand, and radical changes in technologies often cause significant transformations in business activities. It took the emergence of newer transportation and communication technologies (e.g., railways, the telegraph, the telephone) and newer sources of energy (e.g., coal) to catalyze the growth of the modern multiunit enterprise. [65]

IT-enabled transformation can be viewed at multiple levels: individual, process, occupation, organization, firm or business unit, industry, or country.

Transformations at the individual level are evident from cradle to grave—from the moment a baby is born to who will have access to a person's passwords after his or her death, and even presence in Second Life (see Appendix 1.A). Like death and taxes, IT appears to be a force that escapes none. As individuals, we consumed nearly 34 GB of information every day in 2009, an increase of approximately 350% over nearly three decades. [66] This is far more information than we consumed even ten years back or what our parents' generation did or our predecessors ever thought was possible.

Certainly, this is far beyond what James Rothschild could ever imagine. In 1850s, James Rothschild complained that it was a "crying shame that the telegraph has been established," because that suddenly allowed anyone to get news. [67] Rothschild worried that the telegraph would create a situation in which people would have "too much to think about when bathing," which he did not consider a good thing. Rothschild was a businessman who built a banking empire using private couriers on ponies; his empire grew as he moved from one European city to another to profit from market-moving news about business and trade. The telegraph, with its capability for instant communication, threatened this business model and was a disruptive force. Rothschild was not alone in his view of adapting to new technologies, particularly when it also threatens a person's living (Al Gore, for example, has made a similar point about opposition to science regarding climate change). Later, Western Union and AT&T demonstrated similar resistance to changes and innovations. AT&T argued against new handsets because they could potentially disrupt or explode its network. That did not happen; in fact, the world of telecommunications witnessed significant innovations after 1984 when AT&T was finally broken up.[68]

At the process level, transformation is evident in breaking with the silos of the past. Most progressive firms define their key business processes in cross-functional terms rather than in terms of functional areas, something that was common until the late 1980s, just before enterprise resource planning (ERP) systems became more widespread in the 1990s.

At the occupation level, IT is destroying old occupations and creating others. For example, there is less need for travel agents, secretaries, or price checkers in today's world. The term "word processor" now means a software program like Microsoft Word, but it used to be an occupation that employed thousands of workers. IT has also created new occupations. For example, someone has to police entries on eBay or Match.com for offensive or objectionable items, images, or nudity.

At the industry level, the Internet has affected industry structure by creating new industries (e.g., online auctions and digital marketplaces such as eBay) and, more important, has reconfigured existing industries (e.g., distance education, distant tutoring, video rentals, online banking). Earlier, I discussed how industry boundaries are becoming fuzzier, with some prominent examples including Apple and Google. IT is blurring the distinction between "atoms and bits," breaking with the need to trade off between reach and range, informing physical and information processes and value chains, and making conventional value chains irrelevant.[69]

At the organizational level, IT has transformed virtually every functional area, from accounting (from a firm-level annual to a customer-level daily or transactional basis), to marketing (customer-level profitability or customer lifetime value), to human resources (LinkedIn) and procurement (reverse auctions).

At the national level, the U.S. economy has been transformed by IT. Other countries are also witnessing a similar revolution. Among emerging economies, the Indian economy is undergoing a significant transformation enabled by information and communication technologies. [70]

3.3 Phases in Transformation

What are different phases in transformation? How do transformations begin?

Transformations have at least three phases: trigger, experimentation and shakeout. Typically, most transformations are have their trigger or origin in technology, consumer tastes, regulation, and entrepreneurial activity prompted by leaders, entrants or competition. Regarding technology as a trigger, the changes brought about by information technology are evident across virtually all sectors of the economy. [71] Changes in consumer tastes explain the transition from CDs to iTunes. Deregulation of the airline industry in the United States brought significant changes in its wake. Evidence from emerging economies such as China and India also indicates the transformational role of government regulation (or lack thereof) in business activities. Some people anticipate significant transformations in the U.S. health care system in the wake of implementing the Obama Administration's proposed health care reforms. The role of entrepreneurs is evident in the changes brought about by Steve Jobs, arguably entrepreneurs often use newer technologies or combinations of existing technologies to their advantage to bring about transformations.

The prime focus here is on technology. Day and Schoemaker (2000b) distinguish between emerging and established technologies, arguing that emerging technologies have a much greater ambiguity regarding technology, infrastructure, markets/customers, and industry than established technologies. [72] But it must also be recognized that technology alone is insufficient to bring about a transformation. Successful transformations require managerial choices and actions. For example, almost all the technologies related to FedEx's business were already in place, but it took Fred Smith to develop a business model around those technologies. Apple's iPod is another example of technology being combined with managerial choices and innovations.

The most important transformation triggers are those that affect the relative position of players. Dramatic changes in relative position do not come from operational excellence alone; operational excellence only shifts the productivity frontier. Truly transforming changes confront existing companies with difficult trade-offs; if there are no trade-offs, such a technological change merely shifts the productivity frontier.

The next phase after the trigger phase is experimentation, which involves a trial-and-error search for a new formula for competitive success. In this phase, many players compete for key markets with alternative technologies and standards. Alliances act as information conduits, and capital providers, such as venture capitalists, play an important role in this phase, which is characterized by risk and a lack of information. The dilemma is whether to improve relative position but undermine future industry structure. The RFID, smartphone, e-book reader, and movie rental markets are just some that are currently in this phase.

The experimentation phase is followed by a shakeout phase, in which a dominant pattern emerges, only to be thwarted again by another trigger. Arguably, the online music industry experienced a shakeout after Apple entered with iPod and iTunes, making it a dominant player in the retail music space.

3.4 Managing Emerging Technologies and Transformations

Incumbents have always had a difficult time navigating transformations that involve emerging technologies. IT has made that even more difficult. History provides some excellent examples of this phenomenon. As discussed previously, James Rothschild complained back in the 1850s about the telegraph because that suddenly enabled anyone to get news, leading to his worry that people would have "too much to think about when bathing."

In 1887, Western Union, by then a dominant telegraph company, brushed off the threat posed by the telephone and turned down the chance to buy Bell's patent on telephone. The inventor himself saw the patent only as an "improvement on the telegraph."[73] Others have also fallen prey to such tendencies. The *New York Times*, for example, doubted television's "commercial value" in 1927. The jet engine was dismissed by the National Academy of Sciences as being impractical. The transistor was initially viewed as a way to develop better hearing aids for the deaf.

Likewise, AT&T resisted innovations for a long time and tried to avoid competition even for telephone sets for as long as it could until antitrust laws caught up with the company in the 1980s. AT&T was slow to recognize the significance of mobile phones in 1980s and 1990s because of a consulting report that predicted low demand for cell phones. According to an article, AT&T relied on a McKinsey report which predicted fewer than 1 million wireless users by 2000, the report was remarkably off and there were about 740 million actual users of wireless users in 2000.[74] More recently, local phone companies in the United States missed a chance to dominate the market for consumer broadband through their slow rollout of DSL because of their focus on more profitable landlines and T1 lines.[75] In contrast, cable companies moved much faster because they were worried about the threat from satellite television.

IBM has a history of such resistance behavior: It decided not to enter the mainframe business initially because of a 1948 forecast about a very low demand for computers (less than a dozen or so) based on the amount of computing done in the world at that time. It had a difficult time entering the PC business, and when it did, it made choices that later haunted the company. It also did not recognize Xerox's potential and refused to buy it; and it passed an opportunity to buy 10% of Intel's equity.[76]

Encyclopedia Britannica, a company founded in 1760s, lost to Encarta when Microsoft bundled it with its offerings. Borders outsourced its digital book-retailing strategy to Amazon.com, only to realize its mistake much later.

The same story plays out in the music industry (Tower Records), film industry (Kodak), and most recently with Microsoft in the browser and search business. Kodak, founded in 1880 and rated among the five most valuable brands in the world until the 1990s, built one of the first digital cameras in 1975 but failed to morph its business model in time.[77] The worldwide camera sales showed negligible quantities of digital cameras in 1995 but more than 20 million in 2005, overtaking sales of conventional film cameras. Microsoft reportedly killed its search engine project called Keywords in 2000 after two months of experimentation, before Google figured out a way to combine search with advertising, fearing that this new business "would cannibalize other revenue streams."[78] It also thwarted plans to buy Overture in 2003, which was eventually bought by Yahoo. Some suggest that Yahoo too made a mistake early on when it preferred its lower quality search to better performing Google search because it wanted surfers to stick around on its own website even if that did not provide the most relevant search results to users.

Not all the missteps related to emerging technologies and industry transformations can be blamed on managerial arrogance or ignorance. Industry changes happen slowly at times and are brought about by forces that are below incumbents' radars.[79]

Do incumbents always lag when it comes to emerging technologies? The answer is "no," and to understand this, some make a distinction between sustaining and "disruptive" innovations. I must forewarn the readers that despite the hype that "disruptive innovations" have received, there are significant questions about the underlying ideas and the key premises, and stories in the trade press have also provided anecdotal evident against the hype associated with the label "disruption".[80]

Incumbents are usually good at managing transformations that pertain to sustaining technologies, Tushman and Anderson (1986) characterize such technologies as "competence-enhancing." These are the technologies that current dominant customers value. Even if there is a radical discontinuous change in these technologies and it does not threaten the business models of incumbents, chances are that incumbents will find a way to succeed with such transformations.[81]

More difficult, however, are the transformations that pertain to what are known as "disruptive" innovations, or "competence-destroying."[82] According to proponents of theory of disruptive innovation, disruptive innovations are those whose performance trajectory is typically below the current market needs and far below the performance trajectory of the sustaining innovations. Typically, these innovations are not valued by mainstream customers, and they have lower profit margins initially. Disruptive innovations arise because of a simple dynamic: Technologies almost always improve more quickly than the ability of humans and markets to absorb those technologies.

Think about the percentage of the Microsoft Excel program's features that you actually use. Excel was not always as sophisticated as it is now; it started with relatively rudimentary functionalities. Because Excel is so much more complex than the needs of most customers, it has created an opportunity for Google to offer its relatively simple Google Docs for those who do not need more sophisticated functionalities. In that sense, Google Docs is a disruptive innovation for Microsoft because it would be difficult for Microsoft to give away Excel for free, although of late Microsoft is trying to counter that threat by incorporating some Google Doc–like features into Office 2010 and Office 365. In the same way, open-source software, such as Linux (operating system) and MySQL (relational database), pose significant challenges for Microsoft and Oracle, respectively (MySQL has now been acquired by Oracle).

Disruptive innovations are different from radical discontinuous sustaining innovations. The latter make quantum improvements in the technology trajectory but do not create heart-wrenching trade-offs for incumbents in the same way that disruptive innovations do. For example, Internet explorer (a browser) was a radical but sustaining innovation for Microsoft, but Java is disruptive because it makes Microsoft's operating system less valuable.

The "disruptive" part here refers to a technology's potential to disrupt the way current industry players make money and limit their ability to thwart entrants that are not vested in current industry practices or business models. That is one of the critical downsides of disruptive innovations—namely, it brings new types of competitors that have no regard for the current set of rules. Incumbent music players had a difficult time dealing with Apple because Apple was not vested in $15 music CDs. Blockbuster had a difficult time competing with Netflix because Netflix was not wedded to the idea of charging late fees, and its business model did not depend on late fees.

Appendix 2.A shows some recent examples of emerging technologies that may lead to industry transformations or appearance of new business models.

3.4.1 Managing transformations as incumbents

Incumbents and in particular large organizations such as the ones in Fortune 500 rankings contribute a high share of GDP, but they also suffer from high mortality rates and difficulty in transforming themselves. The Fortune 500 firms accounted for more than 70 percent of the GDP of the United States in 2014, based on 2015 rankings. It is said that incumbents tend to suffer from "baby elephant syndrome" which refers to the idea that baby elephants that are chained in circuses in their early days find it hard to overcome the imaginary constraints of those chains even when they grow much larger in size.[83]

Organizations are no different, what makes them successful at one time also creates notions that they are unable to overcome even when such notions become irrelevant. For example, more than 50% Fortune 500 firms in 1995 list were off that list in 2015. Examples of companies such as Kodak, Blockbuster, Borders and A&P are a sobering reminder of the difficulties in transforming organizations. IT has made managing disruptive technologies (particularly those related to IT) even more difficult by blurring the distinction between "atoms and bits," breaking with the need to trade-off between reach and range, informing physical and information processes and value chains, and making conventional value chains irrelevant.[84]

How should incumbents approach emerging technologies, and what are some critical questions they must ask? Proponents of theory of disruption offer some prescriptions. First, determine whether the technology is competence-enhancing versus competence-destroying, or what Christensen calls as sustaining versus disruptive innovations. This can be done by considering the performance trajectories of technologies and the absorptive capacity of the market. One clue, according to some, is that marketing and finance personnel rarely support disruptive technologies because their incentives are more closely aligned with success of existing business, while technical personnel do.[85] Disagreements between these two groups can alert managers to the disruptive potential of a technology.

Second, incumbents should determine the strategic significance of a disruptive technology by asking the right questions of the right people. According to Christensen, the right question is whether the slope of improvement in a disruptive technology will overtake the slope of performance improvement demanded by the mainstream market—not whether the slope of improvement in a disruptive technology will overtake the slope of sustaining innovations in an existing technology. The right people are customers in fringe markets, not lead customers. These customers may be located currently in emerging markets, such as China and India, and/or at the bottom-of-the-pyramid and beyond the radar screens of managers. Although serving these customers can be challenging, they can provide opportunities for creating disruptive innovations for developed markets.[86]

Third, the initial market for an emerging technology must be located. Market research is sometimes not helpful for new products, as the examples of Xerox, Polaroid (100,000 total projected demand over the life cycle), and IBM show. Instead, one should locate and create the initial market for an emerging technology and then experiment rapidly, iteratively, and inexpensively with both the product and the market, as Amazon.com did.[87]

Finally, some argue that an independent organization should be used to build a business based on a disruptive technology. Note that it is not necessary to have a separate organization if the new technology is a sustaining technology or is so financially attractive that current organization will support it anyway. A separate organization is necessary when the disruptive technology has a lower profit margin than the mainstream business and serves unique needs of a new set of customers. A new organization helps create excitement about small orders and lower profits, while at headquarters big orders and profit margins may be needed to turn heads. A new organization also avoids other problems. For example, Kodak, before George Fisher, kept electronic imaging dispersed and mixed with chemical imaging, and its policies did not allow the hiring of better-paid IT employees because they would need larger salaries than chemical employees, who held sway at the moment.[88] Too much organizational separation should also be avoided because separation does not allow a new organization to benefit from the strengths of the parent, as the example of Xerox's PARC lab proves. IBM's personal computer division is another example of where there may have been too much separation.[89] It may be worthwhile to keep the disruptive organization independent even if it is successful at what it does. While reintegrating a unit back into the company may work for sustaining technologies because of scale and scope logic, it often fails for disruptive technologies because of arguments about which groups get certain resources. As Bower and Christensen (1995, p. 53) argue, "For the corporation to live, it must be willing to see the business units die. If the corporation doesn't kill them off itself, competitors will."

As I noted earlier, there remain fundamental questions about the very notion of "disruptive" innovations and underlying definitions, unit of analysis, rigor of research and predictive or prescriptive power. Hence caution is necessary to avoid over-interpreting recommendations or prescriptions coming from proponents of "theory" of disruption. Regardless of the validity or otherwise of the ideas related to disruption, managers must scan new technologies and think carefully about developing new capabilities and creating new organizational structures and incentives to make informed decisions on pilot programs or seed investments to avoid surprises.

A review of research and analyses of some cases suggests that established firms suffer from at least three traps when they face emerging technologies: (1) delayed participation and sticking with the familiar, (2) a reluctance to fully commit, and, (3) lack of persistence. Examples of companies such as Kodak, Borders and Barnes & Noble lend credence to these traps. For example, Borders and Blockbuster delayed investments in technologies and website to compete with the threat from Amazon.com and Netflix. Kodak had a hard time imagining a film-less future even though it invented the first digital camera in 1975. It stuck to its existing business model for far too long and failed to commit to new business models. Barnes & Noble did not show persistence and exited e-reader business prematurely only to re-enter again, even though it invested in that business before Amazon.com did.

How should firms deal with these traps? Day and Schoemaker suggest some solutions to deal with these traps: widening peripheral vision and creating a learning culture, staying flexible in strategic ways, and providing organizational autonomy First, firms should invest in widening peripheral vision, and creating a learning culture. This will require scanning emerging technologies, assessing their significance and launching pilot projects to be familiar with them. Second, firms should stay flexible in pursuing new and abandoning obsolete strategies and business models. However, these decisions should be data-driven and not based on superficial analyses and driven by fads such as pursuit of outsourcing due to mimetic tendencies or blindly following advice of consultants with a narrow view. Finally, providing organizational autonomy to new businesses based on emerging technologies may be a sensible idea if such ideas are hard to nurture within the enterprise due to turf-wars or lack of incentive alignment.[90]

3.4.2 Managing transformations as entrants

If incumbents have a difficult time managing disruptive technologies, so do entrants. They must decide between two ways of framing how they approach the disruptive innovation: technical framing and marketing framing.

Technical framing involves improving the features such that they become more acceptable to mainstream customers. Conversely, marketing framing would involve taking current technology as given and finding relevant unserved or underserved customer segments that are not catered to by the incumbents. Bottom-of-the-pyramid markets in emerging economies, but also in developed economies, are well suited for marketing-focused framing of disruptive innovations. General Electric, Panasonic, Tata Motors, and 3M are among some of the prominent companies that are trying to use reverse innovations or innovations in bottom-of-the-pyramid markets.

Technical versus marketing framing matters for competitive success. Some people argue that one reason for Kodak's failure was that it framed the issue as a technology problem to make digital camera performance similar to that of silver halide film. In contrast, entrants such as Canon were trying to sell what they had and thus framed the issue as a marketing problem. Similarly, Apple's Newton failed because of technology framing, whereas Palm Computing succeeded because of its marketing framing, which emphasized making do with simple, low-end applications.

3.5 A Four-Step Approach to Manage Emerging Technologies and Transformations

In what follows, I outline a four-step process for managing transformations.[91]

The first step involves conducting an industry analysis. The goal in this phase should be to identify potential triggers and distinguish transitory changes from those that are likely to be enduring.[92] For example, when the Internet came along, some people initially felt that artists in the music industry would go direct and that would weaken the power of music labels. That did not happen. A study of the music industry over the last hundred years would have shown such an outcome to be unlikely. Instead of a proliferation of music labels and artists on the Internet, industry structure did not change much, and if anything, it became more concentrated.

The second step involves focusing on the threat of substitute products and services. Here, it is necessary to pay particular attention to emerging technologies that are likely to be "competence destroying" or challenge the business model disruptive because these are the most difficult to cope with as an incumbent. However, for entrants, starting with these technologies can provide an important edge over incumbents, if the entrant can figure out whether a technology or marketing framing makes the most sense. Such markets are frequently at the bottom of the pyramid in emerging economies, but they also exist in developed economies.

The third step involves choosing a strategic posture. Do you want to shape, adapt, or reserve the right to play?[93] Some people advocate shaping strategies, which are becoming more viable due to changes in IT infrastructure, and mobilize several players for risk/reward sharing.[94] If shaping does not work, a choice should be made about what type of participant to be. Depending on risk appetite, a firm can be an influencer (e.g., Bank of America's early influence on the Visa shaping platform), a hedger (e.g., advertisers that participate in both Google AdSense and Microsoft's advertising platform), or a disciple (Dell's exclusive commitment to Wintel platform). When managing emerging technologies, be mindful of your behaviors and actions. Are you creating situations in which price becomes the key consideration, or are you allowing scope for differentiation and competing on non-price attributes? What is done in the early stages can shape the industry evolution and longer-term success.

The fourth step involves choosing portfolios of strategic actions and moves.[95] There are essentially three choices: big bets, options (selective flexibility and experimentation), and "no-regrets" moves. If you think you have a better grasp of the future than your competitors, go for the big bets, but beware that you could lose everything. This was the path that Sony followed to promote its Blue-ray standard to success when it was competing with HD-DVD standard promoted by Toshiba (Sony did lose an earlier battle for its Beta or Betamax standard against VHS standard promoted by JVC for videocassette recorder).[96] If you are less sure, consider launching three or four initiatives to hedge your bets. If you are not sure at all and neither are your competitors, invest in multiple small experiments with little attachment to any one experiment.

3.6 Chapter Summary

This chapter defined industry transformations and distinguished them from a more evolutionary change. The role of technology was discussed, particularly emerging technologies in industry transformations and why incumbents have a difficult time dealing with "competence destroying" or "disruptive" innovations, a particular class of emerging technologies.

How incumbents and entrants should think about IT-enabled transformations was also discussed. Avoid traps such as delayed participation and sticking with the familiar, a reluctance to fully commit, and lack of persistence. Some of the key prescriptions are to stay curious and keep abreast of new technologies, calibrate your response to them carefully, launching pilot projects or "dabbling" in new technologies to reduce technical uncertainties, and pay attention to timing because it is sometimes possible for a technology to be ahead of the market. In such cases, "waiting" may be appropriate till necessary complements or "killer apps" emerge.[97]

While this chapter provided some useful concepts to work with when it comes to thinking about emerging technologies and making sense of transformations, remember that no two transformations are alike, and heuristics based on the past or from a different context may not hold in future. So be prepared to navigate in new waters and to learn as you go along.[98] It may be worth remembering that in the end, technologies themselves rarely change or transform anything, it is thoughtful leadership and managerial actions that drive positive change. It may need some "craziness" and determination. Apple's "Think Different" commercial in 1997 is a particularly apt reminder: The people who are crazy enough to think they can change the world are the ones who do."

Part 2

Govern IT

Chapter 4: Governance of Digital Resources

"The road to hell is paved with good intentions."

—Source Unknown

Chapters in Part 1 focused on how to synchronize IT and strategy, how to develop strategies for digital goods and digital markets, and how to manage emerging technologies, IT innovations, and transformations.

Next comes the task of execution. Even if firms come up with the most brilliant plans and have the best intentions, they are only about as good as their execution, as the opening quotations to this section indicate. And the successful execution of plans requires attention to details. However, managers cannot attend to all the details and micro decisions themselves; thus, they must define how those micro decisions will be made in a way that is consistent with the organization's strategy. That is what governance does. Governance, as the link between strategy and execution, can help synchronize execution with strategy.

4.1 Why and What of Governance

Poor governance has been implicated in many failures and scandals involving businesses, universities, Wall Street, and even Vatican. Consider a few examples of poor governance resulting in failures, sometimes catastrophic. Enron was a very successful company in 2001; it had more than $100 billion in revenues and was declared one of the "most admired" companies several years in a row. Yet it almost suddenly failed, arguably because of poor governance. The financial crisis of 2008 was blamed on poor governance. Toyota's CEO cited the disconnect between the company's quality image and operational emphasis on growth as having led to massive recalls in 2010. Even the massive BP oil spill in the Gulf of Mexico in 2010 can be added to this list, in light of media reports suggesting problems in internal governance at BP. Finally, the ignition switch related problems at GM that led to massive recalls can be considered a manifestation of poor governance.

Among IT related examples relating to poor governance, dozens of companies restate their earnings, partly because of poor integration of their IT systems. Sometimes, firms put together their consolidated statements by combining data from hundreds of interlinked Excel sheets. The tragedy of 9/11 was partly blamed on poor governance of IT systems in the federal government. John Antioco, the former CEO of Blockbuster, blamed board's digital ignorance and dysfunctional governance for its subsequent bankruptcy. MF Global had a hard time tracing hundreds of millions of dollars of customer money that went missing during its bankruptcy filing in 2011 due to "dozens of gaps in policies, procedures and technology."[99]

More recently, Meg Whitman, H-P's CEO in 2012, blamed inadequate investments in "internal software systems that could provide her and other executives with necessary intelligence about how the business is performing" as a reason for poor performance of the company.[100] H-P cut its IT budget from about 4% of revenue to 2% of revenue under Mike Hurd, one of the previous CEOs.[101] It also cut its R&D budget from about 5% to 2.4% during the same period ($3.7 billion over revenues of $73 billion in 2003 to $3 billion over revenues of $126 billion in 2010), while IBM spent close to 6%.[102] HP also wrote off billions of dollars that it spent to acquire

Autonomy, which some blame on poor board governance and lack of due diligence. Ultimately, the company was split in 2015.

Governance plays an important role in successful execution of a digital strategy; some argue that part of the reason for Wal-Mart's problems in digital space is its inability to manage the tension between revenue-focused online engineers at its Walmart.com office in California and cost-driven logisticians in Arkansas.[103] Clearly, governance choices matter when it comes to strategy and competitive performance.

Some of these failures may be the result of bad intentions on the part of some players (malfeasance), and others may be the result of incompetence (misfeasance) or honest people making mistakes. Governance seeks to address malfeasance and misfeasance. Governance also seeks to ensure that all decisions address key strategic issues and the relative emphasis that the organization seeks to achieve with respect to revenues, costs, and innovation.

Like strategy, governance can also be viewed at multiple levels such as the corporate level, the division level, the functional level, and the project level. The focus here is on the governance of IT resources and decisions within a firm. [104]

4.2 How to Govern IT: The 4D (Decision, Department, Dollar, Delivery) Framework

I organize the discussion of IT governance into four major headings, or the 4D framework of IT governance.[105] The 4Ds are as follows:

1. Governance of *Decision* rights related to IT (technical/managerial and centralized/decentralized),
2. Governance of IT *Department* or function,
3. Governance of IT *Dollars* (IT spending, prioritization, justification, and accountability), and
4. Ways to organize the *Delivery* of IT services (make, buy, or rent).

Figure 4.1 graphically depicts the 4D framework. I discuss the first two Ds (decision rights and department) in this chapter and devote Chapters 4 and 5 to the third and fourth D (dollars and delivery), respectively.

4.3 Governance of Decision Rights Related to IT

The first D of IT governance refers to decision rights. There are two parts to such decision rights: structure and process. The structure for decision rights seeks to answer the question of what decisions must be made and who will make those decisions. The process part deals with how those decisions will be made in practice.

Figure 4.1: The 4D Framework for IT Governance

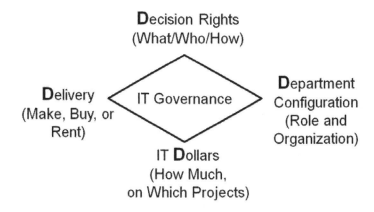

Each organization needs to figure out how to create structures and processes to allocate decision rights within the organization and ensure a balance between decision rights and accountability. Frequently, organizations struggle in dealing with accountability for decision-making pertaining to global versus local, center versus business unit, function versus function and inside versus outside partners issues.

Paul Rogers and Marcia Blenko propose a useful framework for dealing with these issues by articulating primary roles in decision-making processes: recommend, agree, perform, input and decide, denoted by acronym RAPID. The ultimate decision-maker should typically be the one who is also accountable for performance and follow-through. [106]

Contextualizing the above ideas to IT governance, we discuss decision rights for IT governance in terms of what the key IT decisions are, who will take those decisions, and how the decisions will be made.

I begin with a discussion of the key decisions related to IT. Broadly, these can be classified as managerial and technical decisions (see Figure 4.2).

Figure 4.2: What to Decide: Key IT Decision Types

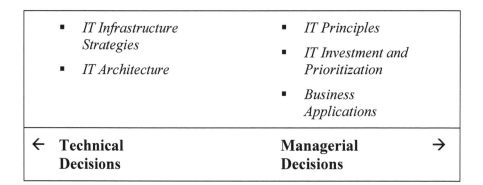

Among decisions that are managerial in nature, organizations need to decide on IT principles (whether IT will focus on revenues, costs, globalization, standardization, innovation, and so forth), funding and prioritization of IT investments, and ownership and responsibility for business applications. Among decisions that are more technical in nature, firms need to decide on issues related to IT architecture (major technology choices for data integration and standardization in core business processes) and IT infrastructure (what services will be shared, how they will be allocated, how they will be priced with associated service-level agreements, and the extent to which the organization will outsource or offshore its IT and other IT-enabled processes).

These categories of decisions can be approached and implemented in a centralized, decentralized, or hybrid manner (see Figure 4.3).

Figure 4.3: How to Decide Based on Degree of Centralization

↑	
Centralized Approach	▪ *Business Monarchy* ▪ *IT Monarchy*
Hybrid Approach	▪ *Federal: Corporate and Business Unit with or Without IT* ▪ *IT Duopoly: IT and One Other Group (Top Management or BU)*
Decentralized Approach	▪ *Feudal: Each Business Unit Decides Independently*
↓	

Centralized decision making may be done only by executives ("business monarchy") or only by high-level IT employees ("IT monarchy"). A completely decentralized approach will allow business units to decide everything for themselves, as in a feudal manner. Hybrid approaches may be federal (when corporate and business units come together with or without IT's involvement) or an IT duopoly (when IT collaborates with either top management or the business unit). One can also visualize a state of anarchy in which no one knows how decisions are to be made and there is no consistent approach.[107]

Based on the types of IT decisions (managerial versus technical) and extent of their decentralization, a decision-decentralization matrix can be created to document current IT governance and then opportunities to improve on this structure. Weill and Ross's (2005) work provides a good example of such an approach (see Figure 4.4 for several options for governance of decision rights).

Figure 4.4: Options for Governance of Decision Rights Based on Types of Decisions and Degree of Centralization

	Technical Decisions	Managerial Decisions
Centralized Approach		
Hybrid Approach		
Decentralized Approach		

Depending on how centralized or decentralized the decision making is, organizations need to come up with appropriate coordinating mechanisms to address alignment. This can be done through the creation of decision-making structures (e.g., steering committees), alignment processes (e.g., chargeback arrangements, service-level agreements, or postimplementation audits to track business value), and formal communications (CIO's office or similar clearing house function).

4.4 Six Principles for Governance of Decision Rights Related to IT

In practice, the IT governance in an organization depends on a variety of factors.[108] Although research till date makes it hard to suggest "the best" model of IT governance for a particular organization, based on what is known about successful practices, managers should keep in mind the following six principles to design governance of decision rights.[109]

First, create an intentional but simple and minimalist design for IT governance taking into account an organization's strategies and goals, and leave the rest to exceptions. For example, governance arrangements may allow business units more autonomy if a firm is focusing on revenue growth, while they may focus more on consolidation and standardization if the firm is focusing on cost reduction. The firm may design a more flexible governance if it is pursuing multiple objectives at the same time or its different business units have varying objectives and strategies.

The key idea here is to start low and in an incremental manner. At the same time, the goal is also to prioritize key objectives for IT by ensuring a robust discussion of different trade-offs and potentially conflicting metrics and actions that different business units or departments may be pursuing.

Second, use governance arrangements for other resources if feasible. For example, if an organization already has mature governance arrangements for, say, engineering or R&D, then those structures can be leveraged. Although that may work for smaller organizations, separate structures and processes may be needed for IT decisions in large organizations.

Third, decide about degree of centralization and governance based on the synergy versus autonomy trade-off. Avoid micromanagement because it can prove suboptimal. For example, it may not make sense to specify a university-wide questionnaire for judging student satisfaction across all colleges and all courses if student expectations from the courses differ significantly across colleges or classes. Likewise, customer satisfaction surveys and some IT systems across a global multidivisional enterprise can differ.

Fourth, ensure board-level leadership, clear ownership, and broad-based executive involvement. Use of interlocking tiered governance at the enterprise, division, and geography/business unit level can help achieve this objective.

Fifth, evolve IT governance in response to changes in external environment, economic conditions and strategies. However, aim for evolution (not revolution) in the implementation of IT governance to allow time for an organization to absorb new governance processes slowly. Because governance is not an end in itself, be willing to grant exceptions to business units to let them cope with change in a flexible manner. This is related to the first point regarding starting with a minimalist design that is easy to understand and then gradually building on that.

Finally, IT governance, like any other governance, is not a substitute for thoughtful and engaged leadership. A good governance system can possibly help to reduce downside risks and power the probability of taking bad decisions, but absent a thoughtful leader governance may not be enough to improve performance. If properly utilized, a good governance system can improve the effectiveness of a leader's actions.

4.5 Governance of IT Department

The second D of IT governance refers to the configuration and role of the IT department. The IT department is a major player in ensuring the successful management and use of IT, the other important stakeholders being executive management, business management, and external vendors.

4.5.1 IT Department: Cost Center or Profit Center?

There are many ways to organize an IT department within a firm. One useful way of thinking about the role of the IT department is to use an approach based on the notion of management accountability.[110] This approach ties governance to the financial discipline and strategy of the organization. Drawing on this approach and the concept of responsibility centers, it is possible to think of at least four options to organize an IT department.

First, an IT department can be organized as a cost center. Most firms fall into this category. If organized as a cost center, firms have the choice to charge all expenses to corporate or allocate these expenses partially or wholly to the business units. In this approach, there is no distinction between prices and costs because pricing of IT services is frequently done to achieve cost recovery. This approach is less effective if business units have no control on their consumption of IT resources or are not incentivized for more prudent use of IT. More often, if allocations are to business units, it is done on the basis of criteria other than the use of IT resources, such as the number of people in a business unit, revenues of business units, or assets.

A second option is to organize the IT department as a profit center. Very few organizations (e.g., Cemex, Charles Schwab, USAA), have experimented with this approach, despite significant potential merits of considering this option.[111] In this approach, business units are charged prices for business functionalities enabled by IT (e.g., per statement price for bank customers, per customer price for a bank), not based on machine units or actual costs. Using the profit center approach can lead to faster adoption of new technologies and help to balance demand for IT resources with the supply of IT resources in an economically disciplined way. However, despite these potential advantages, the profit center concept is not for every organization, because it requires significant IT maturity and sophisticated accounting systems to track costs and charge prices in a transparent manner. It also presumes that IT department is efficient in delivering IT services.

The other two options are perhaps not as practical, but at least worth a discussion. For example, A third option is to organize IT department as an investment center, similar to how R&D is organized in many firms. To the extent that IT investments are similar to R&D investments, in that they create a platform for innovation and intangible assets that can be monetized, this approach has some conceptual merits. However, unlike R&D, IT is much more intimately connected to day-to-day business processes and operations; thus, the investment center concept has limitations for IT. Likewise, a fourth option is to organize the IT department as a revenue center, similar to how marketing and sales are organized in many firms. Few organizations, however, have done so, even though IT plays a significant role in the revenue generation activities of many firms.

4.5.2 IT Department: CIO Reporting Structure

Increasingly, firms rely on chief information officers (CIOs) to lead the IT function and shape business strategy. However, not all firms have a formal CIO position. According to a Wall Street Journal article, about 17% of the CIOs are members of the company's executive leadership team in 2015.[112] Even if firms have a CIO, their reporting relationship varies across firms: in some firms CIO reports to CEO, while in other firms CIO reports to CFO or some other executive. In this context, one can pose two questions: (1) Should there be a formal CIO position, and how does presence or absence of a formal position influence a firm's IT investments and firm performance? and (2) Who should the CIO report to?

Academic research provides some answers to these questions. Research by Jee-Hae Lim, Kunsoo Han and Sunil Mithas answers the first question and suggests that CIO position has a significant impact on IT investments: firms with a formal CIO position make higher levels of IT investments, compared to firms without a formal CIO position.[113] They also find that firms that have a CIO obtain higher performance from their IT investments, compared to firms without CIOs. Their additional analyses indicate that CIO position has significantly stronger impacts in IT intensive firms than in non-IT intensive firms, in terms of both its impact on IT investments and the moderating effect on the effect of IT investments on firm performance.

Research by Rajiv Banker, Nan Hu, Paul Pavlou and Jerry Luftman answers the second question. They studied the effect of CIO reporting structure on strategic positioning and firm performance and find that firms that align reporting structure with strategic positioning have superior firm performance. Their work suggests that a CIO-CEO reporting structure works well only for differentiators and a CIO-CFO reporting structure works well only for cost leaders. [114]

Although these are important findings, it is possible for some progressive firms to not use a formal CIO position or title. For example, at one point Zara did not have anyone with the CIO title and yet the company was considered an exemplar in its IT practices by some. You dont need a CIO if the CEO is willing to play that role (some claim to do so despite many other demands on CEO's time). I was told by two CIOs that influence of the person heading the IT function may be more important than the title itself or the authority to spend IT dollars. [115] Likewise, not all CIOs may be ready to lead their organization to pursue a differentiation strategy, there may be astute CFOs who may have a good understanding of the strategic role of IT to make CIO-CFO relationship work even for a firm that chooses to pursue a differentiation strategy. Similarly, even if a firm pursues cost reduction strategy, it may not be a good idea for CIO to report to CFO if there are concerns about financial discipline in the organization. [116] Once again, context matters when it comes to making governance decisions.

4.6 Chapter Summary

This chapter introduces a 4D framework for IT governance focusing on decisions, department, dollars, and delivery of IT services. I began by asserting that governance is the lynchpin between strategy and execution, but many firms have failed to manage IT and other initiatives properly because of their lack of attention to governance issues. I then discussed some frameworks and principles for making sense of the governance of decision rights and configuration of the IT department in an organization. When it comes to decision rights, firms should create a minimalist, tiered and evolutionary design and decide degree of centralization based on synergy versus autonomy tradeoff. Ideally, decision rights should be allocated in such a way that stakeholders responsible for long-term success of the organization have a say or even a veto right on substantive decision and actions (or non-actions). When it comes to configuring an IT department, think hard on how you want to balance demand for and supply of IT resources through chargebacks or prices. Also, depending on an organization's strategy and the types of competitive environment and risks it faces, should the CIO report to the CEO or some other executive?

Chapter 5: Allocating Digital Resources and Prioritizing IT Projects

"IT can have an unlimited budget, as long as one of the functions or business teams is willing to allocate the money."

> —John Chambers, CEO of Cisco (quoted in McAfee, McFarlan and Wagonfeld 2006, p. 4)

"There is no bank where companies can deposit IT investments and withdraw an 'average' return."

> —Erik Brynjolfsson (1994)

"A negative relationship between use and performance should not be immediately interpreted as an example of low business value from IT. It is quite possible that technology may help raise average performance by improving results for the lowest performing groups. There may be little market potential left for high performing companies and individuals."

> —Henry Lucas (1993, p. 367)

The third D of IT governance refers to IT dollars. As noted previously, firms spend significant amounts of money on IT, and governance of these decisions essentially requires answering three questions: how much overall to spend on IT, how to fund across different types of IT projects, and how to prioritize within an investment type.

5.1 Overall IT Spending

IT spending varies considerably across industries. For example, health care, consulting and business services, and banking and financial services industries spend considerably more on IT than, say, the automotive, chemical, or construction industries. Also, IT investments vary over time for the same industry.

Figure 5.1 shows that industries vary substantially in trends and year-to-year fluctuations of IT investments. Even within an industry, there is a significant variation in IT spending across firms. This is not to say that spending more money on IT is always wise. It is certainly possible to overspend on IT. According to one estimate, firms wrote off approximately $130 billion of IT purchased between 2000 and 2002.[117]

Figure 5.1: Trends in Annual IT Investments in Selected Industries (Source: Mithas, Tafti, and Mitchell (2013))

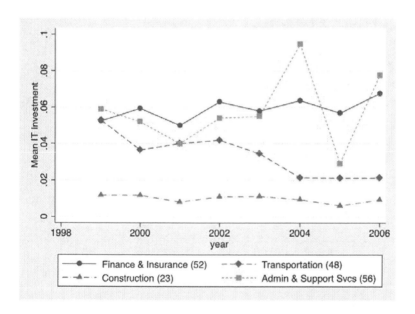

There are at least two approaches to setting overall levels of IT expenditures. The first approach can be characterized as the "John

Chambers" approach, named after the CEO of Cisco whose quotation opens this chapter. This approach grants IT "an unlimited budget" contingent on one of the functions or business teams being "willing to allocate the money" as such.[118] An alternative approach can be characterized as the "Rich-Con" approach, named after a company that reportedly minimized its spending on IT and, in the end, was bought over by another company.[119] Borders and Blockbuster are examples of firms that appear to have floundered because they did not make sufficient investments to keep up with emerging threats in their industries. H-P is another recent example where Mike Hurd cut IT budget from about 4% of revenue to 2% of revenue, leading Meg Whitman to blame such reduced investments for deficiency in "internal software systems that could provide her and other executives with necessary intelligence about how the business is performing."[120]

How should managers choose between the unlimited budget approach (the John Chambers example) and the cost minimization approach (the Rich-Con example)? A firm's overall IT spending depends on its historical IT spending (firms that have accumulated underinvestments in IT or what some call "technical debt" should make up for that eventually), information-processing needs, strategic posture, and external competitive environment. Firms need to decide about the overall amount of their IT investments, taking into consideration their strategic posture, IT strategy, the information intensity of the industry, industry turbulence, competitive intensity, industry growth, and other players' competitive moves. Typically, firms that are trying to achieve both revenue growth and cost reduction will need to invest more in IT for higher profitability and shareholder value.

Although the optimum level of IT investments will vary depending on a firm's unique business strategy and its competitive environment, managers should guard against the temptation to spend as little as possible on IT resources, especially if a firm's competitive strategy focuses on differentiation, customer service, and ambidexterity. Academic research provides some insights on how industry conditions influence IT investments. Broadly speaking, research suggests that firms tend to diverge from the industry norm in their IT investments and allocations toward outsourcing under higher industry turbulence, and converge toward the industry norm under higher industry concentration and higher industry growth.[121] Figure 5.2 shows a summary indicating how industry turbulence, industry concentration, and industry growth influence IT investments and IT outsourcing.

Figure 5.2: How Industry Factors Drive IT Investments and Outsourcing Allocations

Industry Conditions	IT Investment Tendency	IT Outsourcing Tendency
Industry turbulence	Divergence from the norm	
Industry concentration		Convergence toward the norm
Industry growth	Convergence toward the norm	Convergence toward the norm

The right levels of IT investments should be derived on the basis of the information needs of the business model and the business processes of the firm. Firms should also guard against metrics such as IT investment as a percentage of sales or IT spending per employee and benchmarking those with respect to competition, because these metrics may not always be helpful for generating strategic insights. For example, a steel company interested in positioning itself in its competitive space might do well by achieving the lowest per ton cost of hot metal or steel. That may sometimes require incurring relatively higher IT costs per ton of hot metal or steel to drive down costs in other functional areas.[122] Just achieving the lowest IT costs per ton of hot metal may not be useful if that low cost results in wasteful use of resources in other areas.[123] Indeed, CIOs should not be punished for high IT investments if such investments make a firm more competitive in the long run and help to save costs in marketing or R&D for which CIO may not get credit if the focus is only on reducing IT investments. Therefore, firms should be careful in devising metrics they use for different types of investments. Ideally, firms should try to reduce their overall costs by reducing non-value adding costs, and mandating uniform targets for cost reductions across all types of investments may not be a prudent approach to achieve that goal.

5.2 Funding, Ownership, and Accountability of IT Projects

To make sense of funding and ownership of IT investments, it is useful to have a portfolio approach. This approach requires classifying IT projects on some dimensions and managing them both within a particular class and across different classes of projects.

Ross and Beath (2002) propose a classification scheme based on strategic objectives and technology scope. Strategic objectives can emphasize short-term profitability or long-term survival and growth. Likewise, technology scope can be distinguished based on whether the project is a shared infrastructure or a business solution.[124]   They classify IT projects into four types on the basis of their strategic objectives and technology scope: process improvement, experiments, renewal, and transformation.   Process improvement projects and experiments focus on business solutions; while the former emphasize short-term profitability, the latter emphasize long-term growth and survival. Renewal and transformation projects are part of shared infrastructure; while the former relate to short-term profitability, the latter relate to long-term growth and survival.

In general, projects dealing with business solutions (process improvement projects and experiments) should be funded by business units, and shared infrastructure projects (renewal and transformation projects) should be funded by corporate with some contribution from the business units. Having said that, in general, transformation projects, and sometimes even experiments, should be funded by corporate to ensure that the longer-term interests of the corporation do not get overlooked and remain underfunded because of business units' focus on short-term profitability. A similar approach should apply to ownership of projects and accountability for their success.

There are other ways of classifying IT projects, such as in terms of whether they contribute to revenue growth, cost reduction or both. Regardless of the terminology used, firms should ensure a healthy balance among different types of projects in their portfolio, realizing that, in practice, it can be difficult to distinguish one type from the other and that one type can lead to another type. [125]

After an organization has a good understanding of its projects' classification schemes and how much money can be allocated to each bucket in a year based on its cash flow situation and strategic needs, it must then prioritize IT projects within each investment type and select the most promising projects to fund that year, deferring others to the following year or eliminating them from consideration. To do so, an organization will need to pay attention to the governance of valuation and justification approaches, which I discuss next.

5.3 Valuing and Justifying IT Projects

IT projects differ from conventional projects (e.g., think of a project like constructing Hoover Dam or a building project) in several ways. IT projects are inherently risky because of technical and market uncertainties, and they have very little salvage value because of firm-specific nature of such investments. However, they are often modular and often one does not have to commit to a massive project upfront as one would do for say Hoover Dam. The modularity of IT projects and the ability to repurpose or change their scale after allowing for resolution of some technical or market uncertainty provides some additional ways of thinking about valuing and managing IT projects.

I discuss four ways of valuing and justifying IT investments: net present value (NPV)/internal rate of return (IRR), a decision tree, real option value, and the counterfactual approach. This discussion will also shed light on some of the unique characteristics of IT projects which make some approaches more appropriate than others depending on the specifics of a particular case.

5.3.1 NPV/ IRR Approach

The NPV or IRR approach uses a discounted cash flow method to calculate the net present value of all the negative and positive cash flows in today's dollars. The higher the NPV, the better the project is; negative NPV projects are usually considered value destroying and therefore are candidates for elimination. The IRR approach is closely related to NPV, but instead of present value, the emphasis is on calculating the internal rate of return of the project to determine whether it crosses the hurdle rate set by the organization.

One of the things to remember about the NPV approach is that you can get any numbers you want depending on the assumptions involved. As a conscientious manager, it is your job to figure out how realistic these assumptions are. You need to know how sensitive NPV is to reasonable changes in assumptions; you must ask tough questions regarding underlying assumptions and, when necessary, ask for calculations with more realistic assumptions. Remember, a lot of technical knowledge about IT is *not* necessary to ask intelligent questions about IT investments.

While useful as an initial step, the NPV and IRR approaches have been criticized for having restrictive assumptions. The NPV approach assumes that the NPV for the do-nothing option is zero (no investment, no gain), which is an unrealistic assumption. If an organization does nothing while its competitors move ahead in technology, the do-nothing option can have a negative NPV which may far exceed the negative NPV of "doing something." Think of Blockbuster's or Borders' continued inaction which ultimately led to their bankruptcy. Therefore, a firm should be willing to fund a project whose NPV is greater than the negative NPV of doing nothing. [126]

The NPV approach also does not map well onto how organizations undertake and fund IT projects. Real-life IT projects are often undertaken in a sequence. They do not require all investments to be made upfront. For example, Amazon.com did not create its massive infrastructure to handle transactions across its many departments on day one. It started with books and gradually entered other businesses. Had it done an NPV analysis of its entire project on day one, it would have probably never started. Sunil Mittal, the founder and CEO of Bharti in 2011, once remarked that he would not have entered the telecommunications business had he known initially the amount of money and deep pockets that the business would require.[127]

5.3.2 Decision Tree Approach

The decision-tree approach can be used to assess IT projects that involve sequential investments in IT. Rigby and Ledingham (2004) illustrate a useful way to calculate value and cost of CRM using a decision-tree approach. In their hypothetical example of a company called "Ace Grocery," the firm has 1000 customers, and each customer is worth $1,000. According to a survey, 20% of customers planned to switch, and a consultant says that 50% of the potential defectors can be retained with a $100 reward. If the company buys a CRM system costing $50,000; it will correctly identify 60% of potential defectors but will identify 30% of loyal customers as potential defectors.

In this scenario, it is possible to evaluate four options. The first option is to do nothing. A second option is to give $100 to everyone. The third option is an imaginary scenario of implementing a CRM solution that would correctly identify 100% of the potential defectors and loyal customers. Let us first evaluate the value of these three options as below:

- *Do Nothing*: Customer Lifetime Value (CLV) = 1000 customers × $1,000 – 200 customers × $1,000 = $800,000.
- *Give $100 to everyone (and lose 50% of the 20%)*: CLV = 1000 customers × ($1,000 – $100 reward) – 100 customers × $1,000 = $800,000.
- *Buy a perfect CRM system—reward just the right customers (i.e., potential defectors) and retain 50% of them*: CLV =

(1000 − 100) customers × $1,000 − 200 customers × $100 reward = $880,000.

Based on the analyses thus far, the most that one should be willing to pay for a perfect CRM should be $80,000 ($880,000 − $800,000) only if the CRM system yielded perfect information—that is, if it correctly classifies defectors without wrongly classifying loyal customers. One should be willing to pay much less for an imperfect or "actual" CRM system.

The fourth and final option refers to actual CRM implementation. What is the value of this option?

- *Buy an actual CRM system*: CLV = 1000 customers × $1,000 − $100 to 120 correct potential defectors − lose 60 of these × $1,000 − lose 80 potential defectors wrongly classified as loyals × $1,000 − $100 to 240 wrongly classified loyal customers − $50,000 cost of CRM = $774,000.

Note that the fourth option is the least valuable among the above four options. Giving $100 to everyone or not doing anything are equally good options, but giving $100 may induce loyal customers to buy more or at least will not make them feel shortchanged, so the firm may prefer this option. Alternatively, the firm may prefer the fourth option if vendor were to offer actual CRM system for $10,000, instead of $50,000.

The decision-tree approach takes into account the sequential nature of IT investments to some extent. However, it does not account for risks associated with IT projects. In addition, the decision-tree approach requires precise estimates of probabilities for each event, something that is rarely known in practice.

5.3.3 Real Option Value Approach

Real option value (ROV) approach avoids some of the limitations of the NPV and decision-tree approaches. It recognizes that firms can defer some investments to the future after learning about the outcomes of pilot projects.[128] In doing so, not only can firms gain by earning interest on the principal that they did not have to invest upfront, but they also avoid the loss of the entire principal if the pilot shows that the project is not worth undertaking. It also provides a nice language and vocabulary to describe the uncertainties involved in projects. For example, managers can classify projects into growth options (scale-up, switch-up, or scope-up), defer/learn options, and abandonment options (scale-down, switch-down, or scope-down). It helps managers to split projects into must-do and may-do elements to maximize flexibility. It forces managers to more explicitly account for variance of cash-flows in their calculations, something that is not accounted for in NPV calculations as clearly.

Even if managers do not use option valuation, option thinking can help them to recognize and value real options, and cope with resolvable uncertainties because only then options have a value. Managers should also be willing to act on new information by increasing their commitment, engaging in course correction, or cancelling a project altogether. Flexibility is worth something only when you can do something differently based on new information.

However, the real option approach has its own limitations, arising from the threat of competitive preemption and loss of dividends. If a firm decides to pilot a project, while competitors go ahead with a full-throttle implementation, the firm may be preempted. It is like continuing with endless courting to hedge your bets, which can backfire if somebody else proposes before you get around to doing that. In this sense, the real option approach is like dating—it allows for greater flexibility, but if you always date, you may never be able to settle with a partner. In addition, while piloting projects, you do not reap the full benefits that would have accrued if you had gone ahead with the full project. Owning options on a stock deprives you of the dividends on the stock.

Some criticize real option approach because IT projects are not tradable the way stocks are, hence they question borrowing that method from finance literature to IT context. Therefore, while the real option approach has its merits and can be a useful way of looking at IT investments, this approach should be used as a complement to other approaches, not as a substitute. [129]

5.3.4 Counterfactuals and Intangibles

Finally, a counterfactual approach allows an organization to assess the value of an IT project by comparing potential outcomes (value with IT project versus value of not undertaking the project). For example, using a counterfactual approach, we may want to know customer satisfaction of a firm with CRM if it had not adopted CRM. [130] Unlike the associational relationships, or a comparison of performance at time t with some prior time $t - 1$ (as in "before-and-after" study designs), the notion of causality in the counterfactual or potential outcomes framework views causal effect as a contrast or a comparison between two potential outcomes at a given time t corresponding to a treatment or intervention that can be applied to each unit.

This way of assessing causality comes close to answering the counterfactual questions that executives face. For example, executives contemplate a comparison between two scenarios: one in which a firm invests in an IT or some other strategic intervention and one in which the firm does not. This view informs many strategic considerations. Barney (2002, p. 162) notes that a firm's resources and capabilities "are valuable if, and only if, they reduce a firm's costs or increase its revenues compared to what would have been the case if the firm did not possess those resources." Likewise, Porter (1987, pp. 45-46) notes, "Linking shareholder value quantitatively to diversification performance only works if you compare the shareholder value that is with the shareholder value that might have been without diversification."

To fix ideas, consider Figure 5.3, a hypothetical data set of six Fortune 500 firms, which have either implemented CRM ($z = 1$) or not ($z = 0$) and corresponding customer satisfaction of these firms on a scale between 0 and 100. How will we infer the effect of CRM on customer satisfaction based on this limited data? A naive approach may be to simply take average of CRM and non-CRM firms to discover that non-CRM firms have customer satisfaction scores which are higher by 2 points compared to CRM firms.

Figure 5.3: CRM Intervention and Customer Satisfaction

Firm	CRM	No-CRM
A	62	
B	70	
C	78	
D		65
E		70
F		81
Naïve Average is E(Y=1|Z=1) or E(Y=0|Z=0)	70.0	72.0

Notes: Naïve Average Difference is E(Y=1\|Z=1) Minus E(Y=0\|Z=0).

However, it is hard to argue that this naive difference is causal effect of CRM because of the fundamental problem in causal inference, which is that we do not observe an individual subject (i) in two possible states (0 and 1) with associated outcomes (Y_{i0} and Y_{i1}). Jay Barney (2002, p. 189) describes this fundamental problem of causal inference as follows: "[A] firm cannot compare its performance with resources and capabilities to itself without these resources and capabilities."

In our context, assessing the causal effect of a treatment such as CRM is difficult because we cannot observe the customer satisfaction of a firm if they had not acquired CRM, and vice versa. More generally, for any type of treatment z, *individual causal effects* (ICE) are defined as contrasts between potential outcomes. However, because ICE is a firm-specific quantity, this firm-specific quantity can never be observed because, each firm undergoes only one of the possible treatment values. In our hypothetical example, each firm will experience either CRM implementation or not, but not both. Thus, only one of the potential outcomes is observed for any given firm, therefore, we cannot calculate ICE due to the fundamental problem of causal inference.

Physical sciences avoid this fundamental problem of causal inference by making *homogeneity* and *temporal invariance* assumptions. For example, the *homogeneity assumption* enables a physicist to assume that Oxygen Atom 1 and Oxygen Atom 2 will respond to the presence or absence of a treatment in exactly the same way. He can expose Atom 1 to the condition to observe $Y_1(1)$, and withhold the condition from Atom 2 in order to observe $Y_2(0)$. Then, by the *homogeneity assumption*, the difference between the two observed responses gives a causally valid estimate of the individual causal effect.

Turning to *temporal invariance*, consider the effect of a drone's wing size (small $z = 0$ versus large $z = 1$) on length of flight time. We can use the same unit (just one drone) to observe both potential outcomes: the drone's flight time with the small wings $Y(0)$, and flight time with the large wings $Y(1)$. Since the drone is exposed to each condition sequentially, what we observe are the potential outcomes that are influenced by both wing size and time. The temporal invariance assumption says that there can be no effect of time, so that the difference between the two observed responses is a valid estimate of the causal effect of the individual causal effect of small versus large wing size on flight. Another way to state the assumption is that there are no *carry-over effects*, or that the response at time 2 is in no way affected by the exposure at time 1.

Unfortunately, these assumptions are untenable when it comes to individuals or firms. The homogeneity assumption is usually untenable because any two Fortune 500 companies, for instance, are likely to respond differently to CRM implementation. The effect of CRM on customer satisfaction can depend, perhaps, on a firm's business sector, its location. This fact has nothing to do with confounding, which refers to alternate explanations of observed effects. Even in an ideal setting, in which the presence or absence of CRM is randomly assigned to all Fortune 500 companies so that confounding is eliminated or reduced substantially, heterogeneous causal effects are still likely to exist. Like the homogeneity assumption, the temporal invariance assumption also can be indefensible: a company's exposure to CRM at time t1 may have prolonged or delayed effects on customer satisfaction at later points in time, whether or not the company continues to implement CRM. As a result, it is not clear whether taking the difference in responses at two points in time (one exposed and the other not exposed) represents the true effect of CRM, a temporal effect, or some combination of the two.

The critical insight and breakthrough came when the *fundamental problem of causal inference* was reformulated as a problem of missing data. A statistical solution to this missing data problem can be attempted by reformulating the problem at the population level by defining the average treatment effect for a randomly selected subject from the population, which presupposes that treatment and control groups are similar in all respects on both observed and unobserved characteristics (the nature of data collection for observational studies often fails to meet the assumption of the random treatment of assignment). Although we cannot estimate individual causal effect for each firm due to the *fundamental problem of causal inference* and missing data for each entity, we can estimate the *average causal effect (ACE)* in the population of interest if we can somehow find clones that can supply us missing data for the treatment that a firm did not undergo.

Figure 5.4 shows an augmented table where we pretend to know the potential outcomes for customer satisfaction had the companies implemented CRM ($z = 1$) or not ($z = 0$). Now, with imputed data for missing values of counterfactuals, we can assess the average causal effect of implementing CRM on customer satisfaction as 7.3.

The last column in Figure 5.4 describes the individual causal effect for each company, which is simply the difference in the level of customer satisfaction among the two treatment settings. From Figure 5.4, Firm C will not benefit from implementing CRM as much as Firm A will. Also, for Firm F, implementing CRM hurts the company in terms of customer satisfaction ($ICE_C = -3$).

Figure 5.4: Counterfactual Analysis for Effect of CRM on Customer Satisfaction

Firm	CRM	No-CRM	ICE
A	**62**	*50*	*12*
B	**70**	*60*	*10*
C	**78**	*70*	*8*
D	*77*	**65**	*12*
E	*75*	**70**	*5*
F	*78*	**81**	*-3*
			7.3
Naïve Average is E(Y=1|Z=1) or E(Y=0|Z=0)	**70.0**	**72.0**	-2.0
Average is E(Y=1) or E(Y=0)	73.33	66.0	7.3

Notes: Bold numbers are observed, italicized numbers are imputed values for clones. Naïve Average Difference is E(Y=1|Z=1) Minus E(Y=0|Z=0). ACE is E(Y=1) Minus E(Y=0).

The counterfactual approach, if done carefully, illuminates the causal questions that are inherent in justifying an IT project. Politicians frequently use this approach to justify decisions ranging from going to war to overhauling health care to contain costs.[131] Smart managers also use such language to their advantage. However, it is important to know the limitations of this method, the principal one being that counterfactuals cannot be verified.

We now turn to consideration of projects where it is hard to quantify the value created by IT in terms of monetary values or tangible benefits. Although it is important to think about tangible benefits from IT projects, managers should also pay attention to many intangible benefits enabled by IT such as such as customer satisfaction, product variety, innovation and patents. In particular, customer satisfaction has been identified as an important intangible and leading measure of firm performance. [132]

A research study that analyzed the link between IT investments and customer satisfaction suggests that IT investments had a positive association with customer satisfaction; the relationship is stronger in the 1994–1996 period and for manufacturing firms than it was for the 1999–2006 period and for service firms. Interestingly, IT investments have a negative association with profits in the 1994–1996 period but a positive association in the 1999–2006 period. These findings show how firms can use potential improvements in customer satisfaction as a justification for returns on their IT investments. Because customer satisfaction has an effect on the market value of firms, chief information officers and IT managers can use potential improvements in customer satisfaction as a justification for returns on their IT investments. [133]

The quantitative assessment of the intangible value created by IT investments through improvement in customer satisfaction can be particularly useful when firms realize the importance of investing in IT to improve their customer satisfaction and yet find it difficult to justify such investments using traditional metrics such as return on investments. Because IT has stronger effect on perceived quality than on perceived value, and perceived quality appears to have stronger effect on customer satisfaction than that of perceived value, managers may be better off directing their IT systems to improve customization and reliability of consumption experience than reducing costs, particularly for firms that aim to improve customer satisfaction through superior quality. Furthermore, improvement in perceived quality can act as a leading indicator of a firm's customer satisfaction, and by tracking such measures, managers can monitor whether their IT investments are likely to improve customer satisfaction and market value.

5.3.5 Section Summary

To summarize this section, the key point to remember is that no single approach is likely to be perfectly suited to assessing all types of IT projects. Managers need to tailor their valuation and justification approach while considering their strategic objectives and technology scope. A variety of approaches should ultimately be used to triangulate the most likely value of an IT project.

Some leading firms, such as P&G and Wal-Mart, use a combination of these approaches. They assign different weights to tangibles, intangibles, and risks of not undertaking the project to assess a project relative to other projects. They recognize that IT projects have both tangible and intangible benefits. Intangible benefits may be difficult to quantify, but they are no less important. For example, IT can help firms improve their customer satisfaction, first-mover advantage, learning, experimentation, innovation, and organizational capabilities, and there is significant evidence that these intangibles, in turn, result in profitability and shareholder value.[134] Justifying IT projects on the basis of intangible gains is particularly important for customer relationship management (CRM), knowledge management (KM), and sometimes even ERP projects.

5.4 Chapter Summary

This chapter focused on the governance of IT dollars, which constitutes a large percentage of an organization's discretionary investments. I discussed some ways of thinking about how an organization should determine its overall IT spending and how it should create a portfolio of IT projects and define their ownership, funding, and accountability. Then, I discussed various approaches to value and justify IT projects. Together, these concepts should help managers align the governance of IT dollars to achieve their strategic objectives.

Chapter 6: Delivery of IT Services: In-house, Outsource, or Offshore?

"Geography is history."

—Raman Roy, quoted on "60 Minutes", 11 Jan 2004

"What goes around, comes around."

—Thomas L. Friedman, in the "The World is Flat" (2005, p. 29)

The fourth D of IT governance refers to the delivery of IT services. One of the major decisions that firms face is related to the degree to which they will rely on their business partners and suppliers. At one end, firms can decide to make everything themselves, as Ford did in the early 1900s, or they can outsource their production to third-party vendors, as Nike, Boeing, Microsoft, Cisco, and Apple do.

These issues also apply to IT-related decision making. Firms can hire their own IT workers and develop all software internally, they can buy packages from the outside, and they can rely mostly on outside vendors to develop solutions that are most appropriate to the firm.

More broadly, and to the extent that many of today's business processes are enabled by IT, it is important to understand how a firm should decide on the delivery and outsourcing of its IT services. This is because a framework for IT outsourcing can also apply to the outsourcing of business processes such as finance, legal, human resources, and the tasks that knowledge workers perform. [135]

I devote much of this chapter to discussing how firms and managers should consider outsourcing-related decisions from a governance perspective, though I also cover some aspects of delivering IT services in part 3 of the book when I discuss managing IT implementation. Before moving to a discussion of IT outsourcing, it is important to realize that the growth of services and disaggregation are much broader in scope and among some of the major forces that are transforming the global economy. [136]

Services have grown significantly in the last 200 years or so. According to some estimates, services sector employs upwards of 70% of workers in the US and many developed economies. In 1800, when the industrial revolution was just beginning, services and manufacturing each made up approximately 5% of the U.S. economy, and agriculture constituted the remaining 90%. Services and manufacturing grew throughout the 1800s, and by 1900 each represented closer to 25% of the economy, with agriculture making up the remaining 50%. During the 1900s, manufacturing remained relatively constant at about 20%–25% of the U.S. economy, agriculture contracted significantly to less than 5%, and services expanded considerably to 70%–80%.

6.1 Big Picture on Outsourcing and Offshoring

One way to understand outsourcing and offshoring services is to view them as manifestations of a more general phenomenon of disaggregation. [137]

Disaggregation can take two forms: value chain disaggregation and geographic disaggregation. Value chain disaggregation manifests in the form of outsourcing, while geographic disaggregation manifests in the form of globalization and offshoring (see Figure 6.1).

Figure 6.1: Two Dimensions of Disaggregation

Geographic Disaggregation Across **Country** Boundaries		Integrated	Outsourced
Offshore		*International captive operations*	*Outsourced and offshored*
Onshore		*Integrated domestic operations*	*Onshore outsourcing*

Integrated   **Outsourced**

**Value Chain Disaggregation
Across <u>Firm</u> Boundaries**

Outsourcing and offshoring are hot topics and are intimately connected with globalization.[138] Despite appearances to the contrary, some argue that the world is far less globalized now than it was, say, 100 years ago just before the World War I on some measures such as people flows across countries. Despite much progress toward global integration since 1950s, the extent of globalization is less than or close to 10% on many measures of globalization such as percentage of immigrants to population, tourist arrivals, telephone calls and university students of foreign-origin. [139] However, the overall picture looks very different, at least in terms of the percentage of revenues and profits of large U.S. firms. Increasingly, a large percentage of U.S. companies' revenues and profits come from abroad.[140]

Although the outsourcing of services has received a lot of press coverage, it is still only a fraction of the outsourcing of manufacturing; thus, there is significant room for growth in services outsourcing. Services globalization, which has relatively more recent origins, is nowhere near manufacturing globalization.[141] For example, in the U.K. economy, services inputs are only approximately 3% of the nonenergy intermediate inputs, while manufacturing inputs are closer to 30% of the nonenergy intermediate inputs. According to a NASSCOM–McKinsey report in 2005, the potential global IT and business process outsourcing market is approximately ten times the current size, which indicates the tremendous potential for outsourcing and offshoring in the times to come.[142]

Although outsourcing and offshoring generate heated political discussions, their use is undeniably on rise. Beginning with Kodak in the late 1980s, the trend of IT outsourcing continued to gather momentum throughout the 1990s. In today's business environment, it would be rare to find a firm that does not outsource some aspect of its IT, a far cry from the 1970s or 1980s when firms typically handled much of their IT internally. Increasingly, firms are using outsourcing to transform their business processes.[143]

Interestingly, some studies suggest that organizations do not outsource only for cost reasons. Bardhan et al. (2006) find that U.S. manufacturing plants with a "high-quality" strategy tend to engage in greater outsourcing of their production processes; however, they do not find any association between a "low-cost" strategy and outsourcing.

Why is outsourcing becoming a common trend? One reason is the IT-enabled lowering of transaction costs.[144] The cost of communicating across firm boundaries and even across country borders has fallen remarkably in the last 20 years, in sharp contrast to a much slower decline in the costs of land, water, or air transportation. A second reason is the increased capabilities of product and service vendors, particularly those located in emerging economies such as China or India. In addition, globalization, the liberalization of many economies since 1990, and the diffusion of standards (e.g., capability maturity model [CMM]) have played important roles.[145]

While outsourcing can be rewarding, it poses significant risks as well.[146] Boeing ran into difficulties with outsourcing the production of its 787 plane. Some firms have had bad experiences with outsourcing and subsequently have "backsourced" some processes or have outsourced those processes again after learning from their initial mistakes. For example, Dell brought back its customer support function from India to United States after customers complained about difficulties understanding the accents of call center agents and poor customer service. General Motors was once held up as an exemplar of how to outsource IT.[147] However, more recently, GM is trying to reverse its use of outsourcing from 90% in 2012 to only about 10% by 2015.[148] A similar trends is also evident at Target and Bharti Airtel which brought back in-house some of the work they had earlier outsourced to outside service providers such as IBM or Amazon.[149] Often, the reason to keep something in-house is justified based on strategic considerations and to innovate. Bhaskar Bhat, CEO of Titan, notes, "We have benefited a great deal by keeping IT in-house. It is not just about cost cutting. We feel that IT is such a critical function that we don't want to outsource it.... When it is done in-house, the commitment of the people working on the IT project is higher. You can outsource something like travelling, but business driven creative solutions will only emerge when things are done in-house."[150]

Not all backsourcing is driven by poor vendor performance though. Sallie Mae's CEO made remarks about backsourcing to create jobs in the United States when the company was facing increased scrutiny and troubles in 2009. AT&T announced plans to bring jobs back to the United States in 2011, around the same time when its proposed merger with T-Mobile was under consideration, a move that prompted queries from the Federal Communications Commission. [151]

6.2 Why Outsource?

Why do firms outsource IT or other business processes. Broadly, the reasons can be classified into economic and noneconomic factors.

Among economic factors, outsourcing is driven by a comparison of production and coordination costs between in-house production and outsourcing choices. Vendors are likely to have lower production costs because of economies of scale and scope and their ability to utilize IT talent from multiple locations for several clients. IT outsourcing can help to reduce firms' coordination costs and non-IT operating costs (e.g., operational, sales, general and administrative, R&D and marketing costs) by increasing the operational efficiencies of existing processes and freeing up and allowing the reallocation of IT resources.

For example, IT outsourcing can reduce operational costs by improving the operational efficiencies of the existing business processes supported by IT. A case in point is National Account Service Company (NASCO), a Georgia-based service provider for the health insurance industry, which processes over 120 million claims annually. By outsourcing its data center operation to IBM, NASCO could substantially increase operational efficiencies and reduce costs in claim processing.

In addition, by outsourcing such traditional IT services as application development and maintenance, firms can free up their IT resources, especially their IT staff, and reallocate them to more strategic activities that can increase firms' ability to compete and achieve operational efficiencies. A case in point is Campbell Soup Company, which decided to outsource application development/maintenance and computer systems operation to IBM in 2001. By doing so, Campbell's internal IT team could focus on such activities as linking IT strategies to specific business strategies and delivering higher value solutions at an accelerated pace. In particular, the IT team could quickly deploy IT solutions to support new initiatives and innovations, as outlined by various business units. As a result, Campbell could realize significant savings through increased efficiency and productivity.[152]

At times, however, outsourcing may involve higher coordination costs and transaction risk due to a lack of hierarchical control and misaligned incentives. Furthermore, some outsourcing is driven by the need to create a scalable and predictable business model with reduced fixed costs. Outsourcing provides greater flexibility to scale the provision of IT services up or down in accordance with fluctuating business needs and to convert fixed costs into variable costs. Finally, the sometimes "soft allocation" of funds for the internal provision of IT services often does not receive as much scrutiny and discipline as when business units must pay hard dollars and real money to outside vendors.

There are also some noneconomic reasons for firms to outsource IT. These include the access to skilled professionals and a larger market, reduced cycle time due to the ability to "follow the sun,"[153] an emphasis on pursuing core competencies and outsourcing noncore activities, the need to preserve management time, the ability to deal with culture and human resources issues (if the IT department is not perceived as strong within the company), and sometimes simply the need to imitate other successful players.

6.3 What to Outsource?

What are the types of activities that are most suitable for outsourcing or disaggregation across firm boundaries? Apte and Mason (1995) provide a useful framework to think about this issue. They suggest that firms should assess their relative efficiency in performing a service activity and the strategic importance of that activity. Outsourcing makes sense if an organization has low efficiency and the activity is of low strategic importance. If both the relative efficiency and strategic importance dimensions are high, the firm should bring such an activity in-house, even if it was initially outsourced. A firm should organize a service activity as a profit center if it has a high relative efficiency in performing that activity and the activity is of low strategic importance. Conversely, the firm should engage in strategic partnerships when it has a low efficiency in performing a strategically important activity.

While this framework is useful, subsequent research suggests that firms should also think about the extent to which an activity can be codified, standardized, and modularized.[154] Codifiability is the extent to which knowledge can be converted into a form that is suitable for transfer across economic agents, or the extent to which the activities can be described completely in a set of written instructions. Activities with a high proportion of tacit knowledge are less codifiable than those that use explicit knowledge. To use the software development context as an example, the requirements definition phase, which involves the tacit firm- and context-specific knowledge of a client and the varied expectations of its multiple stakeholders, is significantly less codifiable than the programming phase once requirements have been defined and made explicit. The need to achieve codifiability in requirements definition explains why IT service providers frequently maintain a small design team at the client site. Why does codifiability facilitate service disaggregation? Codifiability enables knowledge to be captured, specialized, reduced to a set of instructions, and distributed, which contributes to modifying the spatial organization and division of labor. Codifiability of information enables more loosely coupled contact between the customer and the service provider. Codifiability enables an improved specification of roles, goals, operating procedures, and contractual obligations to facilitate the split of service activities across business units and firm boundaries. Although it may be more difficult to codify some activities with a high proportion of tacit knowledge, they can achieve codifiability as firms achieve greater process maturity and deploy more sophisticated IT systems. The increasing use of offshore locations for activities related to design, research and development (R&D), and innovation testifies to this trend.

Standardizability refers to the extent to which the activities can be performed successfully using a set of consistent and repeatable processes. The consistency of processes applies across different workers, cases, and business units. For example, the occupation of fast-food cashier is more standardizable than the occupation of trial lawyer. Fast-food cashiers can be trained to follow the same process with every customer (greet customers, ask for their orders, enter their orders, etc.). Conversely, a trial lawyer may need to follow a different process for each trial, depending on the issues involved, and two different trial lawyers may follow a different process even for the same trial. Why does standardizability facilitate service disaggregation? Standardizability of a business process enables a firm to communicate more effectively how the business operates, perform handoffs across processes, and benchmark performance. The ease of handoffs applies for processes within an organization and processes across organizations. For example, the Capability Maturity Model, developed by the Software Engineering Institute at Carnegie Melon University, is a process management standard to achieve greater consistency in software development. The CMM certification of a vendor provides assurance about its capability to work effectively in a spatially dispersed manner and has greatly facilitated the growth of outsourcing for software development. Similarly, the spread of ISO 9000 in the early 1990s also facilitated global trade by providing a standard framework to understand vendor business processes and quality levels.

Modularizability is the extent to which the activities can be separated into components so that the components can be performed independently by separate people and then later be integrated. For example, the occupation of technical writer is more modularizable than the occupation of artistic painter. For technical writing, one writer can write a chapter of a user manual, and another writer can write another chapter of a user manual, and both chapters can be placed in the manual. In contrast, it is much more difficult to modularize activities involved in creating an artistic painting because of the interdependence and inseparability of the patterns and visual imageries on a single canvas. Although the idea of modularizability has been extensively used in the manufacturing context to refer to the decomposition of a product into subassemblies and components, its use in the services context is also gaining increasing recognition. Why does modularizability facilitate service disaggregation? The modularization of business processes enables spatially dispersed groups to receive the inputs of incoming business processes and feed the outputs into outgoing business processes in a seamless manner. For example, increasing modularity of software has reduced the cost of coordinating software development and support work among parties by easing the burden of synchronizing, communicating, traveling, monitoring, providing feedback, and enforcing software development contracts. All else being equal, activities that can be easily modularized are more amenable to outsourcing and offshoring.

Because of the significance of the outsourcing decisions, managers should carefully consider their choices. The activities that are core to a business, and those that provide a significant learning and innovation opportunity and potential for creating synergy with other business activities may not be good candidates for outsourcing. Outsourcing is even more risky if the vendor poses a threat of backward integration and if initial outsourcing can thwart development of critical capabilities that may be necessary in the face of changing industry landscape. The outsourcing decisions of IBM (when it launched PC), Kodak and Borders should serve as cautionary tales for managers contemplating what to outsource.

6.4 How to Outsource?

Before I discuss how to outsource, it is important to realize that not all outsourcing arrangements are same. Conventional outsourcing dealing with commodity services typically focuses on getting the lowest bidder among the acceptable ones and monitoring performance using clear and concise specifications. In contrast, in outsourcing alliances, the focus is not on finding the lowest bidder but rather a partner that will deliver new capabilities that are not even specified up front—a situation in which a relationship has to evolve. For such arrangements, choice of supplier becomes much more critical, and the firm needs to consider supplier quality, management fit, stability, culture, size, reputation, and other noncontractible elements. Often, the non-contractible elements of exchange such as trust, responsiveness, flexibility, commitment to quality, technological investments, and information sharing have major impacts on a firm's ability to develop and market new goods and services.[155]

Next, I discuss ways of reducing outsourcing risks through choice of organizational form, location, and contracts.

6.4.1 Reducing risks by choice of location and organizational form

Aron and Singh (2005) argue that outsourcing arrangements should manage two types of risks: operational risk and structural risk. Operational risk is related to the notion of relative economic efficiency and denotes the risk that a vendor may not be able to perform as well as the internal group, at least initially. There are two ways to reduce operational risks: codify work and use effective metrics. By codifying work and developing effective metrics, firms can offshore complex processes that go back and forth.

In contrast to operational risk, structural risk is related to the idea of misalignment of incentives and noncontractibility, whereby a service provider may seem to be in compliance with the legal terms but may cut corners on intangibles that are observable to the client but are difficult to put in a contract.[156] For example, service providers may have different interests, may underinvest in training or employees, may alter the terms of the contract and create a hostage situation, and may even steal intellectual property. Firms can hedge against structural risks by insisting on a clause for service delivery even after the expiration of a contract and under the same terms (e.g., 1.5 times the time it takes to stabilize operations; Lehmann Brothers used such clauses), by splitting business between two suppliers (Bank of America and General Motors do this), and by retaining enough in-house expertise to train new providers for vital processes.

Aron and Singh suggest use of location to combat operational risk and use of organizational structure to respond to structural risk to strike a balance between control/quality of the focal organization and scale/specialization of the vendor. Extended organizational forms, hybrid forms in which a firm works very closely with an outside vendor to achieve specified quality levels and outputs, can help create a "sense-and-respond" type of collaboration. Genpact (previously GE Capital International Services, or GECIS) has two team leaders, one from the client and one from its company, to manage client projects. Research comparing captive, extended, and provider organizational forms suggests that an extended organization may start low but shows the greatest improvement over time and is cost-effective.

6.4.2 Reducing risks by contract choices

Contractual issues are also very important in outsourcing situations. Contracts should be designed to create incentive alignment between buyers and suppliers. Depending on buyer's requirements certainty, volumes and vendor's integrity, options for contracts can vary from firm fixed price to cost plus percentage of costs.[157]

Contracts for standard outsourcing differ from those based on a partnership approach. The latter types of contracts are more like a constitution, insofar as they allow for contract evolution and amendments as business conditions change. Firms should not sign a vendor's standard contract for transformational outsourcing.

Contracts for transformational outsourcing should specifically address three broad sets of issues: performance measurement, incentives, and governance mechanisms.[158] First, firms will need to establish mechanisms for performance measurement and evaluation as part of contract governance. Performance measurement should allow for flexibility and evolution. For example, in the context of cellphone services in an emerging economy the initial percentage of dropped calls and customer satisfaction levels may need to be revised depending on market evolution and competitors' actions. Measurement processes also need to be credible; they should specify who will measure and how to set and update benchmarks.

Second, how will incentives be provided (rewards and penalties)? The contract should be of sufficient magnitude and scope to be of interest to the vendor. It should discuss how revenues or profits will be shared.

Third, governance of the outsourcing arrangement must be considered. Firms need to manage governance at multiple levels and establish rules and criteria for conflict resolution and exit triggers.

The principle of "trust but verify" can serve firms well here. Firms need to think about the type of CIO or in-house staff that will be necessary for a partnership and contract management.[159] Architecture planning is needed—while execution can be outsourced, point of view or strategy should not be outsourced. Firms should retain the ability to scan emerging technologies and be able to engage in continuous learning. Sometimes supplier reputation can be a good hedge as an exit trigger.

6.5 Outcomes of Outsourcing and Offshoring

Outsourcing and offshoring can be beneficial at the overall economy level because parties will engage in an exchange only when there are gains from trade.[160] Doing everything in-house can be extremely costly and time-consuming; thus, outsourcing can be rewarding at the firm level if done carefully.[161] Offshoring involves combining the comparative advantages of countries or geographic locations with firms' resources to maximize competitive advantage.

An interesting question is how value is created and captured across geographies as a result of the disaggregation of value chains.[162] Linden and colleagues estimate the costs and margins of every firm in the value chain for an Apple iPod and an HP notebook computer.[163] They argue that most of the value is captured by players that lead in innovation and branding. For the iPod, Apple's profit is estimated at 36% of the sale price, whereas suppliers in Japan make 12%, suppliers in the United States make 3%, suppliers in Taiwan make 2%, and suppliers in Korea make .4%.

Linden et al. (2011) also study the employment implications, observing that iPod primarily creates services positions in the United States (development and sales) and production positions outside the United States. Furthermore, the U.S. development positions are much more highly compensated than the U.S. sales positions, which in turn are more highly compensated than the non-U.S. positions.

Even if outsourcing and offshoring can benefit economies and firms overall, they can be heart-wrenching and troubling at the level of individual workers. Workers may lose jobs in sectors that are

Digital Intelligence

more prone to outsourcing and offshoring, and their wages will be subject to downward pressure if they have to compete with workers in other, lower-wage countries.[164]Mithas and Whitaker (2007) test the conjecture that IT is a major "flattening" force by examining two implications at the occupation level: (1) a positive association between information intensity of an occupation and its perceived disaggregation potential and (2) a significantly adverse effect in employment and salary growth of information-intensive occupations.[165] Figure 6.2 shows selected occupations covered by the study.

Figure 6.2: Selected Occupations at Different Levels of Information Intensity and Physical Presence Need

		Low	Medium	High
Need for Physical Presence	**High**	Mail carrier Janitor Waiter Home health aid	Construction manager Physical therapist Executive secretary	College professor Registered nurse Air traffic controller Legislator
	Medium	Office clerk	Retail salesperson Real estate broker	Mechanical engineer
	Low		Word processor	Accountant Computer programmer Data entry keyer

Information Intensity

The results indicate support for the former implication but not for the latter. They find that information-intensive occupations are perceived as having a higher disaggregation potential, implying that such jobs are more amenable to offshoring. High information intensity makes an occupation more amenable to disaggregation because the activities in such occupations can be codified, standardized, and modularized.[166] This research suggests that occupations that have greater modularizability are the most susceptible to the flattening effects of IT. However, Mithas and Whitaker's (2007) analysis of actual employment and salary growth for more than 300 U.S. service occupations from 2000 to 2004 does not show adverse effects on employment or salary growth, at least at mean skill levels. On the contrary, the findings show that high-information-intensity occupations that require higher skill levels experienced greater employment growth.

Figure 6.3 shows that, on average (without adjusting for any other covariates), among high-IT-intensive occupations, high-skill occupations have experienced greater salary growth and employment growth.

Figure 6.3: Salary and Employment Growth from 2000 to 2004 for High-IT-Intensive Occupations

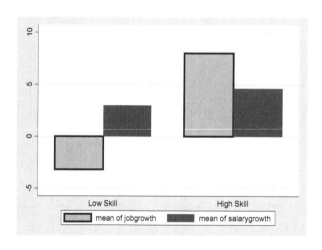

Although high-information-intensity occupations that require higher skill levels experienced a decline in salary growth (relative to occupations that require lower skill levels, after adjusting for a variety of covariates), occupations with a higher need for physical presence also show a decline in salary growth regardless of the skill levels of such occupations. These findings run counter to the media hype that exaggerates the potentially adverse employment and salary consequences of IT-enabled outsourcing and offshoring.

If IT does not flatten the world, what sustains the spikes in the global economy? Mithas and Whitaker's (2007) research implies that skill levels and the need for physical proximity will continue to be frictional forces in the free movement of jobs and equalization of wages. Their findings suggest that occupations with a higher need for physical presence have experienced higher employment growth and lower salary growth. Furthermore, high-skill occupations experienced higher employment growth and salary growth than low-skill occupations.

Figure 6.4 shows that among IT-intensive occupations during the 2000–2004 period, occupations with higher modularizability experienced lower employment and salary growth than occupations with lower modularizability.

Figure 6.4: Salary and Employment Growth from 2000 to 2004 for High-IT-Intensive Occupations by Modularizability

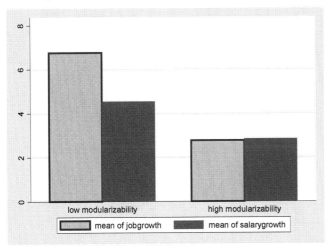

Let us now consider the impact of IT outsourcing at firm level. These days, it is rare for a business not to outsource some part of its information technology function. According to the IT research and advisory company Gartner, global spending for IT outsourcing was projected to reach $287 billion in 2013. What's more, the growth of cloud computing may make IT outsourcing even more common. For many companies, reducing operating costs is a key goal of IT outsourcing, but not all companies realize such savings.

One reason managers may not realize the expected gains from IT outsourcing is because they narrowly focus on only their IT costs. Research suggests that outsourcing IT can also help to reduce other expenses such as sales, general and administrative costs, which are often four to five times IT costs. When managers think of IT outsourcing as a mere substitute for internal IT investments, this narrow focus hides many potential cost benefits. This study, based on data from approximately 300 U.S. companies over the 1999-2003 period, found that a $96.14 million increase in IT outsourcing spending by a company was associated with, on average, a $121.14 million drop in operating costs in other, non-IT functions at the company. [167]

Traditionally, outsourcing and in-house production of IT have been treated as substitutes from a "make-or-buy" perspective based on transaction cost economics. However, to the extent that the internal IT investments of a firm can make it better leverage the expertise and non-contractible investments of its outsourcing vendors, the internal and outsourced IT investments can be complements, as well. This study found that IT outsourcing is not a substitute for internal IT investments, especially investments in personnel.[168] Although outsourcing was associated with a significant reduction in non-IT operating costs, that reduction in non-IT operating costs was greater for companies that made higher levels of internal IT investments.

Figure 6.5 shows the complementarity. The top (bottom) line in the figure shows the slope and intercept of regressing non-IT operating costs on IT outsourcing while fixing the internal IT investment at its mean minus (plus) one standard deviation. The regression line is steeper at the higher level of internal IT investment, and the intercept is smaller at the higher level of internal IT investment. This indicates that greater IT investments are associated with lower non-IT operating costs at a given level of IT outsourcing. This may be because IT outsourcing can increase the operational efficiencies of existing processes and free up resources, thereby allowing resource reallocation. Furthermore, companies' complementary internal investments in IT can make business processes more information-intensive and facilitate coordination with vendors, thereby magnifying outsourcing's cost-cutting effects.

Figure 6.5. Complementarity between IT Outsourcing and Internal IT Investments

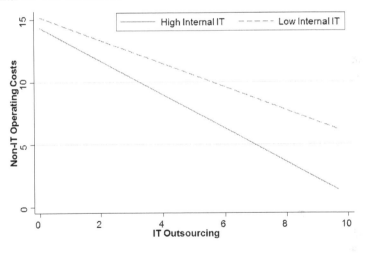

An intriguing finding from the study is that among the various components of internal IT investments (hardware, software, employees, etc.), only investments in employees have a synergy with IT outsourcing in reducing non-IT costs.

Figure 6.6, shows two regression lines: the top (bottom) line in the figure shows the slope and intercept of regressing non-IT operating costs on IT outsourcing while fixing the IT labor spending at its mean minus (plus) one standard deviation. The regression line

Digital Intelligence

is steeper at the higher level of IT labor spending, and the intercept is smaller at the higher level of IT labor spending.

Figure 6.6: Complementarity between IT Outsourcing and IT Labor

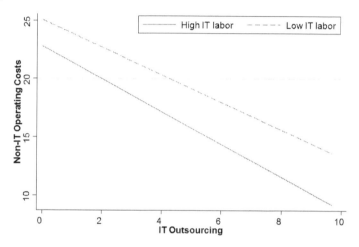

Figure 6.6 indicates that higher IT labor spending is associated with lower non-IT operating costs at a given level of IT outsourcing. This is because IT employees play a critical role in managing and exploiting outsourcing: Not only do they ensure that the vendors keep making investments in the non-contractible aspects of the outsourcing relationship, but they also play the role of a trustworthy liaison between their internal customers (that is, business functions) and vendors.

These findings can assist managers in formulating strategies and allocating budgets. First, managers need to take a balanced approach to their investments in internal systems and outsourcing in order to reap greater benefits in terms of cost savings: Merely substituting IT outsourcing for internal IT will not be very effective. In addition, while managers have mainly focus on the benefit of reducing IT costs when they consider IT outsourcing, they should focus on the impact of IT outsourcing on non-IT costs, which are

136

much larger than IT costs, and formulate strategies for maximizing the savings on these expenses in order to get the most out of their outsourcing spending.

More broadly, benchmarking with respect to competitors on IT budgets alone may be counterproductive. An overemphasis on reducing IT costs may deflect attention from potential opportunities for reducing costs in other areas such as R&D, marketing and sales, and other administrative costs where IT-enabled savings may significantly outweigh any increased spending on IT. Too strong an emphasis on IT cost reduction may overlook this significant point. Managers should remember that it is ultimately the overall costs of a firm that determine its profitability, not just spending less on IT.

Finally, managers need to be careful about the practice of transferring IT employees to the vendor company, which is common in IT outsourcing deals. Internal employees play a critical role in capturing value from outsourcing. Why? It is important to maintain some IT expertise within the firm and having some in-house IT employees to decide which parts of IT to outsource, how to negotiate a mutually acceptable contract with the vendor, how to monitor the outsourcing alliance, how to tailor the outsourcing contract with the passage of time, and finally, how to "backsource" (i.e., bring in-house) a function if the outsourcing contract does not work to a firm's advantage. No matter how well designed a contract is, even if a vendor can make such employees available on contract, a firm still needs some in-house employees who would put the firm's interest ahead of the vendor's interests for the resolution of conflicts due to changes in the business conditions or economic environment, and to ensure that the vendors continue to make investments in the non-contractible aspects of the relationship. Research by Soon Ang and Sandra Slaughter (1998) found that internal IT employees exhibit significantly more organizational citizenship behaviors in terms of extra-role activities and loyalty, compared to outsourced IT employees.

More importantly, internal IT staff can also serve as trustworthy boundary spanners between business functions and the vendor. IT outsourcing typically involves a great deal of knowledge integration activities between the vendor and the client for bridging the knowledge gap (i.e., technical vs. business knowledge) between them. These activities are related to the concept of *boundary spanning, which is important* in both internal systems development and outsourcing context.

Internal IT employees' boundary spanning roles can help their firm capture greater value from IT outsourcing, not only because they understand both the technical and business aspects of the outsourced projects, but also because they have the same objective function and profit motive as their internal business clients, unlike between a firm's and a vendor's employees. For example, internal IT employees can translate the functional domain knowledge of their internal business clients into a language and technical specifications that the technical IT staff of the vendor can understand. Internal IT staff can also help vendors customize their IT solutions to serve the strategic needs of the enterprise. Moreover, these internal IT employees can also ensure a vendor's compliance to such specifications, safeguarding the client firm if a conflict were to arise between what the business clients expected and what the vendor delivered. This is the very reason that GM wanted to "bring in-house some more experience, versatile IT professionals ... who can broker disputes that devolve into finger-pointing or can act as paramedic if something's perilously wrong [in outsourcing]" (Weier 2009), according to its CIO, Terry Kline. Therefore, to get the most out of IT outsourcing, companies should continue to make investments in their own IT professionals and help them improve their skills through continued education, training, and accumulation of relevant industry experience.

6.6 Implications for Policy

From a policy perspective, the results of prior studies suggest that despite the amenability of information-intensive occupations to offshoring, on average, high-information-intensive occupations have not yet experienced a decline in employment or salary growth. Although information-intensive jobs are more likely to be offshored in the long run, there appears to be no current need for policies specifically designed to avoid the migration of information-intensive jobs overseas.

To the extent that developed economies such as the United States and the United Kingdom enjoy a surplus on the whole from the free flow of business services (exports being more than imports) and though the share of service imports is significantly less than that of manufacturing imports (0.9% in 2001 in the United States), any restrictions on global trade in services will only make their current account deficits larger.

At the same time, governments are responsible for ensuring that gains from globalization and trade are allocated equitably and that workers are equipped with education and retraining to cope with macroeconomic forces that affect the jobs and wages of individual workers. One of the disconcerting aspects in this context is that the cost of creating jobs has grown from a few thousand dollars to nearly a hundred thousand dollars over last 30 years.[169] Foxconn (or Hon Hai) employs more workers than Apple, Dell, Microsoft, HP, Intel, and Sony combined. The United States has to find a way to provide meaningful jobs for the masses to maintain social harmony and to avoid the potential downsides of a winner-take-all economy.

Another implication for policy relates to high-skill immigration. It is often tempting to become insular and restrict entry or employment of high-skill foreign-born workers or to delay their citizenship. But succumbing to these temptations would be unwise, particularly if such temptations are based on anecdotes. An academic study of over 50,000 information technology professionals provides evidence to support the benefits of employing highly skilled foreign workers in the United States.[170] Contrary to popular beliefs, this study found that foreign IT workers in the United State earn a salary premium of between 5 and 9% over U.S. IT workers' salaries. Some critics claim that foreign-born workers substitute for U.S. workers; they work for lower wages and depress the wages of U.S. citizens. The finding that U.S. firms pay the foreign IT workers a premium over IT workers who are U.S. citizens implies that these foreign workers are not substituting for U.S. workers. In fact, foreign and

Digital Intelligence

U.S. IT workers may be complements: employing one group enhances the job opportunities of the other.

Why might companies operating in the U.S. pay a foreign worker more than a U.S. Citizen? One explanation may be because of intangible aspects of human capital. A foreign-born IT worker shows flexibility in her willingness to move to a new country and is willing to take a risk that such a move will have real benefits. This worker is highly motivated, and is willing to work flexibly at any location her employer chooses, whether within the US or abroad. Such workers are essential for US companies to compete successfully in today's global economy where about 48% of the revenues of S&P 500 companies came from abroad in 2008. Some attribute the reason for success of U.S. firms in global markets to its dynamic and vibrant high-skill immigrant workforce, in contrast to relatively homogenous labor in Japanese firms. Foreign-born workers also help to create new jobs through their entrepreneurial activities. Others suggest that foreign-born workers enhance innovation in American companies, Universities and the US economy.

What do these findings suggest about immigration policy? First, if foreign-born IT professionals are complements of US workers then expanding visa availability for high-skill foreign workers may be a prudent policy. Second, the need for policy change should consider foreign student enrollment in U.S. universities, a pathway to enter the U.S. workforce. Some have argued for legislation that would grant green cards to foreign students who receive a graduate degree in science, technology, engineer or math from a U.S. university, and one could suggest extending these categories to include business and management. Other proposals that suggest creation of a new visa for entrepreneurs who are able to receive funding from venture capitalists and angel investors should also be considered. We need more companies like Google, Sun Microsystems and Apple, often co-founded by immigrants, to create the next wave of technologies and business model innovations to spur job growth. Interestingly, Steve Jobs, the founder of Apple, was a Syrian immigrant's son, a moot point in light of the ongoing debate on stance toward immigrants and refugees in 2016 US Presidential elections. Among other policy implications, there is a need to educate and train students and workers for the emerging global economy. Policymakers should provide funding and incentives for higher education to educate workers who lose jobs due to the changing occupational mix and skill needs of the economy.

6.7 Implications for Managers

From a firm's perspective, occupations with higher information intensity and a lower need for physical presence are the primary candidates for service disaggregation. By making suitable investments in digital platforms to bring an exogenous shift in the information intensity of business processes, managers can decouple information-intensive activities from activities that require physical presence.

The finding that modularizability partially mediates the relationship between information intensity and disaggregation potential calls for firms to focus on process modularization capabilities. Digital enterprises need to develop process expertise so they can evaluate the interdependencies among service activities, modularize the activities, disaggregate the activities to take advantage of global resources, and reintegrate outputs from the disaggregated processes into the service activity to provide the customer with a seamless experience. This will enable firms to optimize their portfolio of business processes and to locate the processes where they can be performed with greater effectiveness at a lower cost. [171]

Managers should leverage the potential of IT to codify, standardize, and modularize as many business activities as possible and use the geographical distribution of talent and wages to their firm's advantage. If they do not do so, their firms can lose advantage to more nimble competitors, as many manufacturing firms experienced when they did not move quickly enough to relocate facilities and personnel to more cost-effective locations in an earlier phase dominated by globalization of manufacturing.

While managers take these steps to make their firms more competitive, they also need to be mindful of what they need to do to keep them valuable for their firms. Sooner or later, their own occupation will be subject to the same forces of IT-enabled codification, standardization, and modularization that affect other occupations.

What should individual knowledge workers do to become less vulnerable to the potentially undesirable effects of globalization? They should consider investing in higher education degrees that have high returns, such as an MBA.[172] If they have already done so, they should periodically attend short-term executive or continuous education programs. Or they consider acquiring other higher skills or job experiences that make their job and activities less modularizable. For example, they can make themselves more valuable by acquiring a deeper understanding of the linkages and connections between activities and business processes that will provide a competitive advantage to their firms.

Sometimes, acquiring new skills may require switching jobs or industries. Although risky in the short run, such moves across firms or industries may prove advantageous in the long run. As the world continues to globalize and boundaryless careers become more common, knowledge workers need to continuously improve their behavioral skills, customer management skills, and knowledge of foreign cultures to help their firms adapt products and services to meet the needs of a global marketplace in the emerging service economy.

The bottom line is that while managers are busy codifying, standardizing, and modularizing others' jobs, they also need to invest in acquiring newer competencies and skills to keep themselves updated and relevant. If firms value managers' abilities to spot and reconfigure resources, such managers are likely to be in demand, regardless of whether the world becomes flat or remains spiky.

6.8 Chapter Summary

This chapter focused on the fourth D, which pertains to delivery of IT services. Increasingly, firms are relying on outsourcing and offshoring to deliver IT services; thus, the discussion focused on how firms and managers should think about some governance issues in these contexts.

The chapter began with the argument that outsourcing and offshoring represent a trend toward disaggregation across the value chain or country borders and a manifestation of globalization. I then discussed why there is a trend toward outsourcing and some of the risks of outsourcing.

This was followed by a discussion of why firms outsource IT, what can be outsourced, and how that should be done by choosing an appropriate location and organizational form. Finally, I noted some outcomes of outsourcing, along with implications for policy and managers.

Part 3
Manage IT

Chapter 7: Managing Digital Infrastructure

"The bearing of a child takes nine months, no matter how many women are assigned."

> —Frederick P. Brooks Jr., in *The Mythical Man-Month* (1995, p. 17)

"How does a project get to be a year late? ... One day at a time."

> —Frederick P. Brooks Jr. (1995, p. 153)

In the previous chapters, I have discussed how to synchronize IT and strategy and how to govern IT. The focus of this chapter is on how to manage the implementation of IT systems.

As noted earlier, firms spend significant sums of money on IT. Research using data on large global corporations suggests that their IT investments were approximately $15,000 per employee in the 1998–2003 period in constant 2000 dollars.[173] This is about ten times the figure reported by McAfee (2006) for U.S. firms' investment in IT per employee at $1,500 in 1987. On average, U.S. firms tend to spend about 3 percent of their revenues on IT, with some fluctuation around average depending on their strategic posture, industry factors, and economic conditions.

While IT investments can help firms improve their performance, many well-intentioned IT projects fall far short of their goal, as noted previously in the "IT Hall of Shame" (see Chapter 2).

145

Some never finish, others finish too late or too costly, and some never provide the benefits that they were expected to achieve.[174] According to a 2002 KPMG study, approximately 56% of firms had to write off at least one information systems project as a failure during the previous year. Examples of IT failures include botched implementation of healthcare.gov, and loss of customer or user data at organizations such as Target, Sony, hospitals, universities and other government organizations. The goal here is to understand how managers can avoid these IT implementation problems.

7.1 Components of IT Systems

Like other technologies (Arthur 2009), IT is a collection of other subtechnologies. I begin by classifying different components of IT systems. Broadly speaking, most IT can be classified into hardware, software, databases, and networks. Sometimes a fifth component called "vaporware" also exists, and managers need to be able to distinguish vaporware from more useful components of IT systems. That may require "wetware" which is the knowledge that allows an organization to evaluate, use and upgrade technologies over time.[175] Nurturing and developing this knowledge by investing in education and training of business and IT professionals is the responsibility of top management and IT department of an organization.

Hardware refers to anything that can be physically touched. Software refers to computer programs that make hardware do useful things. Databases are specialized software programs that help store and process relevant information about customers, suppliers, employees, products, transactions, and relationships. Networks are what connects pieces of an enterprise together and allows connections with suppliers and customers.

The history of hardware, databases, and networks can be traced to early incarnations of human computing.[176] For example, the abacus was an early form of hardware. Cave paintings and folklore served as databases of human memory. Fire, drum beats, and pigeons substituted for networks. Only software does not seem to have a similar equivalent in human history. It may not be out of place here to mention that even the word "computer" referred to people who solved equations, and it was only around 1945 that the word began to describe machinery.[177]

Next, I briefly review some trends in hardware, software, databases, and networks from a managerial perspective.

7.1.1 Hardware

Hardware is perhaps the least problematic from a managerial perspective because it is characterized by Moore's law and miniaturization. Moore's law refers to an observation in 1965 by Gordon Moore, cofounder of Intel, that the number of transistors per square inch on integrated circuits doubled every year since the integrated circuit was invented. Moore predicted that this trend would continue for the foreseeable future. In subsequent years, the pace slowed down a bit, but data density has doubled approximately every 18 months (the current definition of Moore's law).

Because of Moore's law and significant advances in technology, hardware prices have declined significantly over the years. One gigabytes of memory used to cost about $200,000 in 1980, now it costs only about $100 to buy 1 terabytes of memory. For the sake of comparison, in 1978 a commercial flight between New York and Paris cost $900 and took 7 hours—this should cost a penny and take less than one second if Moore's law applied to airline industry.[178] By another measure, a $4,000 computer of 1987 quality should be worth only approximately $40 in 2007 dollars, based on Brynjolfsson and Saunders's calculations.

Hardware is often based on open standards, which facilitates "plug and play." Taken together, advances in technology and declining prices make hardware ubiquitous, faster, quieter, more intuitive, and user friendly. Increasingly, because of the convergence of technologies, the boundaries between computers, electronics, and appliances are blurring. Increasingly, firms are letting users to bring their own devices (this is known as BYOD or "bring your own device" movement), in contrast to emphasis on standardization of computing equipment till not long ago.

IBM, Sun (acquired by Oracle), HP, Dell, Apple, Intel, AMD, Motorola, and Lenovo are among the major hardware vendors.

7.1.2 Software

Software can be classified into applications software and systems software. Applications software programs directly satisfy specific user needs. They can be personal applications, such as Microsoft Office or OpenOffice, or enterprise systems, such as ERP, CRM, and KM systems. They can be proprietary (developed in-house or outsourced), commercial off-the-shelf (COTS), or open source. Systems software programs serve as intermediaries between hardware and applications software and include control programs (e.g., operating systems, which make hardware more usable and provide functions needed by many applications) and support programs (e.g., utilities, performance monitors, security monitors). Some of the major software vendors include Oracle, SAP, IBM, Microsoft, Apple, Google, Red Hat, Adobe, and Salesforce.

The software development process is labor intensive (vs. the assembly-line approach typical of hardware), slow, and prone to error. As a result, software is often "buggy" and irritating from a managerial perspective. Software is characterized by Linus' law which states that "given enough eyeballs, all bugs are shallow." [179]

Software expenditures have been growing as a percentage of IT budget compared with hardware over the years. Unfortunately, much of the software budget goes toward maintenance costs (approximately 80% of the IT budget), known as the "legacy problem" in the IT world.

There are a few noticeable trends in software. First, there is a trend from in-house development to COTS (e.g., ERP).[180]

Second, there is a trend from proprietary to open source. For example, operating systems used to be proprietary, but there are more choices now as a result of open source.[181] "Open" in open source refers to source code which is open for anyone to see and even modify. Some examples of open source software are Linux (operating system related to Unix), Apache (powers websites), MySQL (Oracle acquired MySQL in December 2009 but promised not to interfere with its open source model to favor its proprietary offerings), and Firefox browser.

The open source movement is gaining wide acceptance in firms and even governments (e.g., China, Massachusetts). IBM supports the open source approach, and Red Hat helps clients use open source software. Even Microsoft appears to be coming around to accepting at least some form of an open source model for some of its software. Among the advantages of open source, it is reliable, cheaper, customizable, and runs on everything from personal digital assistants to mainframes. The open source movement is even spreading to other areas, such as drug development, R&D, and the Human Genome Project. However, there are some issues associated with it, such as how to ensure quality and innovation, how to avoid free riding, protecting intellectual property, its ability to create new things versus being appropriate only for commoditized content, and how to sustain contributors' motivation once the novelty wears off.

Because the word "open" is used in many ways, there is a need to make a distinction among open source, open standards, and open application programming interface (API). Open source is when all source code is open in addition to the compiled code (the code that runs on your system). This is like a restaurant giving away the recipe to its most popular food item or Coca-Cola disclosing its recipe. In contrast, closed source (also known as "proprietary") software releases only the finished, tested, and supported code to the general public. The source code is considered intellectual property, and it is protected by law. Open standards—protocols such as HTTP and XML—are industry-accepted standards. Greater use of open standards facilitates better interoperability among different types of computers and networks. Open API creates an open but structured API to allow developers to significantly customize a piece of software without affecting the overall integrity of the application or system. This provides many of the benefits of open source without the problem of interoperability and integrity.[182]

A third trend in software is toward greater interoperability. There are several approaches to ensure interoperability. Service-oriented architecture (and its variants, such as web services, software as a service, or on-demand) has emerged as a dominant approach. This approach offers several advantages compared with earlier approaches, such as point-to-point connection or middleware (mix-and-match). Web services are technologies that make it easy for computer programs to automatically share information and computing tasks with each other over the Internet. This approach views systems as services (credit check, delivery scheduling), and each system "exposes" a standard interface to other systems. Systems communicate with each other in the context of flexible business processes. These are self-contained, server-based programs designed to perform a single function with interfaces expressed in a standard form (based on XML). They are published in such a way that they can be called on remotely (in general, through HTTP). Amazon Web Services, for example, gives direct access to Amazon.com's technology platform to access catalog data, create and populate an Amazon.com shopping cart, and initiate the checkout process.[183]

Among the prominent business implications of these trends are the conversion of fixed costs into variable costs (pay as you go) and the potential of IT to provide a significant source of revenue.

Among software issues for managers, three are of particular importance. First, there is software evaluation and selection, which includes decisions related to the user base, costs, computing environment, in-house skills, and security.

Second, software licensing has emerged as an important area. Managers need to ensure that software is being used legally, and they must be able to show proof of purchase. Some countries are particularly notorious for piracy and are known as "one-copy" nations. According to some estimates, piracy rates for PC software in China exceeded 75% in 2011.[184] As a result, Microsoft derives only approximately 5% of its revenues from China even though the PC sales in China and the United States are close to 70 million and China has more Internet users (close to 400 million in 2011) than the population of the United States.

Third, managers need to decide when it is a good time to upgrade software; that is, should they wait or innovate? However, it is not always an easy decision, and choice should depend on a firm's business model, how it competes, and what its information needs are.

7.1.3 Databases

Databases are type of software programs that store and manipulate data. For example, databases enable a retailer like Sam's Club to store detailed transaction-level data on millions of customers along with videos of such transactions all the way until customers load their purchases into their cars in the parking lot.

Databases are extremely useful in commercial applications. These programs capture large volumes of data, which in turn are used by analysts (financial, marketing), accountants, auditors, management, staff, sales, and production.

Although flat files, such as Excel, may be good enough for simpler applications, they are not scalable and do not handle deletions, updates, and insertions well. One of the purported reasons for restatement of earnings has been the practice of linking dozens and sometimes hundreds of Excel files and one macro going wrong. Relational databases provide a solution to these problems because facts are stored only once; thus, it is easy to relate data in different tables, facilitating *ad hoc* questions. Many ERP solutions use one integrated database at their core.

The vast explosion of "big data" in recent years, driven by internet activity, mobile technology and the embedding of chips in everyday physical items, is creating a vast digital trail about where we are, what we are doing, what we like and the state and location of physical assets.[185]

This trend of "big data" is associated with 4 V's: Volume (large scale), Velocity (moving or streaming data), Variety (data in different forms, e.g., numerical, text, video) and Veracity (uncertain, inconsistent, imprecise, ambiguous, and sometimes deceptive data, especially from social media and sensors). At the same time, analytics techniques are becoming more powerful, from reporting data to understanding and predicting, and increasingly to optimizing and learning systems that can continually adapt to new conditions. Business analytics combines this powerful combination of data and analytical techniques to automate increasingly complex decisions, far beyond traditional transaction processing tasks into territory which has historically reliant on human judgment.

However, it is not clear if increasingly advanced analytical capabilities create opportunities for radical change in business or just represent an incremental improvement to existing systems. Furthermore previous generations of decision-support technologies have frequently failed to deliver their full potential in practice and many businesses are struggling to make sense of their already large volumes of data.

Are businesses well-positioned to take advantage of the new opportunities created through analytics and big data? The broad conclusion seems to be that business analytics and big data provide radical opportunities to reshape businesses, at least in some industries, but organizational capabilities are relatively in low in all but the biggest companies. This is resulting in many management and implementation challenges and slowing the adoption of tools in practice. [186]

First, although "big data and business analytics" have significant potential, they also have significant limitations and dark side, much like their predecessor technologies. For example, easy availability and manipulation of digital data raises significant privacy concerns for citizens to protect from ill-intentioned or inadvertent misuse of data about them by governments or organizations. To the extent that laws and governance processes are often found lagging or lacking sufficient protection, there is a role for practitioners and academics to come together to inform public discourse in this area and craft prudent policies that protect individual privacy while fostering innovation.

Digital Intelligence

It is also important to note in this context that sheer availability of data and analytics tools does not guarantee that we will suddenly be able to predict everything correctly as the hype would suggest. The case of MIT failing to predict how many students will actually enroll after getting admission offer as late as 2012, and the inability of scientists to predict earthquake incidents in Italy are some sobering reminders. Good data or tools alone will not guarantee that we reach better decisions unless we also equip scientists and managers to pose good questions in the first place or interpret the outputs of data analysis with their deep domain knowledge and judgment that often comes with years of experience.

From a governance perspective, big data and business analytics will require rethinking the role of the CIO and IT department because other functional areas and disciplines. This will also require revisiting some issues such as centralization versus decentralization. For example, businesses need to consider the following key questions when establishing management and governance structures around analytics using the 4D framework that we discussed earlier:

- Decision rights – who will have the decision rights for leading and sponsoring the big data and business analytics projects? To what extent should these decisions be made by business or technology executives and how centralized or decentralized should they be? How should IS, marketing, finance and business executives collaborate on such decisions?

- Department Role and Configuration– what is the role of IT department in developing analytics skills and implementing and exploiting systems? How does it interface with other business units and how are its services charged back to business units?

- Dollars – how much to spend and where should resources be focused? Where is the long-term advantage likely to be e.g. in developing skills?

- Delivery – should businesses recruit and build in-house capabilities for business analytics, retrain existing staff or outsource to specialist providers?

The importance of leadership is essential to success of any analytics effort and there is also a need for a shift in culture: from a culture of Highest-Paid Person's Opinion ('HiPPO') to a data-driven decision-making culture. In many cases, though, senior management do not have sufficient understanding of data to give this leadership. Perhaps more pressure may be needed from sources such as the stock markets to drive change. For example, if institutional and retail investors demand more information from firms and punish or reward them for how they are preparing for big data and business analytics, that can prompt firms to pay more attention to a more prudent approach to their information technology based assets and capabilities. It may also be necessary in some cases to bring in new leaders from outside the organization who have greater experience and understanding of the importance of data and analytics. As businesses gather and exploit more and more personal data, there will be a need to manage customer expectations and compliance obligations.[187]

7.1.4 Networks

Networks can be classified in many ways depending on their reach and specificity. Local area networks (LAN) connect computers within a building. They can be based on client/server architecture in which a server processes requests from clients (e.g., ordering books on Amazon.com's servers) or peer to peer in which all computers are equal (e.g., Napster, Gnutella).

Wide area networks (WAN) connect computers within a city or over longer distances. They can be value-added networks (VANs) or virtual private networks (VPNs). Intranets are networks within an organization. Extranets also connect with suppliers and others business partners.

Digital Intelligence

Internet is a public network of computers worldwide. Electronic data interchange, or EDI, was a protocol to connect firms in the automotive industry originally, but now it is also used in other industries. Electronic marketplaces are networks that connect buyers and suppliers.

Although it used be that different vendors dominated hardware (IBM, HP), software (SAP, Microsoft), databases (Oracle), networks (Cisco), and services (IBM), increasingly there is a trend toward consolidation, as exemplified by the acquisition of Sun Microsystems by Oracle, the acquisition of EDS and 3Com by HP, and the acquisition of Perot Systems by Dell.

Perhaps the most significant trend when it comes to networks is the use of social networks such as Facebook, LinkedIn and Twitter and how quickly they have become part of corporate computing. Networks are characterized by several laws. For example, Metcalfe's law suggests that the value of a one-to-one or transactional network is roughly equal to the square of the number of nodes or users in a network (in its precise form, value is proportional to $[N \times (N-1)]$ which approaches N squared when N is very large). This law is sometimes used to justify high valuations of networked businesses. Others use Reed's law to justify even higher valuations for many-to-many networks whose value is proportional to 2 to the power N when N is very large.[188] There is also Dunbar law which roughly says that humans truly care about 150 people or so and it is very hard to form meaningful relationships with groups larger than 150.[189]

Figure 7.1 shows sales and market capitalization of selected technologies companies in 2011 and 2015. Tech companies often show higher revenue and market cap growth compared to firms in other sectors of the economy. Some of them are among the most valuable companies in the world by market capitalization, despite their relatively young history.

Figure 7.1: Sales and Market Cap of Selected Tech Companies (All values are in Millions USD)

Firm	2015 Sales	2015 Market Cap	2011 Sales	2011 Market Cap
1. Amazon	107,006	251,853	48,077	82,467
2. Netflix	6779.5	38,737	3,204	5,789
3. Facebook	17,928	294,505	3,700	65,000 - 100,000[2]
4. Twitter	2,218	12,587	139	7,700
5. Google (Alphabet Inc.)	74,989	485,487	37,905	199,077
6. eBay	8,592	27,735	11,651	48,246
7. Groupon	3,120	2,254	1,624	10,835
8. Apple	234,988	533,721	108,249	544,140
9. IBM	81,741	128,491	106,916	233,383
10. SAP	20,797	85,474	14,233	47,254.47
11. Microsoft	88,084	412,786	69,943	176,925
12. Oracle	37,473	153,891	35,622	160,969
13. Intel	55,355	138,980	53,999	113,744
14. Cisco	49,589	134,161	43,218	59,066
15. Comcast	74,510	139,998	55,842	118,187
16. HP	103,355	18,850	127,245	47,017
17. Xerox	18,045	9,456	21,900	18,874
18. Dell	58,100[1]	NA	61,494	24,382

Notes: For 2015, annual sales information was collected from Thomson for the period ending Dec 2015, and market capitalization information is as of 20 February 2015 (from Thomson). For 2011, annual sales information was collected from Bloomberg for the period ending Dec 2011, and market capitalization information is as of 14 March 2012 (from Bloomberg). [190]

According to a Bloomberg Businessweek article in 2014, Facebook was on track to reach a market capitalization of $150 billion from its IPO in the shortest amount of time in about 1.5 years (fewer than 30 companies had achieved a market cap of $150 billion by 2014). It took other companies far longer: IBM took about 83 years, Intel and Apple about 27 years each, Amazon 17, Oracle 14, Microsoft 11, Cisco 9, Google 3.[191] These tech companies often receive admiration or criticism for their business practices and policies related to human resources and how they make use of or protect customer data.

7.2 Major Eras in Computing and the Challenges of "Legacy" Management

For most people, the Information Age dawned when *Time* magazine named "The Computer" its Person of the Year in 1982, long before it named humans (i.e., "You") as its Person of the Year in 2006. However, the history of "information" is more ancient and complex.[192] Some have assigned "information technology scores" to the Eastern and Western world going as far back as 9300 BC.[193] However, using Carl Sagan's (1977) Cosmic Calendar, in which the 15 billion year lifetime of the universe (since the Big Bang) is compressed into the span of a single year and the first human appeared as late as 10:30 p.m. on December 31 of this Cosmic Calendar, our current notion of information technology is as old as what happened in the first one second of New Year's Day.

The more recent evolution of computing can be understood in at least four major phases dating back to the 1960s.[194]

The first phase, which lasted until about 1980, can be subdivided into the "mainframe era," and "mini era" (1965–1980). The mainframe era lasted until about 1965, and was largely led by IBM. At that time, much of the software came bundled with hardware. COBOL and ASCII were two of the more well-known software languages of this era—they are still used. The "mini era" (1965–1980) was led by the Digital Equipment Corporation, although IBM and HP also sold miniframe computers. This was an exciting age for the development of computing. Unix came along in 1969, and Microsoft, Apple, Oracle, and 3Com were founded between 1975 and 1979. ARPANET (Advanced Research Projects Agency Network) came along in 1969. As mentioned previously, in the early 1970s, Xerox's PARC lab had many of the key technologies that eventually came to revolutionize computing in products introduced by other companies such as Microsoft and Apple.

Digital Intelligence

The second phase, the "PC era," lasted from 1980 to about 1995. IBM transformed the computer industry with its PC, which had a radically new modular architecture. Although its decisions created waves of innovations, some of those innovations did not go well for IBM, and IBM eventually exited the PC business altogether in the early 2000s. The major players in this era were Microsoft, Apple, Sun, Compaq, and Dell. Cisco (1984) and AOL (1989) were founded in this period.

The third era, called the "networked era," began around 1995, with Netscape's browser that brought computing to laypeople. Client–server computing became dominant, and in the early 2000s, peer-to-peer computing, which many identify with Napster and BitTorrent, continued to revolutionize computing.

The fourth era, called the "mobile era," began around 2002, and this era is characterized by significant diffusion of social (e.g., Facebook, LinkedIn, Twitter), location-based (e.g., Google Maps), cloud computing, big data and business analytics, and mobile computing.

In the early days of computing, there was a separation between scientific computing and commercial computing. The arrival of the IBM 360 series in the mid-1960s helped bridge scientific and commercial computing—until then, advances in scientific computing led advances in commercial computing. Then, commercial computing and consumer technology remained segmented for a while, but more recently, thanks to the efforts of Steve Jobs and other pioneers, developments in consumer technology have begun to drive the expectations of corporate customers. Even in business settings, there is now an expectation for easy-to-use and always-available software applications similar to what consumers are able to experience on their smartphones or tablets.

The nature of IT services and their production function has undergone significant changes since mid-1990s in at least three ways. First, use of Internet-era open standards and service-oriented architecture facilitates a relatively seamless integration of disparate systems, thus reducing the complexity of overall IT infrastructure.

Open standards, such as the ones based on XML, allow for greater flexibility in establishing automated communication between firms, and can be contrasted with proprietary or bilaterally-established standards such as Electronic Data Interchange (EDI) which require substantial firm-specific investments on the part of one or both partners leading to potential inflexibility in disconnecting or switching to new partners, or in changing the scope of the relationship. Many IT implementations after 1998 or so relied on such systems and that made IT infrastructure of firms more IT flexible because such systems allowed business partners to more easily connect, engage and establish automated communication. Before 1998, many firms were still using legacy pre-Internet-era IT systems, and these systems did not allow as much connectivity and integration as the open standards–based systems that emerged subsequently. Second, firms made much greater use of package applications such as ERP and CRM systems in the post-1998 period. Although these commercial off-the-shelf enterprise systems still require significant investments in process design, workflow planning, and development by vendors, they require relatively less effort in roll-out phase at a customer's end compared with the fully proprietary and custom-made software development projects that were more prevalent earlier. Finally, firms made significant use of IT outsourcing and offshoring services to leverage enhanced software development quality and reduced labor costs at vendor firms located abroad. Mani et al. (2013) report that more than 90% of the 100 largest outsourcing contracts by contract value signed during 1996-2005 in their sample belonged to the period after 1998.[195]

More recently, there has been a trend toward cloud computing, which has pit cloud providers, such as Amazon.com, Google, and Microsoft, against traditional infrastructure makers, such as IBM, Oracle, EMC, and HP. Even companies such as Netflix and Zynga use cloud computing to handle spikes in demand. Cloud's attraction lies in its "pay-by-the-drink" pricing, which helps save fixed investments and capital expenditures. [196] Cloud also empowers users to try services without going to the IT department with justifications. However, cloud is not for everyone, as some companies discovered when Amazon.com suffered a major outage in

2011. There are also liability and legal issues, particularly if data involve European customers.

Considering this relatively recent history of computing—and realizing that many firms such as Bank of America, CEMEX, Johnson & Johnson, and Tata Steel have been in business longer than the first mainframe computers came along—it is easy to understand how some firms might have IT systems from various eras coexisting in an organization. Many of these systems work perfectly well, although no one knows how to rewrite the programs because the programmers are no longer around to consult and no one kept manuals. All this keeps managers on their toes trying to figure out how they can minimize risk to their organization if some hardware or software becomes obsolete and is no longer supported by a vendor. This is what is known as the "legacy" problem in IT circles.

7.3 Managing the Three Types of IT

IT rarely provides competitive advantage in and of itself; as such, it is like other general-purpose technologies, such as steam engines, electricity, transistors, and lasers. It needs complements in the form of organizational innovations, such as better-skilled workers, teamwork, redesigned processes, and new decision rights (or governance), to make it more successful.

McAfee (2006) argues that different types of IT have different relationships with these complements, and he suggests another way of classifying IT components: functional IT, network IT, and enterprise IT.

1. Functional IT (FIT) makes the execution of standalone tasks more efficient (e.g., Word, Excel, CAD). It enables productivity and optimization, focuses on discrete tasks, has no complements, and is mostly optional.
2. Network IT (NIT) allows people to interact but does not define how they should interact (e.g., e-mail, instant messaging, wikis, blogs, Web 2.0). It allows interactions and collaboration. Unlike FIT, NIT brings complements such as better-skilled workers, teamwork, redesigned processes, and

new decision rights but allows users to implement and modify them over time. Like FIT, it retains the feature of optional use.

3. Enterprise IT (EIT) focuses on business processes (e.g., ERP, CRM, KM, EDI, SCM [supply chain management]). It imposes complements and defines tasks, sequences, standardization, and monitoring. Typically, it is mandated and is more top-down (unlike NIT, which percolates from the bottom).

McAfee (2006) suggests that executives need to play three roles. They must (1) help select technology, (2) nurture adoption, and (3) ensure exploitation. These roles need to be tailored to technology, and managers need to stop viewing IT projects as technology installation, instead understanding such endeavors as business projects or organizational change.

When it comes to IT selection, two approaches can be used: the outside-in approach or the inside-out approach (e.g., Cisco, Zara). The inside-out approach focuses more on enabling role of technology to support business strategy, while an outside-in approach may focus more on the capabilities of technology per se to create or execute new business strategies. For IT adoption, FIT requires persuasion and not mandate, NIT requires norm setting for use, and EIT needs forceful intervention. For IT exploitation, FIT requires encouraging experimentation, NIT requires facilitation and emergence, and EIT makes adoption more difficult though its exploitation is easier. EIT often requires FIT as complements (e.g., ERP plus BI [business intelligence]) for identifying customer propensity to leave and cross-selling).

7.4 Managing IT Projects

IT snafus are very common. The Standish Group claims that 50%–70% of IT projects fail, and there are many examples across sectors and industries, as we saw earlier in the "IT Hall of Shame."[197]

McFarlan (1981) argues that the majority of these projects can be managed in a better way by understanding the drivers of risk for individual IT projects and for a portfolio of IT projects and then matching an appropriate management approach to a project. First, managers should assess the risks of individual IT projects.[198] Project risk is a function of project structure, experience with technology, and project size. Project structure is a function of the degree to which users are clear about their requirements and how stable such requirements are. Technology requirements for executing a project can also be classified in terms of familiarity with technology and availability of skills for those technologies.

Second, evaluating risks at the project level is a useful place to begin, but firms also need to assess risk at the IT project portfolio level to assess whether there are too many or too few risky projects in the portfolio.

Third, managers should use a contingency approach to manage different types of projects. Projects characterized by high structure–low technology have the lowest risk and are the easiest to manage, but they are also the least common. Usual project life cycles and project management approaches work relatively well for these types of projects.

High structure–high technology projects require technical leadership and internal integration to ensure that the project team operates as an integrated unit. These projects do not require much external integration or linkages with users because of high structure.

Low structure–low technology projects require effective user involvement, and low structure–high technology projects require leadership with technical expertise and an ability to communicate with users.

In general, firms use some defined process or method to execute IT projects. These approaches are termed "systems development life cycle," or SDLC, and they apply to the three major ways of developing systems: custom design and development, system selection and acquisition, and end-user development.[199]

Digital Intelligence

The classic SDLC (also known as the waterfall approach) can be broadly classified into two major activities: development activities (which include requirements definition, functional design, technical design, programming, testing, and implementation) and postlaunch activities (which include operation and maintenance). Among advantages of the classic SDLC approach, it is familiar, it is natural, it is thorough, it produces a quality product, it scales to handle large projects, and it limits the developer's risk. However, it also has disadvantages; namely, it assumes that systems can be well specified, it assumes technology is well-understood and sequential and has a long cycle time, and it involves substantial administrative work.

To overcome these disadvantages of classic SDLC, firms use some variants of classic SDLC such as outsourced development, rapid application development and package implementation. However, some still find the Plan-Design-Build approach in Waterfall development to be too restrictive, and increasingly firms are using Agile Life Cycle Models that emphasize a Speculate-Collaborate-Learn approach.

Agile software development methods (such as extreme programming or XP, Scrum, and feature-driven-development or FDD) stress on the importance of interactions among software developers and customers, developing working software early on, and continuously incorporating changes instead of detailed upfront planning. In XP, programming is often done in pairs. Scrum specifies particular roles within a development team such as a scrum master (responsible for establishing the scrum work mode and eliminating impediments), product owner (who represents the internal customer of the scrum team and defines development targets), and software developers (responsible for the actual development work). Scrum teams follow an iterative work mode defined by a sprint—a time period with a length of one to four weeks and daily standup meetings. FDD emphasizes developing software feature by feature in an iterative manner. [200]

Advantages of custom development include unique tailoring, flexibility, and control. Advantages of purchasing include faster rollout, knowledge infusion, economically attractive possibilities

163

(economies of scale of vendor), and high quality. Hybrid models such as "buy and make" involve customizing an ERP. Often, firms prefer to "configure" ERP systems by adopting recommended business processes embedded in the ERP software, instead of "customization" which requires writing new code that may not work if an organization were to upgrade to newer versions of the ERP software.

Increasingly, IT systems are also being created through end-user development, in addition to the other two major approaches (i.e., custom design and development and system selection and acquisition).

More recent research has suggested some useful tips for IT project implementation. McAfee (2003b) identifies five pitfalls of IT implementation: inertia, resistance, misspecification, misuse, and nonuse. He suggests that some of these pitfalls can be managed by thoughtful choices about five areas: the level at which a project is managed (high or low), optimal management style (top down or consensus), project scope (limited or comprehensive), timing (big bang or phased), and the extent of organizational preparation (basic or extensive).[201]

7.5 Chapter Summary

This chapter provided an overview of different components of IT systems and their historical evolution to explain how "legacy" comes into being. Then, I discussed classification of IT systems as FIT, NIT, and EIT (i.e., functional, network, and enterprise IT) and implications for managing them. Finally, I discussed how managers should assess risks of IT projects and tailor their implementation approaches accordingly.

Chapter 8: Managing Digital Enterprise Systems

"Modern multiunit business enterprise did not make its appearance before the 1840s for technological reasons."

—Chandler (1977, p. 49)

The history of modern multiunit business enterprises dates back about 170 years, but much of what we currently observe in modern enterprises in terms of enterprise systems is as recent as 30 years, beginning in the 1980s.[202] In this chapter, I discuss some major types of enterprise systems and how managers should think about some strategic and implementation issues related to these systems.

8.1 Enterprise Resource Planning (ERP) Systems

8.1.1 Why ERP systems?

Enterprise systems are the systems that companies use to run their business processes. The genesis of enterprise systems can be traced to Europe and the manufacturing industry.[203] Until about the late 1980s, most firms viewed IT from a functional-hierarchical perspective. These systems were isolated from each other and involved a lot of rekeying of data and many inconsistencies. Increasingly, firms began to connect systems with one another, beginning with the manufacturing function.

In contrast to the functional-hierarchical perspective, a new business process view emerged in the early 1990s.[204] A business process defines the way work is organized, coordinated, and focused to produce a valuable product or service. It represents sets of activities and concrete work flows of material, information, and knowledge that transcend the boundary between sales, marketing, manufacturing, and R&D. ERP systems helped facilitate the business process view of managing enterprise information systems. Later, Y2K spurred the adoption of ERPs because most companies needed to upgrade their hardware and software systems to make their IT systems year-2000 compliant, and ERP provided a natural path to migrate to.

Enterprise systems have a single comprehensive database at their center. Their principal characteristics include modularity, data integration, and configurability. They operationalize the vision of a single, one-face enterprise that has integrated systems across functional areas and automatically triggers business processes with shared data and visibility. These systems enable connections with upstream and downstream partners and can facilitate standardization and interoperability across units.

ERPs offer several advantages, such as efficiency, responsiveness, knowledge infusion, and adaptability. For example, Nestlé USA was paying 29 different prices for vanilla to the same vendor in 1997 before its ERP implementation, a situation that was rectified after ERP was implemented. However, ERP systems also have limitations, such as the trade-off between standardization and flexibility, questions about whether the "best practice" is really the best, strategic clash, complexity, high cost, and risks.   SAP, Oracle (which acquired JD Edwards, PeopleSoft, and Siebel), and Microsoft are among some of the major vendors of ERP. These vendors are moving ERP products to web services and service-oriented architecture.

Among companies for which ERP implementations have been successful are Cisco and Digital China. However, several other firms have had difficulties implementing ERP systems, including FoxMeyer Drug, Rich-Con Steel, Nestlé USA, Hershey, Nike, Dell,

California State University, and the University of Michigan. Dow Chemical abandoned a mainframe-based ERP after spending a half billion dollars and seven years and then started implementation using a client/server-based ERP. Kmart wrote off $130 million after a failed implementation.

Beyond their strategic impact, ERPs also affect organization and culture. On the one hand, they can lead to more centralization through greater standardization. On the other hand, they can lead to decentralization through empowerment. Some companies use ERPs to create more uniform practices across the globe, while others allow different practices across the globe.

8.1.2 Strategic issues in ERP implementation

In general, one should be mindful of six key issues when managing ERPs. [205] First, begin with a strategy, and decide whether standardization or differentiation makes more sense. Revisit and reengineer business processes before automating them. Try to identify and target high-value processes first. Applying the Pareto principle and recognizing that 20% of your business processes may be driving 80% of your business may help.

Conventional SDLC used to ensure visiting business processes first and then figuring out a software solution. ERP reverses this paradigm: Firms tend to modify business processes to suit software. However, keep in mind that the generic processes coded in the software may conflict with differentiation and flexibility. A company like Apple need not worry because of its strong brand, but other companies that compete on flexibility and service need to think about that trade-off. Compaq decided to invest in custom forecasting applications to integrate with the ERP vendor's system; it cost more but ultimately aligned better with the shift in strategy of build-to-order. Air Products decided not to implement because it did not want to lose cost advantage. A good practice is to focus on the "enterprise" and not so much on the "systems."

Second, decide whether to use a single vendor solution or best of breed. Dell started implementation in 1994 but abandoned it in 1996 and went for best of breed.

Third, when it comes to implementation, it is important to choose between big bang, phased, pilot, and parallel approaches. Each approach has its merits and drawbacks. Shinsei bank, for example, used a parallel modular approach to implement its enterprise systems in the early 2000s.

Fourth, establish new roles, consolidate fragmented responsibilities, and design appropriate incentives. Fifth, provide visibility to the effort. Establish cross-functional teams and appoint high-level champions. Sixth, manage consultants, and do not let your company be a training ground for rookies. Ensure knowledge transfer from consultants to internal staff. Finally, despite all the care you take, be ready for surprises. Keep in mind that enterprise systems are not a panacea by themselves.

8.2 Customer Relationship Management (CRM) Systems

8.2.1 Why CRM?

Peter Drucker once remarked that a business has only two functions to perform: innovation and marketing. Tesco, a U.K.-based retailer, is an example of a company that has taken this advice about marketing to heart. In 2006, Tesco had 31% market share in the United Kingdom, compared with 16% of Wal-Mart's Asda chain in groceries. The key to Tesco's success is its Clubcard program, which has a database of about 12 million consumers.[206]When Wal-Mart entered the U.K. market, Tesco targeted people who were most likely to defect to Wal-Mart's low prices. It identified 300 items that these shoppers buy frequently, and by targeting its promotions to these buyers and these items, it was able to ward off the competitive threat of Wal-Mart. Tesco introduced the clubcard in 1995, and it analyzes the data generated by the clubcard on 15 million shopping baskets every week. It classifies customers into six segments and scores each product on 50 dimensions to identify similar baskets. On the basis of this analysis, it issues quarterly coupons to customers for products they are likely to buy. Approximately 15%–20% of these coupons are redeemed compared with the 1%–2% industry norm. P&G, Coke, and Kimberly-Clark buy analyses based on Tesco's data.

Unfortunately, not many companies do such a great job with their customers. Indeed, there are even some firms that go so far as to fire their customers, as Sprint reportedly did.[207]

CRM is even more important in the face of increasing customer choice, fierce competition, and overcapacity in production. The percentage of new car buyers who bought the same brand that their household historically owned has declined significantly from approximately 75% in 1986 to only 20% in 2009.[208]CRM is applicable not only to business-to-consumer but also to business-to-business relationships. The goal of CRM programs is to use technology to become a mass customizer and one-to-one marketer at the same time.[209] Together, mass customization and one-to-one marketing help create a learning relationship between a producer and a consumer as the two interact and collaborate further.

Broadly speaking, there are at least five reasons companies initiate CRM or loyalty programs. The first is to keep customers from defecting. For example, Sprint's airline miles act as golden handcuffs. A retention strategy is more profitable than an acquisition strategy because selling to a new customer costs six times more than selling to an existing customer, and dissatisfied customers complain on average to six to eight people.

A second reason is to gain greater share of wallet or consolidation of purchases. Amazon.com, Wyndham, Best Buy, Hilton, and Starwood use these strategies.

A third reason is to prompt or encourage additional purchase. For example, different levels of benefits associated with silver, gold, and platinum for air miles tend to achieve this effect. Amazon.com also uses this strategy by recommending other items of potential interest.

A fourth reason is to gain customer knowledge and insight into customer behavior, as Tesco does in the United Kingdom. Wal-Mart, Harrah's, Capital One, RBC Royal Bank, Best Buy, and

Seven-Eleven Japan also conduct analyses of customer behavior at the individual or more aggregate levels. Firms can also involve customers in innovation processes to translate their needs into new products. For example, Sony developed PlayStation2 in collaboration with customers.[210]

Finally, CRM programs can be used to make money. For example, American Airlines' AAdvantage Program makes money by selling miles to customers of Citibank, Kellogg, and USA Today, and it works as a profit center during times when the airline suffers.

Use of CRM programs can also help firms improve their customer satisfaction, which in turn can generate higher stock returns at lower risk and make the firms more valuable to investors. [211] Academic research suggests that managers dont understand their customers in at least two important ways. Managers systematically overestimate the levels of customer satisfaction and loyalty, and the levels of antecedents such as expectations and perceived value. In addition, among managers' understanding of the drivers of their customers' satisfaction and loyalty, managers underestimate the importance of customer perceptions of quality in driving satisfaction and of satisfaction in driving customers' loyalty and complaint behavior.[212]

At a fundamental level, a key idea in CRM is to recognize that some customers are "more equal" than others and that it is necessary to separate the "angels" from the "devils." Continental Airlines uses its enterprise data warehouse to identify its most valuable customers. Best Buy tries to identify the "devils," who buy products, apply rebates, return purchases, and then buy back the same product at returned-merchandise discounts, or those who load up on loss leaders; such customer visits account for 100 million out of 500 million each year. While the Pareto principle often works, be aware of long-tailed distributions in today's digital economy, as Amazon.com and Netflix show. [213]

In most cases, CRM can help in the domain of one-to-one marketing[214]—the holy grail of marketing. One-to-one marketing requires four steps: (1) identify individual customers, at least the most valuable ones; (2) differentiate customers by value and need and by channel members and other intermediaries; (3) interact with customers with cost efficiency and effectiveness; and (4) customize.

The first two steps (identification and differentiation) are internal and part of analysis, while the next two steps (interacting and customizing) are external, visible to customers, and part of execution or action. In general, it is advisable to start small and then assess the situation and set priorities.

8.2.2 Strategic Issues in CRM Implementation

To manage CRM efforts the right way, it is necessary to be mindful of five strategic issues.[215] First, are the CRM efforts strategic? Apply CRM only to areas that are most strategic and vital to the company's competitiveness. Piccoli (2007) suggests a useful framework for developing a CRM strategy based on theoretical repurchase frequency and degree of customizability. Situations characterized by high theoretical repurchase frequency–high customizability (e.g., B2B business) may benefit from a personalization strategy. High theoretical repurchase frequency–low customizability situations (e.g., hotels, retail) may be appropriate for a rewards strategy. Situations characterized by low theoretical repurchase frequency–high customizability (e.g., wedding reception) may benefit from an acquisition strategy. Low theoretical repurchase frequency–low customizability situations (e.g., a budget hotel in Bahamas) may not justify developing a CRM strategy or significant investments. The unobtrusiveness of data collection should also be considered. For example, it may be alright to collect social security numbers and other personal (sensitive) information in a hospital setting, but asking for this same information in a guest satisfaction survey would clearly be inappropriate.[216]

Second, where does it hurt most? An entire CRM cycle does not need to be done all at once. Instead of creating a broad CRM program, focus on targeted efforts. McDonald's launched a $1 billion initiative it called "Innovate" to enhance customer service at 30,000 locations around the world in 2001; the company cancelled the project after a $170 million write off in 2003 and then relaunched more targeted initiatives that appear to have paid off. Learning and building incrementally can be a helpful advice.

Third, do you need perfect data? To this end, calculate the cost and value of information. Make a distinction between "good enough" versus "perfect" information: Perfect real-time information is expensive, and a firm may not be able to react to that. For example, in the case of hotels, availability of rooms may need perfect information, but customer opinions about carpets can be approximate and may be done in a batch mode.

Fourth, where do we go from here? A narrowly focused program can reveal new opportunities adjacent to the CRM cycle, to upstream and downstream links, and to related business units. Integrate with other systems, such as ERP, because data analysis is key. Research shows that firms learn more about their customers if their systems have better supply chain integration.

Finally, be aware of privacy issues and the fine line between value-added services and annoying, intrusive actions. Even if an organization knows intimate details about a customer in a hotel or retail context, that by itself does not mean that such information should be used indiscriminately and without care.[217]

Note that business issues should be addressed before technology. Just because you *can* does not mean that you *should* implement a CRM solution. Keys to successful implementation are strong executive leadership, careful strategic planning, clear performance measures, coordinated program of technology, and organizational change management.

8.3 IT for Knowledge Management (KM) and Innovation

8.3.1 Why KM systems?

In this section, I consider another class of enterprise system that is related to the effective management of human resources and, in particular, the knowledge that these resources have and how that can be leveraged for innovation. The importance of knowledge management is clear in the quote attributed to Thomas Huxley (1825-1895), an English Biologist, who once remarked: "The great end of knowledge is not knowledge but action" (quoted in Blair 2002, p. 1028). Drucker argues that knowledge is the new basis for competition in today's economy and Romer suggests that knowledge is the only unlimited resource that grows with use. The importance of knowledge work has grown over last few decades as the composition of the economy has changed from an agrarian economy to an industrial economy and now to a knowledge or innovation economy.[218]

Knowledge creation is an individual activity, but it also has an organizational or collective component. Individual knowledge translates into collective learning in a culture that shares and communicates information more frequently.[219] Increasingly, knowledge of who you know and who you are related to (your social network) is recognized to be just as important as what you know.

Knowledge can be classified in several ways. One dominant scheme is to classify knowledge on the basis of how explicit or tacit it is. The distinction between tacit and explicit knowledge suggests four patterns for creating knowledge. The first is tacit to tacit, which works primarily through socialization. More recent research suggests that guided practice, guided observation, guided problem solving, and guided experimentation can lead to deeper knowledge and understanding.[220]The second is explicit to explicit, which works through combination and can create new knowledge. However, more exciting possibilities for knowledge creation are when tacit knowledge becomes explicit through articulation or when explicit knowledge becomes tacit through internalization. These four types of processes create a knowledge spiral, the end product of which is new explicit knowledge.

Consulting companies were among the first organizations to grapple with the complexity of KM, but KM is not entirely new; it has been used in family businesses and by master craftsmen for centuries. [221] However, the complexity of KM has increased because of globalization and dispersion of the workforce—it is no longer possible for people to share the same watercooler or cafeteria once an organization becomes very large. Besides, keeping track of people's expertise is difficult because employees are often reluctant to share their knowledge for the fear of losing their value. According to an estimate, approximately 20% of the American workforce was set to retire by 2008, making it necessary to capture their knowledge and make it accessible to other employees.

Turning now to innovation, innovations are easier to identify than define. For example, Apple's iPhone is an innovative product, but innovation can also occur along other dimensions. It can depend on an organization's perspective and encompasses not only a new product, service, or process but also a new idea, method, brand, business model, offering, customer segment, or delivery and revenue channel. Innovations also vary in terms of outcomes: they can be industry leading, inimitable, and take years to conceptualize. Ultimately, the definition of innovation is relative to a company's current processes, culture, and goals—what might be characterized as innovative in one context might be commonplace in another.

There was a time when firms innovated mostly within their boundaries using R&D. Steve Jobs remarked in 1998 that "Innovation has nothing to do with how many R&D dollars you have."[222] There does seem significant variation in the money firms spend on R&D: companies like Facebook and Qualcomm spent slightly more than 20% of their revenues on R&D in 2014, while Apple spent 3.5% and Google 15%. Some argue that Apple does a better job of integrating innovations of its suppliers. Other companies find customers as valuable sources of innovation. These observations suggest that in today's interconnected world, firms gain a competitive advantage by not only their own R&D but also by leveraging knowledge and expertise of their business partners. The inward-focused R&D approach to innovation has now given way to a broader view that also encompasses open innovation and the notion of "Connect and Develop" or C&D.

8.3.2 Strategic Issues in Implementing IT Systems for KM and Innovation

IT plays an important role in both R&D and C&D strategies for innovation management. The choice of KM strategy depends on several key factors, such as how a company creates value, how it turns a profit, how it manages people, and its global context.

How should managers approach KM strategy? First and foremost, competitive strategy should drive KM strategy. The choice of KM strategy will also require answers to more questions such as: (1) Do you offer standardized or customized products? (2) Do you have a mature or innovative product? (3) Do your people rely on explicit or tacit knowledge to solve problems?

In this context, it is useful to be aware of two broad approaches for making knowledge accessible: codification and personalization.[223] The codification (person to document) approach seeks to transfer explicit knowledge and makes use of databases and repositories. For example, Andersen Consulting (now Accenture) and Dell share knowledge objects as part of the codification approach. Companies such as Anderson Consulting also use other strategies, but the degree of emphasis on codification is higher.

The personalization (person to person) approach seeks to transfer both explicit and tacit knowledge through physical face-to-face meetings, electronic conferences, directories, "people finders," and investments in networks of people. It also uses electronic document systems not as knowledge objects but to get up to speed and to know who has worked in a particular area. HP, Bain, the Boston Consulting Group, and McKinsey are some of the companies that use this approach.

If a company creates value by dealing with similar problems time and again, the codification approach with knowledge reuse may be appropriate. However, if a company creates value by dealing with novel or one-of-a-kind problems, the personalization approach may be more appropriate. Why? The codification approach relies on economics of reuse and a high ratio of consultants to partners (30:1), while the personalization approach uses expert economics, a 7:1 ratio of consultants to partners, one-to-one training and customization, and significantly higher fees. The implications for managing people also differ: The codification approach requires different hiring, training, and rewards criteria than the personalization approach. More implementors, or "undergraduates," may be needed in codification, and more inventors, or "MBAs," may be needed in personalization in a consulting organization.

Some argue that successful firms use one dominant strategy and the other in a supporting role, and straddling or putting equal emphasis on both codification and personalization rarely works and can lead to overinvestment. However, if straddling is unwise, so is an exclusive focus on one strategy, leading to the recommendation to use the 80/20 rule. However, others suggest that firms can use a mix of strategies successfully, and both codification and personalization approaches may be used within a particular KM system.

Two additional complications arise from the existence of multiple business units in a company and from the commoditization of knowledge over time. Tightly integrated business units should focus on only one strategy. CSC Index demonstrates that to benefit most, KM strategy needs to change as products mature over time. Most benefits accrue from a KM strategy if it is coordinated with human resources, IT, and competitive strategy.

Firms should also determine how to deploy IT to support their innovation strategy across geographies, considering that the developing world doesn't approach innovation in the same way as the developed world due to economic and cultural differences. [224] Among economic factors, developing economies with large populations face significant resource constraints. Innovators in the developing world search for new ways of providing products and services of comparable quality at affordable prices. It's this quest for affordable "good enough" but basic products and services that defines the bulk of innovations in the developing world. For example, in India, the Jaipur Foot prosthetic limb provides the necessary functionalities starting at approximately US$30. In contrast, in the US, a prosthetic foot costs approximately $8,000, and the sophisticated Deka prosthetic arm costs approximately $100,000.

Likewise, service innovations in emerging economies make extensive use of IT not only to make the processes more efficient but also to increase the reach of service delivery to increase business volumes aimed at scale and scope economies. One example is open-heart surgery, which costs approximately $2,000 at the Narayan Hrudayalaya hospital in India and somewhere between $20,000 and $100,000 at most US hospitals. Such cost reductions are not only due to rethinking capital investments and redesigning business processes but also using sophisticated but low-cost and reliable IT systems that provide real-time information to physicians and administrators about all costs and revenues. Turning now to cultural factors, most developing countries, have a nonlinear (many different ways rather than linear or one best way) culture, where the innovation process is often unstructured and leverages intuition and emotions (as opposed to a well-planned, and structured approach to innovation). An example is the operational design of aisles and billing counters at Big Bazaar in India, which resemble flea markets as opposed to stores such as Carrefour or Walmart in the developed world, which are relatively well-organized and streamlined. The collectivist culture in these societies relies on the "follow your heart" approach—instead of relying on focus groups or formal market research.

These economic and cultural differences help to develop a global innovation strategy framework for identifying and developing an innovation approach in terms of the framework's two dimensions—*innovation processes* and *innovation goals*. The innovation process describes how the innovation is carried out—varying from a well-planned, structured and methodized approach by firms in developed countries to that of an unstructured, intuition-driven, contingent approach by firms in developing countries. The innovation goal, on the other hand, describes the kind of expected output from the innovation, ranging from opportunity-based solutions in developed countries that focus on augmented products and services to meet latent needs to necessity-based solutions in developing countries that focus on basic or core products and services.

1. Good-Enough Emergent: This strategy is employed by emerging economy firms to produce Tata Swach (a$20 water purifier) and Tata Nano ($2,500 car). Firms in developed markets are increasingly focusing on such a strategy to tap the market potential in developing economies. For example, P&G's Gillette developed an 11-cent razor blade to compete in the Indian market. Firms with this innovation strategy should have flexible processes and supporting IT architecture focused on a personalization approach for knowledge management. Furthermore, the IT function also needs to work on making the processes more efficient and cost sensitive, composed of standardized, cost-effective, and preferably modular components.

2. Good-Enough Structured: Walmart and McDonalds used this approach to reduce the cost of operations. More recently, similar principles have been employed by the service industry in the developing world. For example, Devi Shetty, a cardiac surgeon at Narayana Hrudayalaya, appears to draw inspiration from Ford and Walmart in his effort to design affordable heart surgery for the masses. Similarly, Aravind Hospital in India incorporated the McDonald's model to offer cataract surgery for the masses. The IT systems in such organizations are geared to provide standardized cost-saving solutions, focused on a codification approach for knowledge management, while leveraging economies of scale and scope.

3. Augmented Structured: This strategy combines a structured innovation process with the goal of achieving augmented products or services that respond to latent needs of customers. Generally, firms like Jaguar, Mercedes, and BMW follow this strategy, and firms in developing countries are trying to enter this segment through acquisitions (for example, Tatas Motors acquired England-based Jaguar, India's Mittal Steel acquired Europe's Arcelor, and China's Lenovo acquired US-based IBM). In this approach, IT can be used to create precise sophisticated components. Moreover, IT is also used for structuring and aiding the innovation process through a codification knowledge management approach.

4. Augmented Emergent: This innovation strategy requires striving for excellence with an emergent and intuition-driven innovation process. Whereas the products resulting from such innovation can bring in a high return, they're also prone to high rates of failure. Google and 3M appear to experiment in an unstructured way to come up with innovative products. Google Earth and Google mail emerged from this kind of an innovation strategy. Management of this innovation strategy is by far the most complex and the role of IT in such an innovation is contingent on the requirements of the innovators and leverages a personalization strategy for knowledge management.

5. Mixed Approach: In addition to the four strategies just described, there are some successful firms that appear to have ambidextrous innovation strategies in that they pursue multiple approaches simultaneously. General Electric, has come up with specialized solutions—such as low-cost x-rays machines and other medical equipment for developing countries—while focusing on the developed world markets. IT in such organizations must be highly flexible, especially in terms of knowledge management and sharing. Also, the firms must be sensitive to the fact that the same IT systems that work in the developed world might not work in the developing countries. Generally, such firms segregate the operations based on geographies, but useful knowledge is shared extensively to promote innovation.

Using this framework, organizations around the world can tailor their innovation approaches and consequently their IT strategy. It also enables managers to identify weaknesses and plan their IT and innovation strategies accordingly. For senior executives, the framework can provide useful implications for how to think about their competitive strategies (differentiation, cost-leadership, or focus), knowledge management strategies (personalization versus codification), human resource strategies (for example, hiring inventors versus implementers), governance of their digital resources, and types of IT applications (such as IT tools for idea generation, analysis, collaboration, innovation management, measurement, experimentation, sharing and replication) and innovation platform an organization should use.

In summary, KM implementation raises several strategic issues.[225] First, it is important to choose the KM strategy and codification and/or personalization approach based on competitive strategy and related considerations about the pace of knowledge evolution, and the extent of knowledge reuse. Increasingly firms and organizations are using prediction markets and crowdsourcing for KM. Prediction markets are market-based mechanisms to elicit ideas and evaluate them. Crowdsourcing relies on the idea that sometimes outsiders can also create effective knowledge for an organization. Selecting the right innovation approach is essentially figuring out where the right knowledge resides (inside the organization or outside the organization) and what incentives are needed to elicit and utilize that knowledge. Firms will need to decide the extent to which they will use a combination of internal and external sources for idea generation and idea selection.

Second, it is important to manage the three processes of knowledge creation, development, and reuse carefully. The knowledge hierarchy strategy works well for rapidly changing knowledge to substitute expert knowledge for the novice knowledge. The knowledge market works well when knowledge evolves slowly and the goal is to augment the knowledge of experts. The knowledge community is a hybrid of knowledge hierarchy and knowledge market and views knowledge as a communal resource. This strategy works better for moderately changing knowledge to augment the knowledge of experts.

Third, you need to overcome the paradox of KM to capture the "right" knowledge and get people to share their knowledge and use others' knowledge. The paradox of KM is that those who can give the most are the least likely to benefit from giving. To solve this fundamental problem requires a careful consideration of four factors: (1) Incentivize potential contributors to share their knowledge, (2) create an architecture for participation in the KM program, (3) create mechanisms for integrating contributions into a coherent whole, and (4) train employees to select appropriately. This will require making it easy to find the knowledge (knowledge inventory or map) and develop critical thinking abilities to evaluate knowledge from different sources.

Finally, it is important to continuously monitor and evaluate benefits—but quantification can be tricky.

8.3.3 Case Example: Tata's Corporate Innovation Strategy

Managing innovation in a large and global enterprise is a complex task and firms are increasingly using a variety of strategies and technology tools for managing innovation. Here I discuss Tata Group's corporate innovation strategy and explain how it provides high-level direction and support while allowing significant room for creativity and autonomy to individual companies and business units spread worldwide in multiple industry sectors to devise their competitive or functional innovation strategies. This example clarifies the role of disciplined autonomy to meet innovation challenges across industries and geographies. [226]

Although Tata Group has a long history of innovations across its companies over the past 100 years or so, few systematic attempts were made to actively and systematically manage innovation at the corporate level. In 2007, Tata Group set up the Tata Group Innovation Forum (TGIF) to plan and roll out group-level initiatives to help Tata companies innovate. In a way, TGIF became responsible for the corporate innovation ecosystem at Tata Group. Major TGIF activities fall into four broad areas: create capacity for innovation, measure innovation, facilitate innovation, and recognize and reward innovation.

Creating Capacity for Innovation: TGIF uses three mechanisms to build capability for innovations: innovation workshops, learning missions, and dissemination of innovation-related literature and case studies. First, TGIF organizes workshops with leading innovation experts to introduce the concepts of and tools for innovation. Second, TGIF organizes innovation missions—visits to some leading firms outside India to understand their innovation processes. Finally, dissemination efforts—facilitated by the Tata Management Training Centre through research and

181

training—focus on innovation culture and tools in executive programs, and on publications that trace the history of innovations in the Tata group and review best practices from elsewhere.

Measuring Innovation: Tata Group uses a questionnaire called InnoMeter to measure the "as-is" state of innovation. Broadly, it asks respondents to indicate their assessment of strategic clarity, resource availability, the extent of empowerment, expectations, and processes for tracking and rewarding innovation efforts. It also has some perceptual measures for the success of innovation efforts, such as how quickly innovations could be rolled out or the extent to which they led the industry. The outcome of the InnoMeter generates creative tension and lets the company identify areas it must address to make its innovation value chain more robust.

Facilitating Innovation: Tata Group uses IT to fuel its innovation efforts and improve idea generation and selection. Tata InnoVerse is an in-house social networking platform with Facebook-like features as well as features similar to Google prediction markets that helps Tata companies augment the innovation life cycle that starts from ideas. Some companies have used this platform to pose vexing problems coming from CEOs as part of a "Challenges Worth Solving" (CWS) program. In 2015, 17 Tata companies were using this system with promising results in engaging employees in creative problem solving and idea evaluation. InnoVerse had more than 54,000 enrolled users who generated more than 46,000 ideas and 470,000 impressions either organically or through more than 640 challenges; the platform helped to select more than 2,340 ideas, of which more than 340 were implemented. More than 40 percent of these ideas came from employees of other Tata companies. The group is working toward enhancing this platform to track and develop selected ideas for subsequent commercialization.

Recognizing and Rewarding Innovation: Tata group initiated the process of celebrating innovations across group companies through a program called Tata InnoVista. The goal was to recognize innovators and encourage innovations in companies, share the levers companies use to identify and execute innovation projects, and create a culture of risk taking. Tata InnoVista has four award categories: promising innovations (successfully implemented innovations that have provided benefits); "dare to try" (serious and audacious attempts to innovate that couldn't be completed successfully, to encourage the culture of risk taking); leading-edge proven technologies (for new technologies that have yet to be commercialized); and design honor to highlight the importance of design in all products and services.

How should one assess the impact of innovation initiatives? In terms of economic value, the estimated potential benefit of 43 finalist InnoVista innovations in 2014 is approximately US $1 billion annually, according to Mukund Rajan, brand custodian and chief ethics officer at Tata Sons. Although the methodology for calculating economic value is in a nascent stage, roughly 20 percent of the benefits relate to revenue gains, whereas 80 percent relate to cost reduction initiatives.

Among noneconomic parameters, the group has achieved some success in creating a culture of risk taking with its "dare to try" category: it received only 12 entries from six companies in this category in 2007, but participation increased to 248 entries from 31 companies by 2013. Another important benefit is the development of a commonly understood language; every employee knows how and when to contribute to their company's or group's innovation efforts. Innovation is no longer seen as a job only for R&D, and employees across all functional areas participate in innovation projects. Some within the group argue that innovation's true value should be judged not only by how much visibility it has but also by the fraction of the world's population it touches and the difference it makes in the quality of life for people at the base of the pyramid. Many of the innovations in Tata Group (such as Tata Swach and Ace) had perhaps lower visibility or hype but a significantly large potential impact in terms of their footprint (the population they were intended to touch. In contrast, some other innovations (such as Apple's products) had higher perceived impact, even though they touched mostly top-of-the-pyramid consumers in most markets. The group has made progress in the last few years to improve its culture of innovation. By removing the stigma associated with failure and bringing salience to innovation efforts to bring similar attention as that given to economic measures, it's now moving toward addressing the "process" part of innovation through better tracking and measurement. Some of these refinements could address both effectiveness and efficiency considerations.

How is IT helping to drive innovation at the Tata group? We can discern the use of IT for innovation to help with learning (by disseminating other companies' innovation approaches), measuring (deploying the InnoMeter tool), facilitation (through Tata InnoVerse to build a community of innovation evangelists and facilitate the discovery and development of new ideas), and recognition (through InnoVista competitions that are managed using an IT platform). The use of IT to sustain corporate innovation programs suggests that an enterprise's digital, innovation, and global strategies should be viewed as part of its broader portfolio of interdependent strategic choices to transform itself and to meet the product, process, and business model innovation needs of its customers across the globe.

8.4 Chapter Summary

This chapter provided an overview of different types of enterprise systems and issues that come up in managing them. Increasingly, ERP systems also encompass the functionality that used to come with CRM or KM systems. Despite some differences across these types of systems, they share a similarity in the sense that use of these systems requires managers to make strategic choices that are consistent with business strategy—a theme that recurs across all the chapters of this book. Strategic considerations relate to standardization and differentiation for ERP systems, customization and purchase frequency for CRM systems, and codification and personalization for KM systems (in addition to choice of internal versus external sources). Enterprise systems need to be integrated with other systems or legacy applications and workflows. Implementation approaches vary across systems, and incremental approaches seem to work better for CRM and KM systems. These systems do require changes in roles, incentives, and desirable behaviors. Finally, managers should pay attention to knowledge transfer from consultants to employees, privacy issues, aligning incentives, and evaluating benefits that are linked to strategic goals of the organization.

Chapter 9: Conclusion

"No man ever steps in the same river twice, for it is not the same river and he is not the same man."

—Heraclitus 535-475 BC

"Stay Hungry. Stay Foolish."

—Steven Paul Jobs (quote from his commencement speech at the Stanford University in 2005)

In the previous chapters, I have discussed many useful components of digital intelligence and how to think about managing IT strategically. This chapter offers a summary of what we hope to have learned and where we should go next. I also briefly discuss how some visionaries and managers have used IT to transform their organizations and people's lives.

In discussing the key components of digital intelligence, I have used a framework that rests on three pillars—a basic understanding of how a firm should synchronize its business strategy with its IT strategy, how the firm should govern IT, and how the firm should manage IT infrastructure and implement IT projects.

I have emphasized several themes. First, all managers need to have a vision for IT, and realize that IT can make or break an organization. This is not only true in information-intensive sectors, such as banking, music, book retailing, or newspapers, but also in relatively non-information-intensive sectors, such as cement or steel. For example, CEMEX became a very successful company and the third largest producer of cement in the world in a span of about 20 years, in large part because of its information management capabilities. Conversely, companies such as FoxMeyer Drug, Rich-Con Steel, Blockbuster, Kodak, and Borders had significant difficulties managing IT and dealing with IT-enabled transformations, and some even ceased to exist. The role of IT in the success or failure of an organization is not limited to firms in the private sector or large firms alone. It applies equally well to government, nonprofit sectors, and smaller organizations.

Fortunately, IT can be used strategically to create and sustain a competitive advantage. There is evidence for this in many case studies and large-sample empirical research. CEMEX, Zara, Capital One, Harrah's, and Amazon.com are some of the firms that demonstrate how IT and information-based capabilities can help firms create and capture value. Large-sample empirical studies of global firms also provide evidence suggesting that firms' IT investments can provide significant advantage in terms of profitability and other measures of firm performance.

When I say "all managers," I am referring to both business and IT managers. The failure of Xerox to capitalize on innovations of its PARC lab demonstrates the importance of this theme.[227] If only its business managers in New York had understood the tremendous knowledge and product portfolio their IT people had and provided resources to commercialize them, Xerox could have had market capitalization similar to that of players such as Apple and Microsoft, companies that were inspired, in part, by some of what they saw at PARC. Equally, IT people at Xerox could have done a better job of articulating their technological prowess in business value terms to get a buy-in for their initiatives. Instead of becoming victims of the "translation" problem, managers have a responsibility to acquire basic IT knowledge and skills, or digital intelligence, just as they are expected to have basic literacy or numeracy to be an effective manager. They should invest not only in their own continuous learning and engagement with IT projects, but they should also provide opportunities for their subordinates and colleagues to acquire digital intelligence. Boards would do well to pick key executives for their digital intelligence, as some have started doing.

Second, from a strategic perspective, IT should be an integral part of any strategy discussions. It is the responsibility of senior leaders to develop inclusive but robust strategy development processes that are informed by capabilities of IT but also stretch capabilities of IT to ensure long-term sustainability of an organisation. Senior leaders and managers must understand the duality inherent in IT before they can choose an appropriate digital business strategy and posture. They need to start questioning their conventional-strategy concepts and toolkits, which focus on tradeoffs without recognizing that IT can, at times, help overcome the tradeoffs altogether. For example, IT can help firms pursue both revenue growth and cost reduction, or higher quality and lower costs—things that a purist approach to conventional strategy might not consider. The ADROIT framework discussed in Part 1 of this book can help managers to think about the role of IT in a comprehensive manner to synchronize IT and strategy.

Companies also need to incorporate a bottom-up perspective in strategy formulation by using more sophisticated tools, such as prediction markets. Such tools might help guard against the temptation to rely too much on executive judgment, which can be limited in breadth or simply off the mark. To illustrate, consider Jeff Bezos, who has made many astute digital strategic moves, yet remarked in a 2006 interview, "I guarantee that five years from now, no one will want to be a social-networking company."[228] Jeff was way off the mark in this case.

Third, managers need to scan new technologies to assess their significance and use such technologies to stay relevant and transform their organizations. Even entrepreneurs, and investors can find attractive opportunities if they scan new technologies and anticipate their impact on industries and firms. Scanning of emerging technologies, identifying their strategic significance, and deploying them should not be a one-time exercise; these actions should become a part of a manager's routine because newer technologies are forever emerging. To avoid being Napstered, Amazoned, or Netflixed, successful managers should lead transformations, not wait passively.

Although we focused mostly on IT and IT-enabled changes, a broader theme that managers need to appreciate is that thinking about newer technologies can often reveal new and more effective ways of doing business—even though doing so challenges one to get out of his or her comfort zones and routines, which can become addictive after a while. Viewed as such, technology and change are synonymous; to avoid making sense of newer technologies on an ongoing basis is to avoid change, and that rarely pays off, as the examples of Kodak and Borders demonstrate.

Just scanning new technologies and recognizing their significance is not enough. Leadership matters when it comes to transforming organizations, and top leaders perhaps matter the most as has been realized in several studies of transformation. While technologies or frameworks such as BPR, Six Sigma or Baldrige Criteria can act as 'triggers', unless the leader empowers the organisation and monitors the progress made on these opportunities for improvement, companies are unlikely to achieve success.

Managers also need to recognize that transformations, whether technology-enabled or otherwise, need persistence, management continuity, and eschewing the pursuit of management fads. In other words, sustained performance will require tireless efforts, persistence and refining technologies and their integration with incentive systems and business process to yield desired outcomes. More than relying on the charisma of some leaders, organizations should focus on creating processes that focus on long-term thinking and where continuous improvement, scanning of newer technologies and agile transformations to stay relevant become routine.

Fourth, formulating strategy is rarely enough; deployment is equally important and successful deployment needs attention to governance. Senior managers need to govern IT to align IT systems with a firm's strategy. The 4D governance framework discussed in

189

Part 2 of this book can help managers govern IT decisions, department, dollars, and delivery in a way that is synchronized with the company's strategy.

Managers should make careful choices regarding how managerial and technical decisions will be decided in a centralized, decentralized or hybrid manner considering the autonomy-synergy tradeoffs. How should they configure an IT department to balance supply with demand for IT services and who should the CIO report to? How much should they spend on IT, where and how should they approach justification of IT-enabled business projects? How should they think about delivery of IT services: build, buy or rent? Governance system can help to answer all these managerial decisions and not grappling with them is to abdicate managerial responsibility.

In a way, a solid governance can provide an operating system that ensures disciplined autonomy, providing the discipline in the form of a coherent framework and autonomy in terms of how to interpret the framework based on competitive needs. It also provides a platform for integrating various initiatives just as an operating system allows a variety of applications to be built leveraging a common platform.

This also has implications for the role of corporate boards in discharging their responsibility—not only as a steward to ensure that the firm is held accountable to its acts of commission, but also to hold a firm accountable for acts of omission, such as moving too late in the digital space, as Blockbuster might have done. Recent failures at Yahoo (to vet the CEO's resume), MF Global (to account for hundreds of millions of dollars that went missing), and JP Morgan (to avoid losing billions of dollars in bad bets) suggest there's significant room for improvement in governance in top echelons of decision-making structures. In all three cases, the boards might be faulted for not demanding the information necessary to properly understand the companies' risks, make key hiring decisions, and fully perform their fiduciary duties.

Fifth, IT projects need to be managed carefully with particular attention to technology evolution, firm strategy, business processes, business value, and bottom-line benefit, while ensuring buy-in and business sponsorship whenever possible. They should not be left to "geeks in the back row," as Carly Fiorina, former CEO of HP, once remarked. It is the responsibility of managers to be aware of technology evolution to take informed decisions regarding technology upgrades, how they should help to adopt, diffuse and exploit IT systems, what risk management strategies they should adopt when it comes to implementing various enterprise projects consistent with their strategy.

Finally, it is not just IT systems or "big data" that by themselves can provide business outcomes. Analytics and metrics matter; organisations suffer if they do not have metrics, but they also suffer if they focus on the wrong or narrow metrics to measure success. It is the job of managers to ask critical questions related to data definitions, some upfront thinking about how the data will be analyzed and used to inform business decisions, and then ensuring that over time such data-driven decisionmaking becomes the norm to realize true benefits from the power of information technology systems.

Smart managers with digital intelligence can make a difference through their business and IT leadership, just as others who came before them did. For example, Lorenzo Zambrano used IT to transform CEMEX. José Maria Castellano, an IT manager at Zara, rose to become CEO and used IT for fast fashion. Sunil Mittal of Bharti Airtel capitalized on an IT-enabled opportunity and became a billionaire while transforming a nation. Sam Pitroda made a difference using telecommunications to change India's destiny. In most cases, the key is to be able to identify pain points and do something about them using IT, as Amazon.com, YouTube, and Netflix demonstrate.

We need leaders and managers to do the same to other pressing problems the world faces in areas such as improvement in productivity or quality of services, health care, education, social security, government services, and dealing with climate change, just to name a few. [229]

Services have been particularly notorious when it comes to productivity gains. For example, the output per watchmaker in Geneva is estimated to have risen from about 12 watches to more than 1200 watches per year between the 1670s and the 1970s. Cowen (1996, p. 208) notes the contrast colorfully in the context of performing arts: "Today's string quartet appears hardly more productive than a string quartet in the eighteenth century. In 1780 four quartet players required forty minutes to play a Mozart composition: today forty minutes of labor are still required."

Similar to performing arts, there has hardly been any gains in productivity of services such as education and health care. Health care and education appear to suffer from Baumol's cost disease— that is, the increase in the cost of providing these services exceeds the rise in the cost of living.[230]

How should policy makers, entrepreneurs and managers approach IT in health care? Will a fragmented approach ensure universal connectivity and access similar to what can be witnessed in the financial services sector? What complementary policies and changes are needed to institutionalize a system that is fair and equitable for all? Similarly, education is another area that can significantly benefit from IT-enabled delivery to make it more affordable and accessible. Despite the potential of IT to transform education, very few leading and established universities have taken thoughtful and deliberate steps to integrate IT with learning and education to make education more affordable or accessible at their campuses.

This phenomenon of Baumol's disease is also noticeable in many public services that have a high proportion of "stagnant" service activities that pose significant challenges in standardization and in which perceived quality requires a significant amount of human labor. Can advances in IT help overcome some of the regressive characteristics of stagnant services?

Government services can benefit significantly with IT-enabled interventions. Prior research in the United States suggests that e-government is lagging its counterparts in e-business when it comes to website design and customer experience. Even worse performance would likely be expected from government agencies in emerging economies, because they have relatively lower levels of resources and human capital. Can politicians and government officials rise to the challenge of providing superior services to their citizens and improving overall trust in government in a cost-effective way using IT?

We introduced some powerful tools and concepts with which to think about IT and to shape and execute strategy. While no article of even a book—and this one is no exception—can provide a definitive answer to the types of problems that executives face, managers need to remember that as they grapple with IT- and business-related issues, they can often influence the answer through their thinking, actions, and initiative. They must continue to stay vigilant about new technologies.

What will you do next week to keep current with technology and to sharpen your digital intelligence? What about a month or a year from now? Which technology on the horizon can eat your lunch, and which technologies can help you grow? Can you stay hungry and stay foolish and use IT to change the world for better, as Steve Jobs did?

Appendix 1.A: IT from Cradle to Grave and Beyond

1. Dating, Marriage, and Related Matters: Websites such as MeetMoi, Match.com, eHarmony, Shadee.com and FastFlirting are facilitating short-term and long-term relationships (Vascellaro 2007). About 2 million Americans met their spouses online (Gamerman 2006). Some use services of wedding planners operating in India to take care of wedding logistics. There are reports of people checking their smartphones while engaging in intimate human activities. Notably, the pornographic industry was a pioneering user of e-commerce, but likely its casualty also. A *Wall Street Journal* story reports about a man potentially cheating on his wife through Second Life (Alter 2007). His wife remarks, "You try to talk to someone or bring them a drink, and they'll be having sex with a cartoon" (p. W1).

2. Parenting: IT has not only enabled outsourcing of the parenting function to some extent through services such as TaskRabbit but also allows parents to track their children using GPS over the phone and even nag them using texting (George 2009).

3. Divorce: IT is also raising questions even when relationships are dissolved—for example, getting off the buddy list, the Facebook friend list, or cell phones (Sharma 2006).

4. Health: IT is increasingly facilitating telemedicine, telesurgery, remote monitoring, and personalized medicine.

5. Politics: IT is being used in elections to target voters, raise money, and attack opponents. Some presidential candidates,

such as Howard Dean, benefitted from the Internet's reach but also suffered badly when a clip of a bad campaign moment went viral. George Allen's Mecaca moment derailed his campaign for senate race in Virginia.

6. Driving: Increasingly, drivers are getting tickets from remote cameras. GPS facilitates driving but has also led drivers to cliffs. IT has also facilitated car sharing and new business models such as Zipcar.

7. Shopping: Online shopping is one of the fastest-growing segments of retail. Increasingly, some firms tout advantages of the so-called "sharing economy" or "renting" (instead of owning) for travel, accommodation and a whole host of products and services.

8. Banking: IT has facilitated online and peer-to-peer banking.

9. Sports: Wii is changing how people play sports and helping keep senior citizens fit in nursing homes.

10. Movies: Netflix has significantly changed the movie rental business using IT.

11. Worship: IT has allowed worshippers to seek forgiveness for sins by e-mail. They can get fruits of worship (or Prasad, as Indians call it) shipped to their homes thousands of miles away.

12. Publishing Books: IT has facilitated rapid growth of the self-publishing industry, as exemplified by iUniverse and CreateSpace (Rich 2009). Publishers are experimenting with simultaneous delivery of books in five formats: hardcover, digital, audio, print-on-demand, and piecemeal (Lowry 2006).

13. Education: IT is transforming education through interactive whiteboards, online portals (such as Blackboard), e-libraries, distance education (e.g., University of Phoenix), and remote tutoring (e.g., tutorvista.com). However, some worry about distractions caused by laptops and mobile devices in class and questionable learning outcomes.

14. Editing: A friend who edits a magazine in India writes editorials on his cell phone. Kapil Sibal, minister of India's Human Resources and Information Technology in 2011 wrote a book of poems on his cellphone (Sibal 2008). Even this book has been copyedited remotely by an editor the author has never met in person.

15. Staying in Touch: Skype, FaceTime, and smartphones are enabling people to stay in touch without any regard for distance.

16. The "Thumbs" People: Some worry that overuse of thumbs and fingers on smartphones might cause their overgrowth over time, but others argue that people who overuse such devices do not fare well due to their distracted driving.

17. New "Days": IT has given us new days, such as Cyber Monday (coined first in 2005), after the Thanksgiving weekend.

18. Vocabulary: IT has created new words such as LOL and Leet.

19. Occupations: IT has created new occupations such as that of a Cyberbouncer at Match.com to prevent offensive content or images from making to the website (Gomes 2003).

20. Work: IT is changing the nature of work. Increasingly, we do our own typing, rendering "typing pools" of earlier years a thing of past. Doctors are beginning to rely on automated alerts to point to any interactions among different drugs when they prescribe medicine.

21. Twitter: Twitter is causing us to thinking in 140 characters or less. Some management schools are asking MBA candidates to write essays within 140 characters.

22. Christmas: Amazon.com filed for a patent that allows gift recipients to convert their gifts into cash based on preset rules and depending on the profile of the gift giver and the nature of the gift item.

23. Taxes: TurboTax and TaxCut have undercut conventional tax return preparation and filing. The IRS even extends deadlines when Intuit users hit online filing snags (Herman and Vara 2007).

24. Death: There are now websites that can send the e-mails that you wanted to send only after your death after confirming your death. They can also provide loved ones access to passwords (Rosenwald 2010).

25. Second Life: A married man uses SecondLife to date a woman in Canada. His wife notes: "The other life is so wonderful: it's better than real life. Nobody gets fat, nobody gets gray. The other person that's left can't compete with that" (Alter 2007, p. W8).

Appendix 2.A: Some Examples of Emerging Technologies and Transformations

1. Automotive: Smaller and more energy efficient vehicles. Arguably, General Motors, Ford, and Chrysler did not pay as much attention to energy efficiency, because U.S. consumers in their main markets did not care as much due to low gas prices. However, changing customer preferences and competition from new and emerging players (e.g., the Tata Nano) in other markets may lead to disruptive innovations. There are some signs of awakening though. General Motors and Segway are planning to produce a two-seater car that can go 35 miles at 35 mile per hour.

2. Rental cars: Services such as Zipcar are making inroads in markets served by conventional rental companies, such as Hertz.

3. Movie rental: Blockbuster could not compete with Netflix.

4. Phone: Voice Over Internet Protocol (VOIP)–based services such as Skype and Vonage threaten business models of conventional operators and world's trillion-dollar telecommunications industry.

5. Cell phones: Pay as you go pricing disrupts conventional players with huge sunk costs. In some emerging markets such as India, firms price phone calls by seconds (not by minutes).

6. Retail banking: ING Direct is taking away the profitable segments of online-savvy customers through its better rates and without making investments in off-line assets.

7. Education and Tutoring: TutorVista threatens conventional tutors. There are debates on the extent and the pace with which information technology will influence various segments of education to lower costs and improve access (Holland 2009; Lucas 2014; Lucas 2016; Mithas and Lucas 2015; Whitaker, New and Ireland 2016) and how online education compares with conventional education in terms of learning outcomes (Means et al. 2010).[231]

8. Hotels: Yotels in Europe allow you to pay by the hour, not by the day.

9. Will mobile phones replace PCs? Bill Gates coauthored an op-ed piece in the *Wall Street Journal* in 2006 with Paul Otellini, the CEO of Intel, arguing the continued importance of PCs even as other personal devices, such as smartphones, become more ubiquitous. Should the computer industry players make inroads into mobile phones because that is where the future growth is? Google and Microsoft are already doing that.

10. Medicine: Will online consultation make visits to doctor's office a thing of past? How might MinuteClinics, which are staffed by registered nurses, threaten the services of full-service hospitals staffed by doctors? Remote monitoring of patients is already a reality, and General Electric has made some acquisitions signaling its move in that direction.

11. Electricity: Piezoelectric crystals help illuminate subway stations and roads. Solar-powered electric lamps as substitutes for kerosene-based lamps in India.

12. Newspaper industry: Craigslist and free news on the Internet have prompted changes in the business model of the newspaper industry.

13. 3D printing: Will 3D printing threaten additive manufacturing of prototypes, mock-ups, and consumer goods? This technology can also change the practice of medicine, and some surgeons are using 3D printed models to plan complex operations. Is it far-fetched to imagine printing of body parts some day?

About the Author

Dr. Sunil Mithas is a Professor in the Robert H. Smith School of Business at the University of Maryland and the author of the books *Dancing Elephants and Leaping Jaguars: How to Excel, Innovate and Transform the Tata Way* (published by Penguin India in 2015 for the Indian subcontinent with the title "Making the Elephant Dance: The Tata Way to Innovate, Transform and Globalize") and *Digital Intelligence: What Every Smart Manager Must Have for Success in an Information Age*. He earned his PhD from the Ross School of Business at the University of Michigan and an engineering degree from IIT, Roorkee. Before pursuing his PhD, he worked for nearly ten years in engineering, marketing, and general management positions with the Tata group.

He was identified as a 2011 MSI Young Scholar by the Marketing Science Institute which selects about 25 such scholars every two years. Sunil is a frequent speaker at industry events for senior leaders. He has worked on research or consulting assignments with organizations such as Johnson & Johnson, Lear, A.T. Kearney, the Tata group, the Social Security Administration, and the U.S. Census Bureau.

Sunil's research focuses on strategies for managing innovation and excellence for corporate transformation and competitive advantage. His work provides insights on the role of technology and other intangibles, such as customer satisfaction, human capital, and organizational capabilities, for improved performance. His research has appeared in premier journals, including *Management Science*, *Marketing Science*, *Information*

Digital Intelligence

Systems Research, MIS Quarterly, Journal of Marketing Research, Journal of Marketing, and *Production and Operations Management.* Some of this work has been featured in business publications such as *Bloomberg, CIO, Computerworld, InformationWeek,* and *MIT Sloan Management Review.* His papers have won best-paper awards.

Contact Sunil at sunil.mithas@gmail.com, or visit http://www.sunilmithas.com

Digital Intelligence

References

Adler, P. S., Goldoftas, B., and Levine, D. I. 1999. "Flexibility versus Efficiency? A case study of model changeovers in the Toyota production systems," *Organization Science* (10:1), pp. 43-68.

Agarwal, R., and Gort, M. 2001. "First-mover advantage and the speed of competitive entry, 1887–1986," *Journal of Law, and Economics* (XLIV:April), pp. 161-177.

Agarwal, R., and Sambamurthy, V. 2002. "Principles and models for organizing the IT function," *MIS Quarterly Executive* (1:1), pp. 1-16.

Agarwal, R., and Weill, P. 2012. "The benefits of combining data with empathy," *MIT Sloan Management Review* (54:1), pp. 35-41.

Aksoy, L., Cooil, B., Groening, C., Keiningham, T. L., and Yalcin, A. 2008. "The long term stock market valuation of customer satisfaction," *Journal of Marketing* (72:July), pp. 105-122.

Allen, B. 1987. "Make information services pay its way," *Harvard Business Review* (Jan-Feb), pp. 57-63.

Alter, A. 2007. "Is this man cheating on his wife?," in: *Wall Street Journal (10 August 2007)*. Washington, DC: pp. W1, W8.

Amiti, M., and Wei, S.-J. 2005. "Fear of service outsourcing: Is it justified?," *Economic Policy* (20:42), pp. 307-347.

Amiti, M., and Wei, S.-J. 2009. "Service Offshoring and Productivity: Evidence from the U.S.," *The World Economy* (32:2), pp. 203-220.

Amram, M., Kulatilaka, N., and Henderson, J. C. 1999. "Taking an option on IT," in: *CIO Enterprise Magazine (June 15, 1999), (accessed 2 Feb 2010), [available at http://www.cio.com.au/article/46963/taking_an_option_it]*.

Andal-Ancion, A., Cartwright, P. A., and Yip, G. S. 2003. "The Digital Transformation of Traditional Businesses," *MIT Sloan Management Review* (44:4), pp. 34-41.

Anderson, C. 2006. *The long tail: Why the future of business is selling less of more*. New York: Hyperion.

Anderson, E. W., Fornell, C., and Mazvancheryl, S. K. 2004. "Customer Satisfaction and Shareholder Value," *Journal of Marketing* (68:4), pp. 172-185.

Anderson, M. C., Banker, R. D., and Ravindran, S. 2003. "The new productivity paradox," *Communications of the ACM* (46:3), pp. 91-94.

Antioco, J. 2011. "How I did it...: Blockbuster's Former CEO on sparring with an activist shareholder," *Harvard Business Review* (89:4), pp. 39-44.

Applegate, L. M., Austin, R. D., and Soule, D. L. 2009. *Corporate Information Strategy and Management: Text and Cases*. Boston: McGraw-Hill Irwin.

Apte, U. M., Karmarkar, U. S., and Nath, H. K. 2008. "Information services in the U.S. economy: Value, jobs, and management implications," *California Management Review* (50:3), pp. 12-30.

Apte, U. M., and Mason, R. O. 1995. "Global disaggregation of information-intensive services," *Management Science* (41:7), pp. 1250-1262.

Aral, S., Brynjolfsson, E., and Wu, L. 2012. "Three-Way Complementarities: Performance Pay, Human Resource Analytics, and Information Technology," *Management Science* (58:5), pp. 913-931.

Aral, S., and Weill, P. 2007. "IT assets, organizational capabilities, and firm performance: How resource allocations and organizational differences explain performance variation," *Organization Science* (18:5), pp. 763-780.

Arndt, M., and Brady, D. 2004. "3M's rising star, available at: http://www.businessweek.com/magazine/content/04_15/b3878001_mz001.htm, accessed 2 July 2011," *Business Week* (12 April 2004).

Aron, R., and Singh, J. V. 2005. "Getting Offshoring Right," *Harvard Business Review* (83:12), pp. 135-143.

Arthur, M. B., and Rousseau, D. M. (eds.). 1996. *The Boundaryless Career*. Oxford, UK: Oxford University Press.

Arthur, W. B. 2009. *The nature of technology: What it is and how it evolves*. New York: Free Press.

Digital Intelligence

Autor, D. H., Levy, F., and Murnane, R. 2003. "The skill content of recent technological change: An empirical explanation," *Quarterly Journal of Economics* (118:4), pp. 1279-1333.

Avison, D., Gregor, S., and Wilson, D. 2006. "Managerial IT unconsciousness," *Communications of the ACM* (49:7), pp. 89-93.

Bakos, J. Y., and Brynjolfsson, E. 1993. "Information technology, incentives and the optimal number of suppliers," *Journal of Management Information Systems* (10:2), pp. 37-53.

Banjo, S. 2013. "Wal-mart's e-stumble, http://online.wsj.com/news/articles/SB10001424127887323566804578553301017702818," in: *Wall Street Journal (19 June 2013)*. Washington, DC: pp. B1, B2.

Banker, R. D., Hu, N., Pavlou, P. A., and Luftman, J. 2011. "CIO reporting structure, strategic positioning, and firm performance," *MIS Quarterly* (35:2), pp. 487-504.

Bapna, R., Langer, N., Mehra, A., Gopal, R., and Gupta, A. 2013. "Human Capital Investments and Employee Performance: An Analysis of IT Services Industry," *Management Science* (59:3), pp. 641-658.

Bardhan, I. R., Whitaker, J., and Mithas, S. 2006. "Information Technology, Production Process Outsourcing and Manufacturing Plant Performance," *Journal of Management Information Systems* (23:2), pp. 13-40.

Barney, J. B. 2002. *Gaining and sustaining competitive advantage*, (2nd ed.). Upper Saddle River, New Jersey: Prentice Hall.

Bartlett, C. A., and Ghoshal, S. 1995. "Rebuilding behavioral context: Turn process reengineering into people rejuvenation," *Sloan Management Review* (Fall), pp. 11-23.

Barua, A., and Mukhopadhyay, T. 2000. "Information Technology and Business Performance: Past, Present, and Future," in *Framing the Domains of Information Technology Management: Projecting the Future... through the past*, R.W. Zmud (ed.). Cincinnati, OH: Pinnaflex Press, pp. 65-84.

Baumol, W. J. 1985. "Unbalanced growth revisited: Asymptotic stagnancy and new evidence," *The American Economic Review* (75:4).

Baumol, W. J. 1993. "Social wants and dismal science: The curious case of the climbing costs of health and teaching," *Proceedings of the American Philosophical Society (250th Anniversary Issue, Dec 1993)*: American Philosophical Society, pp. 612-637.

Baumol, W. J. 1996. "Children of performing arts, the economic dilemma: The climbing costs of healthcare and education," *Journal of Cultural Economics* (20).

Benbya, H., and Van Alstyne, M. 2011. "How to find answers within your company," *MIT Sloan Management Review* (52:2), pp. 65-76.

Bennett, D. 2013. "The Dunbar Number, From the Guru of Social Networks, http://www.businessweek.com/articles/2013-01-10/the-dunbar-number-from-the-guru-of-social-networks," *BusinessWeek* (10 Jan 2013).

Bhagwati, J., Panagariya, A., and Srinivasan, T. N. 2004. "The muddles over outsourcing," *Journal of Economic Perspectives* (18:4), pp. 93-114.

Bilton, N. 2009. "Part of daily American diet, 34 Gigabytes of data," in: *New York Times (10 Dec 2009)*. New York: p. B6.

Birkinshaw, J., and Gibson, C. 2004. "Building ambidexterity," *MIT Sloan Management Review* (Summer), pp. 47-55.

Blair, D. C. 2002. "Knowledge Management: Hype, hope, or help?," *Journal of the American Society for Information Science and Technology* (53:12), pp. 1019-1028.

Blinder, A. S. 2006. "Offshoring: The next industrial revolution?," *Foreign Affairs* (85:2), pp. 113-128.

Boccaletti, G., Loffler, M., and Oppenheim, J. M. 2008. "How IT can cut carbon emissions," *McKinsey Quarterly* (October), pp. 1-5.

Bohmer, R., and Knoop, C.-I. 2006. "The challenge facing the U.S. healthcare system," in: *Harvard Business Publishing (9-606-096)*.

Boston Consulting Group. 2012. "The Internet Economy in G-20: The $4.2 trillion growth opportunity (A Boston Consulting Group Report, March 2012), https://www.bcg.com/documents/file100409.pdf."

Boudreau, K. J., and Lakhani, K. R. 2009. "How to Manage Outside Innovation," *MIT Sloan Management Review* (50:4).

Digital Intelligence

Bradach, J. 1996. "Organizational alignment: The 7-S model," in: *HBS Publishing (9-497-045)*. Boston, MA.

Brandenburger, A. M., and Nalebuff, B. J. 1995. "The right game: Use game theory to shape strategy," *Harvard Business Review* (July-August), pp. 57-71.

Brooks, F. P. 1995. *The mythical man-month: Essays on software engineering* (20th Anniversary Edition ed.). Reading, MA: Addison-Wesley.

Brotman, A., and Garner, C. 2013. "How Starbucks Has Gone Digital, available at http://sloanreview.mit.edu/article/how-starbucks-has-gone-digital/," *MIT Sloan Management Review* (April).

Brown, S. A., Chervany, N. L., and Reinicke, B. A. 2007. "What matters when introducing new information technology," *Communications of the ACM* (50:9), pp. 91-96.

Brynjolfsson, E. 1994. "Technology's True Payoff," *InformationWeek* (October 10), pp. 34-36.

Brynjolfsson, E., and Hitt, L. M. 1996. "Paradox lost? Firm-level evidence on the returns to information systems spending," *Management Science* (42:4), pp. 541-558.

Brynjolfsson, E., Hu, Y., and Smith, M. 2006. "From niches to riches: Anatomy of the long tail," *MIT Sloan Management Review* (47:4), pp. 67-71.

Brynjolfsson, E., and McAfee, A. 2011. "The Big Data Boom Is the Innovation Story of Our Time, available at http://www.theatlantic.com/business/archive/2011/11/the-big-data-boom-is-the-innovation-story-of-our-time/248215/," in: *The Atlantic*.

Brynjolfsson, E., and Saunders, A. 2010. *Wired for Innovation: How Information Technology Is Reshaping the Economy*. Cambridge, MA: The MIT Press.

Bulkeley, B. 2011. "How Cloud Computing Rose From Lehman Brothers' Ashes, available at http://www.cio.com/article/678425/How_Cloud_Computing_Rose_From_Lehman_Brothers_x2019_Ashes," *CIO.com* (11 Apr 2011).

Bustillo, M., and Lubin, J. S. 2011. "Sears has new chief with tech resume," in: *Wall Street Journal (24 Feb 2011)*. Washington, DC: p. B1.

Campos, P. F. 2015. "The Real Reason College Tuition Costs So Much, available at http://www.nytimes.com/2015/04/05/opinion/sunday/the-real-reason-college-tuition-costs-so-much.html?_r=0," in: *New York Times (4 April 2015)*.

Carmel, E., and Agarwal, R. 2002. "The maturation of offshore sourcing of information technology work," *MIS Quarterly Executive* (1:2), pp. 65-77.

Carmel, E., and Espinosa, J. A. 2011. *I'm working while they're sleeping: Time zone separation challenges and solutions*. Nedder Stream Press.

Carmel, E., and Tjia, P. 2001. *Offshoring Information Technology: Sourcing and Outsourcing to a Global Workforce*. Cambridge, UK: Cambridge University Press.

Carr, N. G. 2008. "Is Google making us stupid? Available at http://www.theatlantic.com/magazine/archive/2008/07/is-google-making-us-stupid/6868/," *The Atlantic* (July-August).

Carroll, L. 2004. *Alice's Adventures in Wonderland and Through the Looking-Glass*. New York, NY: Barnes & Noble Classics.

Ceruzzi, P. E. 2003. *A history of modern computing*. Cambridge, MA: The MIT Press.

Cha, A. E. 2005. "In retail, profiling for profit; Best Buy stores cater to specific customer types (17 Aug 2005) " in: *Washington Post*. Washington, DC: p. A1.

Chabrow, E. 2002. "Keep 'Em Happy," in: *InformationWeek (Issue 907, 23 September 2002), available at http://www.informationweek.com/story/IWK20020920S0037*. pp. 20-22.

Chandler, A. D. 1977. *The Visible Hand: The Managerial Revolution in American Business*. Cambridge, MA: The Belknap Press of Harvard University Press.

Chandler, A. D. 2000. "The information age in historical perspective," in *A Nation Transformed by Information*, A.D. Chandler and J.W. Cortada (eds.). New York: Oxford University Press.

Chandler, A. D., and Cortada, J. W. (eds.). 2000. *A Nation Transformed by Information*. New York: Oxford University Press.

Chandler, C. 2007. "Wireless Wonder: India's Sunil Mittal, available at http://money.cnn.com/magazines/fortune/fortune_archive/2007/01/22/8397979/index.htm," in: *Fortune (17 Jan 2007)*.

Charette, R. N. 2005. "Why software fails, available at http://www.spectrum.ieee.org/sep05/1685," in: *IEEE Spectrum*. pp. 42-49.

Digital Intelligence

Chatterjee, D., Richardson, V. J., and Zmud, R. W. 2001. "Examining the Shareholder Wealth Effects of Announcements of Newly Created CIO Positions," *MIS Quarterly* (25:1), pp. 43-70.

Chen, D. Q., Mocker, M., Preston, D. S., and Teubner, A. 2010. "Information Systems Strategy: Reconceptualization, Measurement, and Implications," *MIS Quarterly* (34:2).

Chernova, Y. 2014. "How Opower bested Google, http://online.wsj.com/news/articles/SB10001424052702304819004579487860196985456," in: *Wall Street Journal (8 Apr 2014)*. Washington, DC: p. B2.

Christensen, C. M. 1998. "Disruptive Technologies: Catching the wave (5-699-125)," in: *Harvard Business Publishing*. Boston, MA.

Christensen, C. M., Kaufman, S. P., and Shih, W. C. 2008. "Innovation killers: How financial tools destroy your capacity to do new things," *Harvard Business Review* (January), pp. 98-105.

Christensen, C. M., Raynor, M., and McDonald, R. 2015. "What is disruptive innovation?," *Harvard Business Review* (Dec), pp. 45-53.

Chui, M., and Fleming, T. 2011. "Inside P&G's digital revolution, available at http://www.mckinsey.com/insights/consumer_and_retail/inside_p_and_ampgs_digital_revolution," *McKinsey Quarterly* (Nov), pp. 1-11.

CIO.com. 2006. "25 Terrifying Information Technology Horror Stories, Available at http://www.cio.com/special-reports/horror/index," in: *CIO*.

CIO.com. 2014. "Jaguar Land Rover, available at http://www.cio.co.uk/cio100/2014/jaguar-land-rover/," in: *CIO*.

Clissold, T. 2006. *Mr China: A Memoir*. New York: Collins Business.

Colby, C. L., Mithas, S., Orlando, T., and Norman, E. 2015. "What Drives Successful Product Development and Innovation in the Software Development Process? The Product Development Success Index (PDSI) " *Frontiers in Service Conference*, J. Spohrer, R.T. Rust, A. Rayes and S. Kwan (eds.), San Jose, CA.

Coles, P. A., Lakhani, K. R., and McAfee, A. 2007. "Prediction Markets at Google (HBS Case 9-607-088)," Harvard Business School, Boston, MA, pp. 1-21.

Collins, J., and Porras, J. I. 2004. *Built to Last*. New York: HarperBusiness.

Collis, D. J., and Montgomery, C. A. 1995. "Competing on resources," *Harvard Business Review* (July-August), pp. 118-128.

Collis, D. J., and Rukstad, M. G. 2008. "Can you say what your strategy is?," *Harvard Business Review* (April), pp. 82-90.

Colvin, G. 2006. "The FedEx edge," in: *Fortune (March 20, 2006), available at http://money.cnn.com/2006/03/17/magazines/fortune/csuite_fedex_fortune_040306/index.htm*

Colvin, G. 2008. "Information worth billions (Interview with GE CIO), Available at http://money.cnn.com/magazines/fortune/fortune_archive/2008/07/21/105711270/index.htm," *Fortune* (July 21, 2008), pp. 73-78.

Cooper, J. C. 2008. "The profit squeeze has only begun," *BusinessWeek* (November 24, 2008), p. 12.

Cooter, M. 2011. "CIO Series - Jeremy Vincent, Jaguar Land Rover, available at http://www.cloudpro.co.uk/cloud-essentials/939/cio-series-jeremy-vincent-jaguar-land-rover," in: *CloudPro*.

Copeland, T. E., and Keenan, P. T. 1998. "How much is flexibility worth?," *The McKinsey Quarterly* (2), pp. 38-49.

Courtney, H. 2001. *20|20 Foresight: Crafting strategy in an uncertain world*. Boston, MA: Harvard Business School Press.

Courtney, H., Kirkland, J., and Viguerie, P. 1997. "Strategy under uncertainty," *Harvard Business Review* (75:6), pp. 67-79.

Cowen, T. 1996. "Why I do not believe in the cost-disease," *Journal of Cultural Economics* (20).

Craig, D., and Tinaikar, R. 2006. "Divide and conquer: Rethinking IT strategy," *McKinsey on IT* (Fall), pp. 1-10.

Crovitz, L. G. 2008. "Optimism and the digital world," in: *Wall Street Journal*. Washington, DC: p. A15.

Crovitz, L. G. 2010. "From the Roman codex to the iPad," in: *Wall Street Journal*. Washington, DC: p. A15.

Digital Intelligence

Daemmrich, A. A., and Pineiro, E. 2010. "U.S. healthcare reform: International perspectives," in: *Harvard Business Publishing (9-710-040)*.

Damsgaard, J., and Karlsbjerg, J. 2010. "Seven principles for selecting software packages," *Communications of the ACM* (53:8), pp. 63-71.

Davenport, T. H. 1998. "Putting the enterprise into the enterprise system," *Harvard Business Review* (76:4), pp. 121-131.

Davenport, T. H. 2005. "The coming commoditization of processes," *Harvard Business Review* (83:6), pp. 1-8.

Davenport, T. H., Harris, J. G., and Kohli, A. K. 2001. "How do they know their customers so well?," *MIT Sloan Management Review* (42:2), pp. 63-73.

Day, G. S., and Schoemaker, P. J. H. 2000a. "Avoiding the pitfalls of emerging technologies," in *Wharton on Managing Emerging Technologies*, G.S. Day, P.J.H. Schoemaker and R.E. Gunther (eds.). Hoboken, New Jersey: Wiley, pp. 24-52.

Day, G. S., and Schoemaker, P. J. H. 2000b. "A different game," in *Wharton on Managing Emerging Technologies*, G.S. Day, P.J.H. Schoemaker and R.E. Gunther (eds.). Hoboken, New Jersey: Wiley, pp. 1-23.

Day, G. S., Schoemaker, P. J. H., and Gunther, R. E. (eds.). 2000. *Wharton on Managing Emerging Technologies*. Hoboken, New Jersey: Wiley.

Dehning, B., Pfeiffer, G. M., and Richardson, V. J. 2006. "Analysts' forecasts and investments in information technology," *International Journal of Accounting Information Systems* (7), pp. 238-250.

Dehning, B., Richardson, V. J., and Zmud, R. W. 2003. "The value relevance of announcements of transformational information technology investments," *MIS Quarterly* (27:4), pp. 637-656.

DeLong, T. J., Brackin, W., Cabanas, A., Shellhammer, P., and Ager, D. L. 2005. "Procter & Gamble: Global business services (HBS Case 9-4040124)," in: *HBS*. Boston, MA.

Dennis, A. R., and Vessey, I. 2005. "Three knowledge management strategies: Knowledge hierarchies, knowledge markets, and knowledge communities," *MIS Quarterly Executive* (4:4), pp. 399-412.

Dhar, V., and Sundararajan, A. 2007. "Information Technologies in Business: A Blueprint for Education and Research," *Information Systems Research* (18:2), pp. 125-141.

Dixit, A. K., and Pindyck, R. S. 1995. "The Options Approach to Capital Investment," *Harvard Business Review* (May-June), pp. 105-115.

Dos Santos, B. L. 1991. "Justifying investments in new information technologies," *Journal of Management Information Systems* (7:4), pp. 71-90.

Dragoon, A. 2005. "How to do customer segmentation right (1 Oct 2005), http://www.cio.com/article/12558/Customer_Segmentation_Done_Right_," in: *CIO*.

Dyer, J., Gregersen, H., and Christensen, C. M. 2011. *The Innovator's DNA*. Boston, MA: Harvard Business Review Press.

Earl, M., and Feeny, D. 2000. "How to be a CEO for the Information Age," *Sloan Management Review* (41:2), pp. 11-23.

Edelman, B. 2014. "The market power of platform-mediated networks (9-914-029)," in: *HBS Case Collection*. Boston, MA.

Eisenhardt, K. M., and Sull, D. N. 2001. "Strategy as simple rules," *Harvard Business Review* (79:1), pp. 107-116.

Eisenmann, T. 2007a. "Module Note: Platform-mediated networks: Definitions and core concepts (9-807-049)," in: *HBS Case Collection*. Boston, MA.

Eisenmann, T. 2007b. "Winner-take-all in networked markets (9-806-131)," in: *HBS Case Collection*. Boston, MA.

Eisenmann, T., Parker, G., and Van Alstyne, M. W. 2006. "Strategies for Two-Sided Markets," *Harvard Business Review* (Oct).

El Sawy, O. A., and Pavlou, P. A. 2008. "IT-enabled business capabilities for turbulent environments," *MIS Quarterly Executive* (7:3), pp. 139-150.

Engardio, P. 2006. "Outsourcing: Let's offshore the lawyers," in: *Business Week (Sept 18, 2006)*. pp. 42-43.

Ensign, P. C. 2007. "Book Review- Managing Global Offshoring Strategic: A Case Approach," *Journal of International Business Studies* (38), pp. 207-210.

Digital Intelligence

Escalle, C. X., and Cotteleer, M. J. 1999. "Enterprise resource planning (HBS 9-699-020)," Harvard Business School, Boston, MA, pp. 1-8.

Evans, B. 2009. "Chevron: A tech company in the energy business?," in: *InformationWeek*. p. 12.

Evans, P. B., and Wurster, T. S. 1997. "Strategy and the new economics of information," *Harvard Business Review* (75:5), pp. 71-82.

Farrell, D. 2004. "Beyond offshoring: Assess your company's global potential," *Harvard Business Review* (December), pp. 2-10.

Farrell, D. 2006. *Offshoring: Understanding the emerging global labor market.* Boston: Harvard Business School Press.

Ferguson, N. 1999. *The House of Rothschild: The World's Banker 1849-1999.* New York: Viking.

Fichman, R. G., Keil, M., and Tiwana, A. 2005. "Beyond valuation: "Options Thinking" in IT Project Management," *California Management Review* (47:2), pp. 74-96.

Fletcher, O., and Dan, J. 2011. "Ballmer bares China travails," in: *Wall Street Journal (27 May 2011).* Washington, DC: p. B1.

Florida, R. 2005. "The World is Spiky," *Atlantic Monthly* (296:3), pp. 48-51.

Foerderer, J., Kude, T., Mithas, S., and Heinzl, A. 2016a. "Does Platform Owner's Entry Crowd Out Innovation? Evidence from Google Photos," in: *University of Mannheim, Working Paper.* Mannheim, Germany.

Foerderer, J., Kude, T., Mithas, S., and Heinzl, A. 2016b. "How Deadline Orientation and Product Modularity Influence Software Quality and Job Satisfaction," *Academy of Management Annual Meeting (5-9 August 2016),* M.A. Glynn (ed.), Anaheim, CA: Academy of Management.

Fornell, C., Mithas, S., and Morgeson, F. V. 2009a. "The Economic and Statistical Significance of Stock Returns on Customer Satisfaction," *Marketing Science* (28:5), pp. 820-825.

Fornell, C., Mithas, S., and Morgeson, F. V. 2009b. "The statistical significance of portfolio returns," *International Journal of Research in Marketing* (26:2), pp. 162-163.

Fornell, C., Mithas, S., Morgeson, F. V., and Krishnan, M. S. 2006. "Customer Satisfaction and Stock Prices: High Returns, Low Risk," *Journal of Marketing* (70:1), pp. 3-14.

Fowler, M., and Highsmith, J. 2001. "The Agile Manifesto," *Software Development* (9:8), pp. 28-35.

Frank, H. 2012. *Adventures of a Dean: A primer on business school management.* San Diego, CA: University Readers.

Fredricksen, C. 2011. "Twitter Ad Revenues to Grow 210% to $139.5 Million in 2011, available at http://www.emarketer.com/PressRelease.aspx?R=1008617," *eMarketer (28 Sep 2011)).*

Freeman, R. B. 1995. "Are Your Wages Set in Beijing?," *Journal of Economic Perspective* (9:3), pp. 15-32.

Friedman, T. L. 2005. *The world is flat: A brief history of the twenty-first century.* New York: Farrar, Straus and Giroux.

Gamerman, E. 2006. "Mism@tched.com," in: *Wall Street Journal (April 1-2, 2006).* Washington, DC: pp. P1, P4.

Gardner, H. 2006. *Multiple Intelligences: New Horizons.* New York: Basic Books.

Garvey, M. J. 2004. "Is an MBA worth it?," in: *InformationWeek (Issue number 1012; November 1, 2004),* available at http://www.informationweek.com/story/showArticle.jhtml?articleID=51201467. pp. 31-33.

George, D. S. 2009. "Text, text, text: Parental nagging evolves electronically," in: *Washington Post (6 Sept 2009).* Washington, DC: pp. A1, A6.

Ghemawat, P. 2007. *Redefining global strategy: Crossing borders in a world where differences still matter.* Boston, MA: HBS Press.

Ghemawat, P. 2010. *Strategy and the Business Landscape (Third Edition).* Boston, MA: Prentice Hall.

Gibson, C., and Birkinshaw, J. 2004. "The antecedents, consequences, and mediating role of organizational ambidexterity," *Academy of Management Journal* (47:2), pp. 209-226.

Gillon, K., Aral, S., Lin, C.-Y., Mithas, S., and Zozulia, M. 2014. "Business Analytics: Radical Shift or Incremental Change?, Available at: http://aisel.aisnet.org/cais/vol34/iss1/13," *Communications of the Association for Information Systems* (34:Article 13), pp. 287-296.

Gillon, K., Brynjolfsson, E., Griffin, J., Gupta, M., and Mithas, S. 2012. "Panel--Business Analytics: Radical Shift or Incremental Change?, available at http://aisel.aisnet.org/icis2012/proceedings/Panels/4/," *Proceedings of the 32nd*

International Conference on Information Systems (Dec 16-19), Orlando, Florida: Association for Information Systems.

Ginsberg, B. 2011. *The Fall of the Faculty: The Rise of the All-administrative University and Why it Matters.* New York: Oxford University Press.

Gleick, J. 2011. *The Information: A history, a theory, a flood.* New York: Pantheon Books.

Goleman, D. 1995. *Emotional Intelligence.* New York: Bantam Books.

Gomes, L. 2003. "This cyberbouncer battles to keep it clean at dating-service site," *Wall Street Journal*).

Gottfredson, M., Puryear, R., and Phillips, S. 2005. "Strategic sourcing: From periphery to the core," *Harvard Business Review* (83:2), pp. 132-139.

Greengard, S. 2009. "Are we losing our ability to think critically?," *Communications of the ACM* (52:7), pp. 18-19.

Grimm, C. M., Lee, H., and Smith, K. G. 2006. *Strategy as Action: Competitive Dynamics and Competitive Advantage.* Oxford: Oxford University Press.

Grove, A. 2010. "How America Can Create Jobs, available at http://www.businessweek.com/magazine/content/10_28/b4186048358596.htm," *BusinessWeek* (1 July 2010).

Grover, V., Henry, R. M., and Thatcher, J. B. 2007. "Fix IT-Business relationships through better decision rights," *Communications of the ACM* (50:12), pp. 80-86.

Grover, V., and Ramanlal, P. 1999. "Six myths of information and markets: Information technology networks, electronic commerce, and the battle for consumer surplus," *MIS Quarterly* (23:4), pp. 465-495.

Gupta, S., and Mela, C. E. 2008. "What is a free customer worth?," *Harvard Business Review* (Nov).

Gurbaxani, V., and Whang, S. 1991. "The Impact of Information Systems on Organizations and Markets," *Communications of the ACM* (34:1), pp. 59-73.

Guth, R. A. 2009. "Microsoft Bid to Beat Google Builds on a History of Misses, http://www.wsj.com/articles/SB123207131111388507," *Wall Street Journal* (16 Jan 2009), pp. A1, A8.

Hacker, A., and Dreifus, C. 2010. *Higher education?* New York: Times Books.

Hagel III, J., Brown, J. S., and Davison, L. 2008. "Shaping Strategy in a World of Constant Disruption," *Harvard Business Review* (October), pp. 81-89.

Hagel III, J., and Singer, M. 1999. "Unbundling the corporation," *Harvard Business Review* (77:2), pp. 133-141.

Hagiu, A. 2011. "The last DVD format war (9-710-443)," in: *HBS Case Collection.* Boston, MA.

Hagiu, A. 2013. "Multi-sided platforms: Foundations and strategy (9-714-436)," in: *HBS Case Collection.* Boston, MA.

Halaburda, H., and Oberholzer-Gee, F. 2014. "The limits of scale," *Harvard Business Review* (April), pp. 95-99.

Hambrick, D. C., and Fredrickson, J. W. 2001. "Are you sure you have a strategy?," *Academy of Management Executive* (15:4), pp. 48-59.

Hamel, G., and Valikangas, L. 2003. "The quest for resilience," *Harvard Business Review* (September).

Hamm, S. 2005. "GM's way or the highway," in: *BusinessWeek (Dec 19, 2005).* pp. 48-49.

Hammer, M. 1990. "Reengineering Work: Don't Automate, Obliterate," *Harvard Business Review* (68:4), pp. 104 - 112.

Han, K., Kauffman, R. J., and Nault, B. R. 2011. "Returns to Information Technology Outsourcing," *Information Systems Research* (22:4), pp. 824-840.

Han, K., and Mithas, S. 2013. "Information technology outsourcing and non-IT operating costs: An empirical investigation," *MIS Quarterly* (37:1), pp. 315-331.

Hansen, M. T., Nohria, N., and Tierney, T. 1999. "What's your strategy for managing knowledge?," *Harvard Business Review* (77:2), pp. 106-116.

Hardy, Q. 2011. "At Procter & Gamble, Toothpaste Is Data, available at http://www.forbes.com/sites/quentinhardy/2011/08/03/at-procter-gamble-toothpaste-is-data/," in: *Forbes.*

Hays, C. L. 1999. "Variable-Price Coke Machine Being Tested, http://www.nytimes.com/1999/10/28/business/variable-price-coke-machine-being-tested.html?pagewanted=all&src=pm," in: *New York Times (28 Oct 1999).*

Digital Intelligence

Hays, C. L. 2004. "What Wal-mart knows about its customers' habits (14 Nov 2004), http://www.nytimes.com/2004/11/14/business/yourmoney/14wal.html," in: *New York Times*.

HBR. 2012. "It keeps growing...And growing..." *Harvard Business Review* (Oct), pp. 32-33.

Herman, T., and Vara, V. 2007. "Intuit users hit filing snags," in: *Wall Street Journal (19 Apr 2007)*. Washington, DC: p. D2.

Herzlinger, R. E., and Millenson, M. L. 2008. "Note on accountability in the U.S. health care system," in: *Harvard Business Publishing (9-308-111)*.

Hickins, M. 2012. "IT takes charge at AstraZeneca, http://blogs.wsj.com/cio/2012/05/13/it-takes-charge-at-astrazeneca/," in: *CIO Journal, Wall Street Journal Blog (13 May 2012)*.

Highsmith, J. 2000. "Retiring lifecycle dinosaurs, available at http://www.adaptivesd.com/articles/Dinosaurs.pdf," *Software Testing & Quality Engineering* (July/August), pp. 22-28.

Hindo, B. 2007. "At 3M, A Struggle Between Efficiency and Creativity, available at: http://www.businessweek.com/magazine/content/07_24/b4038406.htm, accessed 4 Apr 2010," *Business Week* (June 11, 2007).

Hirschman, A. O. 1970. *Exit, Voice and Loyalty: Responses to Decline in Firms, Organizations, and States*. Cambridge, MA: Harvard University Press.

Ho, V., Whitaker, J. W., Mithas, S., and Roy, P. K. 2012. "It's What's Inside that Counts: The Role of Social and Psychological Capital in Compensation for Offshore BPO Professionals," *Proceedings of the 32nd International Conference on Information Systems (Dec 16-19)*, F.G. Joey (ed.), Orlando, Florida: Association for Information Systems.

Ho, V., Whitaker, J. W., Mithas, S., and Roy, P. K. 2013. "Success is More Than a Resumé: The Role of Social and Psychological Capital in Compensation for Offshore BPO Professionals," *Proceedings of the ACM SIGMIS CPR 2013 (May 30-June1)*, K.D. Joshi and A. Morgan (eds.), Cincinnati, Ohio: Association for Computing Machinery, pp. 125-133.

Hof, R. D. 2006. "Jeff Bezos' Risky Bet, available at http://www.businessweek.com/magazine/content/06_46/b4009001.htm," in: *BusinessWeek (13 Nov 2006)*.

Holland, K. 2009. "Is it time to retrain B-schools?," *New York Times (March 15, 2009), available at http://www.nytimes.com/2009/03/15/business/15school.html?scp=1&sq=Is%20It%20Time %20to%20Retrain%20B-Schools?&st=cse)*.

Holland, P. 1986. "Statistics and Causal Inference (with discussion)," *Journal of American Statistical Association* (81:396), pp. 945-970.

Holmes, A. 2006. "Federal IT flunks out, available at http://www.cio.com/archive/051506/federal_IT.html," in: *CIO*

Hoover, J. N. 2008. "IT extends Hilton's welcome mat," in: *InformationWeek (16 Sept 2008)*.

Houseman, S., Kurz, C., Lengermann, P., and Mandel, B. 2010. "Offshoring and the State of American Manufacturing," *Measurement issues arising from the growth of globalization (Nov 6-7, 2009)*, Washington, DC: W.E. Upjohn Institute for Employment Research, National Academy of Public Administration.

Huang, P., Tafti, A., and Mithas, S. 2012. "Knowledge Contribution in Online Network of Practice: The Role of IT Infrastructure, Foreign Direct Investment and Immigration," *Proceedings of the 32nd International Conference on Information Systems (Dec 16-19)*, Orlando, Florida: Association for Information Systems.

Hult, G. T. M., Morgeson, F. V., Morgan, N., Mithas, S., and Fornell, C. 2016. "Do managers know what their customers think and why?," *Journal of the Academy of Marketing Science* (Forthcoming).

Icahn, C. 2011. "Why Blockbuster Failed," *Harvard Business Review* (89:4), p. 43.

Im, G., and Rai, A. 2008. "Knowledge Sharing Ambidexterity in Long-Term Interorganizational Relationships," *Management Science* (54:7), pp. 1281-1296.

Immelt, J. R., Govindarajan, V., and Trimble, C. 2009. "How GE is disrupting itself," *Harvard Business Review* (October), pp. 56-65.

InformationWeek. 2012. "2012 InformationWeek (Report ID: R5320912) " in: *InformationWeek Reports, available at reports.informationweek.com*.

Digital Intelligence

Isaacson, W. 2011. "American Icon, available at http://www.time.com/time/magazine/article/0,9171,2096327,00.html, accessed 18 Oct 2011," in: *Time (October 17, 2011)*. pp. 34-35.

Ittner, C. D., and Larcker, D. F. 1998. "Are nonfinancial measures leading indicators of financial performance? An analysis of customer satisfaction," *Journal of Accounting Research* (36:Supplement), pp. 1-35.

Jargon, J. 2014. "Starbucks CEO to focus on digital, http://online.wsj.com/news/articles/SB10001424052702303519404579351140320955988," in: *Wall Street Journal (30 Jan 2014)*. Washington, DC: p. B6.

Javidan, M., Teagarden, M., and Bowen, D. 2010. "Making it overseas," *Harvard Business Review* (April), pp. 109-113.

Jeffery, M., and Leliveld, I. 2004. "Best practices in IT portfolio management," *MIT Sloan Management Review* (Spring), pp. 41-49.

Johnson, A. 2006. "Hotels take 'know your customer' to new level," in: *Wall Street Journal (7 Feb 2006)*. Washington, DC: p. D1.

Johnson, S. 2010. *Where good ideas come from: The natural history of innovation*. New York: Riverhead books.

Jones, G. 2005. *Multinationals and global capitalism: From the nineteenth to the twenty-first century*. Oxford, UK: Oxford University Press.

Kaplan, R. S., and Norton, D. P. 2003. "Lock-in strategies: A new value proposition (HBSP B0309A)," *Balanced Scorecard Report (HBS publishing)*), pp. 3-6.

Kekre, S., Krishnan, M. S., and Srinivasan, K. 1995. "Drivers of customer satisfaction for software products: Implications for design and service support," *Management Science* (41:9), pp. 1456-1470.

Kim, K., Mithas, S., and Kimbrough, M. 2012. "Assessing risks associated with IT investments across industries: Evidence from bond markets," in: *Working paper, Smith School of Business*.

Kim, K., Mithas, S., Whitaker, J., and Roy, P. K. 2014. "Industry-Specific Human Capital and Wages: Evidence from the Business Process Outsourcing Industry," *Information Systems Research* (25:3), pp. 618-638.

Kim, W. C., and Mauborgne, R. 2004. "Blue ocean strategy," *Harvard Business Review* (October).

King, A., and Lakhani, K. R. 2013. "Using open innovation to identify the best ideas," *MIT Sloan Management Review* (55:1), pp. 41-48.

King, A. A., and Baatartogtokh, B. 2015. "How useful is the theory of disruptive innovation? available at http://sloanreview.mit.edu/article/how-useful-is-the-theory-of-disruptive-innovation/," *MIT Sloan Management Review* (Fall), pp. 77-90.

King, J. 2010. "Beyond alignment, available online at http://www.computerworld.com/s/article/348634/Beyond_Alignment," in: *Computerworld*. pp. 21-24.

King, R. 2013. "Why Target decided to ditch Amazon.com, http://blogs.wsj.com/cio/2013/05/20/why-target-ditched-amazon/," in: *Wall Street Journal (May 13, 2013)*. Washington, DC: p. B7.

Kirkland, R. 2013. "Leading in the 21st century: An interview with Hertz CEO Mark Frissora, http://www.mckinsey.com/insights/strategy/leading_in_the_21st_century_an_interview_wit h_hertz_ceo_mark_frissora."

Kleis, L., Chwelos, P., Ramirez, R. V., and Cockburn, I. 2012. "Information technology and intangible output: The impact of IT investment on innovation productivity," *Information Systems Research* (23:1), pp. 42-59.

Kohli, R. 2007. "Innovating to create IT-based new business opportunities at United Parcel Service," *MIS Quarterly Executive* (6:4), pp. 199-210.

Kohli, R., Devaraj, S., and Ow, T. T. 2012. "Does information technology investment influence a firm's market value? A case of non-publicly traded healthcare firms," *MIS Quarterly* (36:4), pp. 1145-1163.

Krugman, P., and Wells, R. 2006. *Economics*. New York, NY: Worth Publishers.

Kude, T., Schmidt, C. T., Mithas, S., and Heinzl, A. 2015. "Disciplined Autonomy and Innovation Effectiveness: The Role of Team Efficacy and Task Volatility," *Academy of Management Annual Meeting (7-11 August 2015)*, J. Humphreys (ed.), Vancouver, BC, Canada: Academy of Management.

Digital Intelligence

Kulatilaka, N. H., and Venkatraman, N. 2001. "Strategic Options in the Digital Era," *Business Strategy Review* (12:4), pp. 7-15.

Kurzweil, R. 2006. *The Singularity Is Near: When Humans Transcend Biology* New York: Penguin.

Lacity, M. C., Feeny, D. F., and Willcocks, L. P. 2003. "Transforming a back-office function: lessons from BAE systems' experience with an enterprise partnership," *MIS Quarterly Executive* (2:2), pp. 86-103.

Lacity, M. C., and Fox, J. 2008. "Creating global shared services: Lessons from Reuters," *MIS Quarterly Executive* (7:1), pp. 17-32.

Lacity, M. C., Willcocks, L. P., and Feeny, D. F. 1995. "IT outsourcing: Maximizing flexibility and control," *Harvard Business Review* (73:3), pp. 84-93.

Landes, D. S. 2005. *The Unbound Prometheus: Technological Change and Industrial Development in Western Europe from 1750 to the Present (Second Edition)* Cambridge, UK: Cambridge University Press.

Lariviere, B., Keiningham, T. L., Aksoy, L., Yalcin, A., Morgeson, F. V., and Mithas, S. 2016. "Modeling Heterogeneity in the Satisfaction, Loyalty Intention, and Shareholder Value Linkage: A Cross-Industry Analysis at the Customer and Firm Levels," *Journal of Marketing Research* (53:1), pp. 91-109.

Lee, D., and Mithas, S. 2014. "IT Investments, Alignment and Firm Performance: Evidence from an Emerging Economy," *Proceedings of the 34th International Conference on Information Systems (Dec 14-17)*, A. Srinivasan, B. Tan and E. Karahanna (eds.), Auckland, New Zealand: Association for Information Systems.

Lee, D., Mithas, S., and Saldanha, T. 2015. "IT Investments, Alignment and Firm Performance: Evidence from an Emerging Economy," in: *Working paper, University of Maryland.*

Leiponen, A., and Helfat, C. E. 2010. "Innovation objectives, knowledge sources, and the benefits of breadth," *Strategic Management Journal* (31:2), pp. 224-236.

Leonard, D., and Swap, W. 2004. "Deep smarts," *Harvard Business Reivew* (September).

Lepore, J. 2014. "The disruption machine, http://www.newyorker.com/reporting/2014/06/23/140623fa_fact_lepore," in: *The New Yorker (June 23, 2014).*

Leslie, K. J., and Michaels, M. P. 1997. "The real power of real options," *The McKinsey Quarterly* (3), pp. 97-108.

Lev, B. 2001. *Intangibles: Management, Measurement, and Reporting.* Washington, DC: Brookings Institution Press.

Levin, R. 2013. "Driving the top line with technology: An interview with the CIO of Coca-Cola, available at http://www.mckinsey.com/insights/business_technology/driving_the_top_line_with_technology_an_interview_with_the_cio_of_coca-cola." *McKinsey Insights and Publications*

Levina, N., and Ross, J. W. 2003. "From the vendor's perspective: Exploring the value proposition in information technology outsourcing," *MIS Quarterly* (27:3), pp. 331-364.

Levinson, M. 2002. "Honeywell Retools Business Processes for CRM, available at http://www.cio.com/article/30972/Honeywell_Retools_Business_Processes_for_CRM," in: *CIO (1 Apr 2002).*

Levinson, M. 2007. "Getting to know them," in: *CIO (May 9, 2007), available at http://www.cio.com/article/print/108409.*

Levy, F., and Murnane, R. J. 2004. *The New Division of Labor: How Computers are Creating The Next Job Market.* New York: Russell Sage Foundation.

Lim, J.-H., Han, K., and Mithas, S. 2013. "How CIO Position Influences IT Investments and Firm Performance," *Proceedings of the 33rd International Conference on Information Systems (Dec 15-18)*, R. Baskerville and M. Chau (eds.), Milan, Italy: Association for Information Systems.

Linden, G., Dedrick, J., and Kraemer, K. L. 2011. "Innovation and job creation in a global economy: The case of Apple's iPod," *Journal of International Commerce & Economics* (3:1), pp. 223-240.

Linden, G., Kraemer, K. L., and Dedrick, J. 2009. "Who captures value in a global innovation network? The case of Apple's iPod," *Communications of the ACM* (52:3), pp. 140-144.

Linder, J. C. 2004. "Transformational outsourcing," *Sloan Management Review* (45:2), pp. 42-58.

Digital Intelligence

Linder, J. C., Jarvenpaa, S., and Davenport, T. 2003. "Toward an Innovation Sourcing Strategy," *Sloan Management Review* (Summer).

Liu, C.-W., Kude, T., and Mithas, S. 2015. "How Strategy and Governance Choices Influence Innovation Success in Software Products and Services," *Proceedings of the 35th International Conference on Information Systems (Dec 13-16)*, T. Carte, A. Heinzl and C. Urquhart (eds.), Forth Worth, Texas: Association for Information Systems, pp. 1-18.

Liu, C.-W., Kude, T., Mithas, S., Colby, C. L., and Orlando, T. 2016. "How Strategy and Governance Choices Influence Innovation Success in Software Products and Services," *Frontiers in Service Conference (June 23-26)*, T.W. Andreassen, E. Breivik and R.T. Rust (eds.), Bergen, Norway.

Lohr, S. 2012. "The age of big data, available at http://www.nytimes.com/2012/02/12/sunday-review/big-datas-impact-in-the-world.html?scp=1&sq=big%20data&st=cse," *New York Times* (11 Feb 2012).

Lowry, T. 2006. "Getting out of a bind: Publishers are testing multichannel delivery to offer readers more choices," in: *BusinessWeek (10 Apr 2006)*. pp. 79-80.

Lucas, H. C. 1993. "The Business Value of Information Technology: A Historical Perspective and Thoughts for Future Research," in *Strategic Information Technology Management: Perspectives on organizational growth and competitive advantage*, R.D. Banker, R.J. Kauffman and M.A. Mahmood (eds.). Harrisburg, PA: Idea Group Publishing, pp. 359-374.

Lucas, H. C. 2014. "Viewpoint: Disrupting and transforming the University," *Communications of the ACM* (57:10), pp. 32-35.

Lucas, H. C. 2016. *Technology and the Disruption of Higher Education: Saving the American University*. San Bernardino, California: CreateSpace.

Lucas, H. C., and Mithas, S. 2011. "Foreign-Born IT Workers in the US: Complements, not Substitutes," *IEEE IT Professional* (13:4), pp. 36-40.

Lucchetti, A., and Steinberg, J. 2012. "MF Global Problems Started Years Ago," in: *Wall Street Journal (29 Oct 2012)*. Washington, DC: pp. C1, C6.

Luehrman, T. A. 1998. "Investment Opportunities as Real Options: Getting Started on the Numbers," *Harvard Business Review* (July-August), pp. 51-67.

MacCormack, A. 2006. "Managing innovation in an uncertain world: Course Overview Note (HBS 5-606-105)," Harvard Business School, Boston, MA, pp. 1-26.

Malone, T. W., Laubacher, R., and Dellarocas, C. 2010. "The collective intelligence genome," *MIT Sloan Management Review* (51:3), pp. 21-31.

Malone, T. W., Yates, J., and Benjamin, R. I. 1987. "Electronic Markets and Electronic Hierarchies," *Communications of the ACM* (30:6), pp. 484-497.

Mani, D., Barua, A., and Whinston, A. B. 2006. "Successfully Governing Business Process Outsourcing Relationships," *MIS Quarterly Executive* (5:1), pp. 15-29.

Mani, D., Barua, A., and Whinston, A. B. 2013. "Outsourcing contracts and equity prices," *Information Systems Research* (24:4), pp. 1028-1049.

March, A., and Garvin, D. A. 1997. "A Note on Knowledge Management (HBS 9-398-031)," Harvard Business School, Boston, MA, pp. 1-20.

Margolies, D. 1999. "Rich-Con steel selling its assets, http://www.bizjournals.com/kansascity/stories/1999/09/13/story1.html?page=all," in: *Kansas City Business Journal (12 Sept 1999)*.

Mari, A. 2013. "CIO interview: Darrell Stein, IT director, Marks & Spencer, http://www.computerweekly.com/news/2240179873/CIO-interview-Darrell-Stein-IT-director-Marks-and-Spencer," in: *ComputerWeekly (20 March 2013)*.

Markides, C. C. 2013. "Business Model Innovation: What Can the Ambidexterity Literature Teach Us?," *Academy of Management Perspectives* (27:4), pp. 313-323.

Martinez-Jerez, F. A., and Narayanan, V. G. 2011. "Teaching Note: Strategic outsourcing at Bharti Airtel Limited (HBS 9-107-003)," in: *Harvard Business School Cases*.

Maruping, L. M., Venkatesh, V., and Agarwal, R. 2009. "A control theory perspective on agile methodology use and changing user requirements," *Information Systems Research* (20:3), pp. 377-399.

McAfee, A. 2003a. "Rich-Con Steel (HBS Case 9-699-133)," Harvard Business School, Boston, MA, pp. 1-10.

Digital Intelligence

McAfee, A. 2003b. "When Too Much IT Knowledge is a Dangerous Thing," *Sloan Management Review* (44:2), pp. 83-89.

McAfee, A. 2004. "Do you have too much IT? ," *Sloan Management Review* (45:3).

McAfee, A. 2006. "Mastering the three worlds of information technology," *Harvard Business Review* (84:11), pp. 141-149.

McAfee, A. 2011. "What every CEO needs to know about the cloud," *Harvard Business Review* (89:11), pp. 124-132.

McAfee, A., Dessain, V., and Sjoman, A. 2004. "Zara: IT for fast fashion (HBS Case 9-604-081)," Harvard Business School, Boston, MA, pp. 1-23.

McAfee, A., McFarlan, F. W., and Wagonfeld, A. B. 2006. "Enterprise IT at Cisco (HBS Case 9-605-015), Revised 2007," Harvard Business School, Boston, MA, pp. 1-13.

McConnell, S. 1996. *Rapid Development*. Microsoft Press:

McDougall, P. 2006. "Dexterity required," in: *InformationWeek (June 19, 2006)*. pp. 34-50.

McFarlan, F. W. 1981. "Portfolio approach to information systems," *Harvard Business Review* (Sept-Oct), pp. 142-150.

McFarlan, F. W., and Nolan, R. L. 1995. "How to manage an IT outsourcing alliance," *Sloan Management Review* (36:2), pp. 9-26.

McGee, M. K. 2007. "Make the management move," in: *InformationWeek (Issue February 26, 2007)*. pp. 51-52.

McKenney, J. L., Copeland, D. C., and Mason, R. O. 1995. *Waves of change: Business evolution through information technology*. Boston, MA: HBS Press.

McWilliams, G. 2004. "Minding the store: Analyzing customers, Bestbuy decides not all are welcome," in: *Wall Street Journal (8 Nov 2004)*. Washington, DC: p. A1.

Means, B., Toyama, Y., Murphy, R., Bakia, M., and Jones, K. 2010. "Evaluation of Evidence-Based Practices in Online Learning: A Meta-Analysis and Review of Online Learning Studies, https://www2.ed.gov/rschstat/eval/tech/evidence-based-practices/finalreport.pdf," US Department of Education (ed.).

Melville, N., Kraemer, K. L., and Gurbaxani, V. 2004. "Information technology and organizational performance: An integrative model of IT business value," *MIS Quarterly* (28:2), pp. 283-322.

Merrill, S. 2012. "With Many Eyeballs, All Bugs Are Shallow, available at http://techcrunch.com/2012/02/23/with-many-eyeballs-all-bugs-are-shallow/," in: *Techcrunch (Feb 23, 2012)*.

Meyer, M. W. 2003. *Rethinking Performance Measurement: Beyond the Balanced Scorecard*. New York: Cambridge University Press.

Miles, R., Snow, C. C., Meyer, A. D., and Coleman, H. J. 1978. "Organizational strategy, structure, and process," *Academy of Management Review* (3:3), pp. 546-562.

Mitchell, R. L. 2012. "Brain drain: Where Cobol systems go from here, available at http://www.computerworld.com/s/article/9225079/Brain_drain_Where_Cobol_systems_go_from_here_," *ComputerWorld (14 March 2012)*).

Mithas, S. 2014. *Dancing Elephants and Leaping Jaguars: How to Excel, Innovate, and Transform Your Organization the Tata Way (http://amzn.com/1503011879)*. North Potomac: Finerplanet.

Mithas, S. 2015a. *Making the Elephant Dance: The Tata Way to Innovate, Transform and Globalize (Kindle version is available at http://www.amazon.in/dp/B012G9MSCA)*. New Delhi: Penguin Portfolio.

Mithas, S. 2015b. "A Saga of Excellence," *Indian Management* (September), pp. 47-50.

Mithas, S., and Agarwal, R. 2010. "Information Technology Governance for Revenue Growth at Johnson & Johnson," in: *Case Study, Robert H. Smith School of Business*. College Park.

Mithas, S., Agarwal, R., and Courtney, H. 2012. "Digital business strategies and the duality of IT," *IEEE IT Professional* (14:Sept-Oct), pp. 2-4.

Mithas, S., Almirall, D., and Krishnan, M. S. 2006. "Do CRM Systems Cause One-to-one Marketing Effectiveness?," *Statistical Science* (21:2), pp. 223-233.

Mithas, S., Almirall, D., and Krishnan, M. S. 2009. "A potential outcomes approach to assess causality in information systems research," in *Economics, Information Systems and Electronic*

Digital Intelligence

Commerce Research II: Advanced Empirical Methodologies, R.J. Kauffman and P.P. Tallon (eds.). Armonk, New York: ME Sharpe, pp. 63-85.

Mithas, S., and Arora, R. 2015. "Lessons from Tata's Corporate Innovation Strategy, available at http://ieeexplore.ieee.org/stamp/stamp.jsp?tp=&arnumber=7077248," *IEEE IT Professional* (17:2), pp. 2-6.

Mithas, S., Jones, J. L., and Mitchell, W. 2008. "Buyer intention to use Internet-enabled reverse auctions? The role of asset specificity, product specialization, and non-contractibility," *MIS Quarterly* (32:4), pp. 705-724.

Mithas, S., and Krishnan, M. S. 2008. "Human Capital and Institutional Effects in the Compensation of Information Technology Professionals in the United States," *Management Science* (54:3), pp. 415-428.

Mithas, S., and Krishnan, M. S. 2009. "From association to causation via a potential outcomes approach," *Information Systems Research* (20:2), pp. 295-313.

Mithas, S., Krishnan, M. S., and Fornell, C. 2005. "Why Do Customer Relationship Management Applications Affect Customer Satisfaction?," *Journal of Marketing* (69:4), pp. 201-209.

Mithas, S., Krishnan, M. S., and Fornell, C. 2016. "Information Technology, Customer Satisfaction, and Profit: Theory and Evidence," *Information Systems Research* (27:1), pp. 166-181.

Mithas, S., and Lucas, H. C. 2010a. "Are Foreign IT Workers Cheaper? U.S. Visa Policies and Compensation of Information Technology Professionals," *Management Science* (56:5), pp. 745-765.

Mithas, S., and Lucas, H. C. 2010b. "What is your digital business strategy?, available at http://ieeexplore.ieee.org/stamp/stamp.jsp?tp=&arnumber=5662565," *IEEE IT Professional* (12:6), pp. 4-6.

Mithas, S., and Lucas, H. C. 2014. "Information Technology and Firm Value: Productivity Paradox, Profitability Paradox and New Frontiers," in *Information Systems and Information Technology (Volume 2),* H. Topi and A. Tucker (eds.). Boca Raton: Chapman & Hall/ CRC Press (Taylor and Francis Group).

Mithas, S., and Lucas, H. C. 2015. "What Will It Take To Create A World-class B-School In India? available at http://www.businessworld.in/article/What-Will-It-Take-To-Create-A-World-class-B-School-In-India-/07-12-2015-88986/," in: *BW BusinessWorld (14 Dec 2015).* pp. 106-108.

Mithas, S., Ramasubbu, N., and Sambamurthy, V. 2011. "How Information Management Capability Influences Firm Performance," *MIS Quarterly* (35:1), pp. 237-256.

Mithas, S., and Rust, R. T. 2016. "How Information Technology Strategy and Investments Influence Firm Performance: Conjectures and Empirical Evidence," *MIS Quarterly* (40:1), pp. 223-245.

Mithas, S., Tafti, A. R., Bardhan, I. R., and Goh, J. M. 2012a. "The impact of IT Investments on Profits, available at http://sloanreview.mit.edu/x/53302," *MIT Sloan Management Review* (53:3), p. 15.

Mithas, S., Tafti, A. R., Bardhan, I. R., and Goh, J. M. 2012b. "Information Technology and Firm Profitability: Mechanisms and Empirical Evidence," *MIS Quarterly* (36:1), pp. 205-224.

Mithas, S., Tafti, A. R., and Mitchell, W. 2013. "How a Firm's Competitive Environment and Digital Strategic Posture Influence Digital Business Strategy," *MIS Quarterly* (37:2), pp. 511-536.

Mithas, S., and Whitaker, J. 2007. "Is the World Flat or Spiky? Information Intensity, Skills and Global Service Disaggregation," *Information Systems Research* (18:3), pp. 237-259.

Mithas, S., Whitaker, J. W., and Tafti, A. R. 2013. "Information Technology and Globalization: Theory and Evidence," in: *Working paper, Smith School of Business, University of Maryland.* College Park, MD.

Mitra, S., Sambamurthy, V., and Westerman, G. 2011. "Measuring IT performance and communicating value," *MIS Quarterly Executive* (10:1), pp. 47-59.

Mittal, V., Anderson, E. W., Sayrak, A., and Tadikamalla, P. 2005. "Dual emphasis and the long-term financial impact of customer satisfaction," *Marketing Science* (24:4), pp. 544-555.

Montgomery, L. 2007. "The cost of war, unnoticed, http://www.washingtonpost.com/wp-dyn/content/article/2007/05/07/AR2007050701582.html," in: *Washington Post (May 8, 2007).* Washington, DC: pp. D1-2.

Digital Intelligence

Morgeson III, F. V., and Mithas, S. 2009. "Does E-Government Measure up to E-Business? Comparing End-User Perceptions of U.S. Federal Government and E-Business Websites," *Public Administration Review* (69:4), pp. 740-752.

Morgeson III, F. V., Van Amburg, D., and Mithas, S. 2011. "Misplaced Trust? Exploring the Structure of the E-Government-Citizen Trust Relationship," *Journal of Public Administration Research and Theory* (21:2), pp. 257-283.

Morris, I. 2010. *Why the west rules--for now.* New York: Farrar, Straus and Giroux.

Mudambi, R. 2007. "Book Review- Offshoring: Economic geography and the multinatinal firm," *Journal of International Business Studies* (38), pp. 206-210.

Murphy, C. 2008. "InformationWeek 500 Trends: Web 2.0, Globalization, Virtualization, And More, available at http://www.informationweek.com/story/showArticle.jhtml?articleID=210601098," in: *InformationWeek.* pp. 29-35.

Murphy, C. 2011. "Chief of the year, http://informationweek.us/news/global-cio/interviews/232200549," in: *InformationWeek (12 Dec 2011).* pp. 21-31.

Murphy, C. 2012. "General Motors Will Slash Outsourcing In IT Overhaul, available at http://www.informationweek.com/global-cio/interviews/general-motors-will-slash-outsourcing-in/240002892 " in: *InformationWeek.* pp. 21-26.

Narasimhan, B. 2013. "IT helped Titan grow: Bhaskar Bhat, available at http://www.cio.in/view-top/it-helped-titan-grow," in: *CIO.in.*

Nash, K. S. 2015. "Target CIO to Reduce Outsourcing, Hire 1,000 in IT, http://blogs.wsj.com/cio/2015/09/18/target-cio-to-reduce-outsourcing-hire-1000-in-it/," in: *Wall Street Journal (Sept 18, 2015).* Washington, DC.

National Research Council. 1999. *Being fluent with information technology.* Washington, D.C.: National Academy Press.

Nelson, R. R. 2007. "IT project management: Infamous failures, classic mistakes, and best practices," *MIS Quarterly Executive* (6:2), pp. 67-78.

Nolan, R. L. 2000. "Information technology management since 1960," in *A nation transformed by information: How information has shaped the United States from colonial times to the present,* A.D. Chandler and J.W. Cortada (eds.). Oxford: Oxford University Press, pp. 217-256.

Nolan, R. L., and McFarlan, F. W. 2005. "Information technology and the board of directors," *Harvard Business Review* (83:10), pp. 96-106.

Nonaka, I. 2007. "The knowledge-creating company," *Harvard Business Reivew* (July-August).

Nunes, J. C., and Dreze, X. 2006. "Your loyalty program is betraying you," *Harvard Business Review* (April:124-131).

O'Reilly III, C. A., and Tushman, M. L. 2004. "The ambidextrous organization," *Harvard Business Review* (82:4), pp. 74-81.

Overby, S. 2004. "USAA: I.T. Incorporated, available at http://www.cio.com/article/print/32260," *CIO (1 May 2004)).*

Overby, S. 2005. "Simple successful outsourcing," *CIO (Oct 1, 2005)).*

Overby, S. 2006. "How to say no to outsourcing, available at http://www.cio.com/article/25356/How_to_Say_No_to_Outsourcing," *CIO (Oct 1, 2006)).*

Parisi, S., Cross, R., and Davenport., T. H. 2006. "Strategies for Preventing a Knowledge-Loss Crisis," *MIT Sloan Management Review* (47:4), pp. 31-38.

Parker, G. G., Van Alstyne, M. W., and Choudary, S. P. 2016. *Platform Revolution: How networked markets are transforming the economy and how to make them work for you.* New York: Norton.

Pavlou, P. A., and El Sawy, O. 2006. "From IT Leveraging Competence to Competitive Advantage in Turbulent Environments: The Case of New Product Development," *Information Systems Research* (17:3), pp. 198-227.

Pavlou, P. A., and El Sawy, O. 2010. "The "Third Hand": IT-Enabled Competitive Advantage in Turbulence Through Improvisational Capabilities," *Information Systems Research* (21:3), pp. 443-471.

Peppers, D., Rogers, M., and Dorf, B. 1999. "Is your company ready for one-to-one marketing?," *Harvard Business Review* (77:1), pp. 3-12.

Digital Intelligence

Philip, J. T., and Sen, A. 2014. "Bharti Airtel's evolving outsourcing strategy, http://www.livemint.com/Companies/v0BPytPnOJMAalnMRWRDAM/Bharti-Airtels-evolving-outsourcing-strategy.html," in: *Livemint (29 May 2014)*.

Piasno, G. P., and Verganti, R. 2008. "Which kind of collaboration is right for you?," *Harvard Business Reivew* (Dec).

Piccoli, G. 2007. *Information Systems for Managers: Texts & Cases* Wiley.

Piccoli, G., and Ives, B. 2005. "Review: IT-dependent strategic initiatives and sustained competitive advantage: A review and synthesis of the literature," *MIS Quarterly* (29:4), pp. 747-776.

Pine, B. J., Peppers, D., and Rogers, M. 1995. "Do you want to keep your customers forever?," *Harvard Business Review* (Mar-Apr), pp. 103-114.

Pitroda, S. 1993. "Development, Democracy, and the Village Telephone," *Harvard Business Review* (Nov-Dec), pp. 66-79.

Pollack, A. 2003. "Who's reading your X-ray? (Nov 16, 2003)," in: *New York Times*.

Popkin, J. M., and Iyengar, P. 2007. *IT and the East: How India and China are altering the future of technology and innovation.* Boston: Harvard Business School Press.

Porter, M. E. 1980. *Competitive Strategy: Techniques for analyzing industries and competitors.* New York: Free Press.

Porter, M. E. 1985a. *Competitive Advantage: Creating and Sustaining Superior Performance.* New York: Free Press.

Porter, M. E. 1985b. "Technology and Competitive Advantage," *Journal of Business Strategy* (5:3), pp. 60-78.

Porter, M. E. 1987. "From competitive advantage to corporate strategy," *Harvard Business Review* (May-June), pp. 43-59.

Porter, M. E. 1996. "What is Strategy?," *Harvard Business Review* (Nov-Dec), pp. 61-78.

Porter, M. E. 2001. "Strategy and the Internet," *Harvard Business Review* (79:3), pp. 63-78.

Porter, M. E., and Millar, V. E. 1985. "How Information Gives You Competitive Advantage," *Harvard Business Review* (63:4), pp. 149-160.

Porter, M. E., and Rivkin, J. W. 2000. "Industry Transformation (9-701-008)," in: *Harvard Business Publishing.* pp. 1-14.

Puri, L. 2007. "The CEO as CIO: An interview with the head of India's top private bank," *McKinsey on IT* (Spring).

Raelin, J., and Balachandra, R. 1985. "R&D Project Termination in High Tech Industries," *IEEE Transactions on Engineering Management* (EM-32:1), pp. 16-23.

Rai, A., Patnayakuni, R., and Patnayakuni, N. 1997. "Technology investment and business performance," *Communications of the ACM* (40:7), pp. 89-97.

Rai, A., Patnayakuni, R., and Seth, N. 2006. "Firm performance impacts of digitally-enabled supply chain integration capabilities," *MIS Quarterly* (30:2), pp. 225-246.

Raisch, S., and Birkinshaw, J. 2008. "Organizational ambidexterity: Antecedents, outcomes and moderators," *Journal of Management* (34:3), pp. 375-409.

Ramasubbu, N., Mithas, S., and Krishnan, M. S. 2008. "High Tech, High Touch: The Effect of Employee Skills and Customer Heterogeneity on Customer Satisfaction with Enterprise System Support Services " *Decision Support Systems* (44:2), pp. 509-523.

Ramasubbu, N., Mithas, S., Krishnan, M. S., and Kemerer, C. F. 2008. "Work Dispersion, Process-Based Learning and Offshore Software Development Performance," *MIS Quarterly* (32:2), pp. 437-458.

Ravichandran, T., Han, S., and Mithas, S. 2012. "How information technology influences innovation output of a firm: Theory and evidence," in: *Working paper, Rensselaer Polytechnic Institute*.

Ravichandran, T., Han, S., and Mithas, S. 2015. "How information technology influences innovation output of a firm: Theory and evidence," in: *Working paper, Rensselaer Polytechnic Institute*.

Raymond, E. S. 2000. "The Cathedral and the Bazaar, http://www.catb.org/~esr/writings/cathedral-bazaar/cathedral-bazaar/index.html#catbmain."

Reed, D. P. 2001. "The law of the pack," *Harvard Business Review* (Feb), pp. 23-24.

Reid, T. R. 2009. *The healing of America.* New York: The Penguin Press.

Reingold, J., Jones, M., and Kramer, S. 2014. "jcpenney: How to fail in business while really, really trying, available at http://money.cnn.com/2014/03/20/leadership/jc-penney.pr.fortune/," in: *Fortune.* pp. 81-90.

Digital Intelligence

Reinhardt, A., Kripalani, M., Smith, G., Bush, J., Balfour, F., and Ante, S. E. 2006. "Angling to be the next Bangalore, http://www.businessweek.com/magazine/content/06_05/b3969409.htm," *BusinessWeek* (30 Jan 2006).

Rettig, C. 2007. "The trouble with enterprise software," *MIT Sloan Management Review* (Fall), pp. 21-27.

Reuters. 2011. "Twitter share auction suggests $7.7 billion valuation, available at http://www.reuters.com/article/2011/03/04/us-twitter-idUSTRE7221JL20110304," *Reuters (4 March 2011))*.

Rich, M. 2009. "Bright passage in publishing: Authors who pay their way," in: *New York Times (28 Jan 2009)*. New York: p. A1.

Rigby, D., Reichheld, F., and Schefter, P. 2002. "Avoiding four perils of CRM," *Harvard Business Review* (Jan-Feb).

Rigby, D. K., and Ledingham, D. 2004. "CRM done right," *Harvard Business Review* (82:11), pp. 118-129.

Rigby, D. K., Sutherland, J., and Takeuchi, H. 2016. "Embracing Agile," *Harvard Business Review* (May), pp. 41-50.

Rivkin, J. W. 2002. "An options-led approach to making strategic choices (9-702-433)," in: *HBS Publishing*.

Roberts, R., and Sikes, J. 2008. "McKinsey Global Survey Results: IT's unmet potential," *McKinsey Quarterly* (November), pp. 1-9.

Rodrik, D. 1997. *Has globalization gone too far?* Washington, D.C.: Institute for International Economics.

Rogers, P., and Blenko, M. 2006. "Who has the D? How clear decision roles enhance organizational performance," *Harvard Business Review* (Jan), pp. 53-61.

Rohwedder, C. 2006. "Stores of knowledge: No. 1 retailer in Britain uses 'Clubcard' to thwart Wal-Mart," *Wall Street Journal* (6 June 2006), pp. A1, A16.

Rose, C. 2012. "Charlie Rose talks to Cisco's John Chambers, available at http://www.businessweek.com/articles/2012-04-19/charlie-rose-talks-to-ciscos-john-chambers," in: *BusinessWeek (19 April 2012)*.

Rosenwald, M. S. 2010. "Website ensure online lives don't disappear with "dearly departed'," in: *Washington Post (25 Jan 2010)*. Washington, DC: pp. A1, A7.

Ross, J. W., and Beath, C. M. 2002. "Beyond the business case: New approaches to IT Investment," *MIT Sloan Management Review* (Winter), pp. 51-59.

Ross, J. W., Vitale, M. R., and Beath, C. M. 1999. "The untapped potential of IT chargeback," *MIS Quarterly* (23:2), pp. 215-237.

Ross, J. W., and Weill, P. 2002. "Six IT Decisions Your IT People Shouldn't Make," *Harvard Business Review* (November), pp. 85-91.

Rottman, J. W., and Lacity, M. C. 2006. "Proven practices for effectively offshoring IT work," *MIT Sloan Management Review* (Spring), pp. 56-63.

Rubin, D. B. 1974. "Estimating Causal Effects of Treatments in Randomized and Nonrandomized Studies," *Journal of Educational Psychology* (66:5), pp. 688-701.

Rubin, D. B. 1978. "Bayesian Inference for Causal Effects: The Role of Randomization," *Annals of Statistics* (6:1), pp. 34-58.

Rubinstein, D. 2015. "Industry Watch: Successful software development, available at http://sdtimes.com/industry-watch-successful-software-development/," in: *SD Times (30 April 2015)*. p. 62.

Rust, R. T., Moorman, C., and Dickson, P. R. 2002. "Getting return on quality: Revenue expansion, cost reduction, or both?," *Journal of Marketing* (66:4), pp. 7-24.

Rust, R. T., Moorman, C., and van Beuningen, J. 2016. "Quality Mental Model Convergence and Business Performance," *International Journal of Research in Marketing* (Forthcoming:http://dx.doi.org/10.1016/j.ijresmar.2015.07.005).

Rust, R. T., and Oliver, R. W. 1994. "The death of advertising," *Journal of Advertising* (23:4), pp. 71-77.

Sabherwal, R., and Jeyaraj, A. 2015. "Information technology impacts on firm performance: An extension of Kohli and Devaraj (2003)," *MIS Quarterly* (39:4), pp. 809-836.

Digital Intelligence

Sagan, C. 1977. *The Dragons of Eden: Speculations on the evolution of human intelligence.* New York: Random House.

Saldanha, T., Mithas, S., and Krishnan, M. S. 2016. "Leveraging Customer Involvement for Fueling Innovation: The Role of Relational and Analytical Information Processing Capabilities," *MIS Quarterly* (Forthcoming).

Sambamurthy, V., Bharadwaj, A., and Grover, V. 2003. "Shaping Agility through Digital Options: Reconceptualizing the Role of Information Technology in Contemporary Firms," *MIS Quarterly* (27:2), pp. 237 - 263.

Satariano, A. 2015. "Apple Is Getting More Bang for Its R&D Buck, available at http://www.bloomberg.com/news/articles/2015-11-30/apple-gets-more-bang-for-its-r-d-buck," in: *Bloomberg BusinessWeek (30 Nov-6Dec, 2015).* pp. 38-39.

Schein, E. H. (ed.) 1992. *The Role of the CEO in the Management of Change: The Case of Information Technology.* Oxford, UK: Oxford University Press.

Schmidt, C. 2016. *Agile software development teams: The impact of agile development on team performance (ISBN 978-3-319-26055-0).* New York: Springer.

Schmidt, C. T., Kude, T., Heinzl, A., and Mithas, S. 2014. "How Agile Practices Influence the Performance of Software Development Teams: The Role of Shared Mental Models and Backup," *Proceedings of the 34th International Conference on Information Systems (Dec 14-17),* A. Srinivasan, B. Tan and E. Karahanna (eds.), Auckland, New Zealand: Association for Information Systems.

Segars, A., and Chatterjee, D. 2010. "Diets that don't work: Where enterprise resource planning goes wrong," in: *Wall Street Journal (23 Aug 2010).* Washington, DC: p. R6.

Shannon, C. E. 1948. "A Mathematical Theory of Communication," *Bell System Technical Journal* (27:July, October), pp. 379-423 and 623-656.

Shapiro, C., and Varian, H. R. 1999. *Information Rules: A strategic guide to the network economy.* Boston, Mass.: Harvard Business School Press.

Sharma, A. 2006. "Love, shift, delete: Saying bye-byte in a digital age," *Wall Street Journal (27 Mar 2006)),* p. A1.

Sharma, R., Mithas, S., and Kankanhalli, A. 2014. "Transforming decision-making processes: A research agenda for understanding the impact of business analytics on organisations," *European Journal of Information Systems* (23:4), pp. 433-441.

Sibal, K. 2008. *i witness: partial observations.* New Delhi: IndiaLinks.

Simon, H. A. 1960. "The corporation: Will it be managed by machines?," in *Management and the Corporations 1985,* M.L. Anshen and G.L. Bach (eds.). New York: McGraw-Hill, pp. 17-55.

Skinner, W. 1986. "The Productivity Paradox," *Harvard Business Review* (July-August), pp. 55-59.

Sood, V., Seth, S., and John, S. 2010. "How Tata Motors turned JLR around, http://www.livemint.com/Companies/UhROXPttBWa40lVOgtS6wL/How-Tata-Motors-turned-JLR-around.html," in: *Livemint (14 Nov 2010).*

Spector, M., and Bellman, E. 2008. "Tata and Ford Reach Deal For Land Rover, Jaguar, available at http://online.wsj.com/news/articles/SB120652768989365191," in: *Wall Street Journal (27 March 2008).* Washington, DC.

Srivastava, S. C., Mithas, S., and Jha, B. 2013. "What is your global innovation strategy?, available at http://www.computer.org/csdl/mags/it/2013/06/mit2013060002.pdf," *IEEE IT Professional* (15:6, Nov-Dec), pp. 2-6.

Stabell, C. B., and Fjeldstad, Ø. D. 1998. "Configuring value for competitive advantage: On chains, shops and networks," *Strategic Management Journal* (19), pp. 413-437.

Stewart, T. A. 1998. *Intellectual Capital: The New Wealth of Organizations.* Crown Business.

Stone, B., and Frier, S. 2014. "Facebook Turns 10: The Mark Zuckerberg Interviews, available at:http://www.bloomberg.com/bw/articles/2014-01-30/facebook-turns-10-the-mark-zuckerberg-interview#p4, accessed 28 Feb 2016," *Bloomberg Business Week* (30 Jan 2014), pp. 46-49.

Sullivan, B. K. 2005. "Men Who Have MBAs Are Highest-Paid in Technology, Study Finds," in: *Bloomberg (May 26, 2005).*

Surowiecki, J. 2004. *The wisdom of crowds: Why the many are smarter than the few and how collective wisdom shapes business, economics, societies, and nations.* New York: Doubleday.

Digital Intelligence

Sutherland, J. 2015. *Scrum: The art of doing twice the work in half the time.* London: Random House.

Swartz, J., Martin, S., and Krantz, M. 2012. "Facebook IPO filing puts high value on social network, available at http://www.usatoday.com/tech/news/story/2012-02-01/facebook-ipo/52921528/1," *USA Today (2 Feb 2012)).*

Swift, R. S. 2000. *Accelerating Customer Relationships: Using CRM and Relationship Technologies.* Prentice Hall.

Tafti, A., Mithas, S., and Krishnan, M. S. 2007. "Information technology and the autonomy-control duality: Toward a theory," *Information Technology and Management* (8:2), pp. 147-166.

Tafti, A., Mithas, S., and Krishnan, M. S. 2013a. "The Effect of Information Technology- Enabled Flexibility on Formation and Market Value of Alliances," *Management Science* (59:1), pp. 207-225.

Tafti, A., Mithas, S., and Krishnan, M. S. 2013b. "The Importance of IT-Enabled Flexibility in Alliances, http://sloanreview.mit.edu/x/54312," *MIT Sloan Management Review* (54:3), pp. 13-14.

Tafti, A., Mithas, S., and Krishnan, M. S. 2015. "Empowering IT Professionals Through HR Practices: Implications for IT Productivity," in: *Working Paper, University of Illinois at Chicago.* Chicago.

Tafti, A. R., Mithas, S., and Krishnan, M. S. 2009. "Complementarities between Information Technology and Human Resource Practices in Knowledge Work," *Workshop on Information System Economics*, Phoenix, Arizona.

Tallon, P. P., Kraemer, K. L., and Gurbaxani, V. 2000. "Executives' Perceptions of the business value of information technology: A process oriented approach," *Journal of Management Information Systems* (16:4), pp. 145-173.

Tam, P.-W. 2007. "CIO jobs morph from tech support into strategy," *Wall Street Journal* (February 20, 2007), p. B1.

Tambe, P. B., and Hitt, L. M. 2012. "The Productivity of Information Technology Investments: New Evidence from IT Labor Data," *Information Systems Research* (23:3 Part 1), pp. 599-617.

Taylor III, A. 2011. "Tata takes on the world: Building an auto empire in India, Available at http://money.cnn.com/2011/04/15/news/international/tata_auto_empire_india.fortune/," *Fortune* (May 2, 2011), pp. 87-92.

Tellis, G. J. 2006. "Disruptive Technology or Visionary Leadership?," *Journal of Product Innovation and Management* (23:1), pp. 34-38.

Tetlock, P. E., and Belkin, A. (eds.). 1996. *Counterfactual thought experiments in world politics: Logical, methodological, and psychological perspectives.* Princeton, New Jersey: Princeton Paperbacks.

The Economist. 2002. "Always-on people, http://www.economist.com/node/949014," *The Economist* (31 Jan 2002).

The Economist. 2005. "The fall of a corporate queen, http://www.economist.com/node/3632638," (Feb 3, 2005).

The Economist. 2006. "Open, but not usual, available at http://www.economist.com/node/5624944," in: *The Economist (16 March 2006).*

The Economist. 2008. "Let it rise (Special report on corporate IT)," in: *The Economist Magazine.* pp. 3-4.

The Economist. 2009. "The information-technology industry revives: Back to the circuit board, http://www.economist.com/node/14704601," in: *The Economist.* pp. 73-74.

The Economist. 2011. "Special report: Personal Technology; Oct 8, 2011, available at http://www.economist.com/node/21531109," in: *The Economist.*

The Economist. 2012. "Technological change: The last Kodak moment? (14 Jan 2012), available at http://www.economist.com/node/21542796," in: *The Economist.* pp. 63-64.

The Economist. 2014. "Super subs, available at http://www.economist.com/news/business/21599370-adobes-bold-embrace-computing-cloud-should-inspire-others-super-subs," in: *The Economist (22 March 2014).* p. 65.

The Economist Blog. 2012. "General purpose technologies: The revolution to come (13 Apr 2012), available at http://www.economist.com/blogs/freeexchange/2012/04/general-purpose-technologies," in: *The Economist Blog.*

Digital Intelligence

Thurm, S. 2007. "Behind outsourcing: Promise and pitfalls," in: *Wall Street Journal (February 26, 2007)*. Washington, DC: p. B3.

Thurm, S. 2015. "Why most firms better get moving: Cisco's John Chambers on digital disruptions ahead', available at http://www.wsj.com/articles/ciscos-john-chambers-on-the-digital-disruptions-ahead-1423540859," in: *Wall Street Journal (Feb 10, 2015)*. Washington, DC: p. R6.

Tian, F., and Xu, S. X. 2015. "How Do Enterprise Resource Planning Systems Affect Firm Risk? Post-Implementation Impact," *MIS Quarterly* (39:1), pp. 39-60.

Tiwana, A. 2014. "Separating signal from noise: Evaluating emerging technologies," *MIS Quarterly Executive* (13:1), pp. 45-61.

Tiwana, A., and Keil, M. 2004. "The one-minute risk assessment tool," *Communications of the ACM* (47:11), pp. 73-77.

Tiwana, A., Konsynski, B., and Venkatraman, N. 2013-14. "Information technology and organizational governance: The IT Governance Cube," *Journal of Management Information Systems* (30:3), pp. 7-12.

Totty, M. 2006. "Business solutions: A new way to keep track of talent," in: *Wall Street Journal (15 May 2006)*. Washington, DC: p. R7.

Trachtenberg, J. A. 2010. "Barnes & Noble names its web chief as CEO," in: *Wall Street Journal (19 Mar 2010)*. Washington, DC: p. B5.

Treacy, M., and Wiersema, F. 1993. "Customer intimacy and other value disciplines," *Harvard Business Review* (71:1), pp. 84-93.

Treacy, M., and Wiersema, F. 1997. *The Discipline of Market Leaders: Choose Your Customers, Narrow Your Focus, Dominate Your Market*. Perseus Publishing.

Tuli, K., and Bharadwaj, S. 2009. "Customer Satisfaction and Stock Returns Risk " *Journal of Marketing* (73:Nov), pp. 184-197.

Tushman, M., and Anderson, P. 1986. "Technological discontinuities and organizational environments," *Administrative Science Quarterly* (32), pp. 439-465.

Twiddy, D. 2007. "Sprint Nextel defends cutting customers," in: *Washington Post (10 July 2007)*. Washington, DC.

Upton, D. M., and Staats, B. R. 2008. "Radically Simple IT," *Harvard Business Review* (March), pp. 118-124.

Vallis, H., and Murphy, C. 2008. "2008 InformationWeek 500 Analytics Report (Sept 2008)," in: *InformationWeek Analytics Reports*.

Vallis, H., and Murphy, C. 2011. "2011 InformationWeek 500 Analytics Report (Sept 2011), available at http://reports.informationweek.com/abstract/186/8354/InformationWeek%20500/2011-informationweek-500-report-and-issue.html, accessed 19 Oct 2011," in: *InformationWeek Analytics Reports*.

Van Alstyne, M. W., Parker, G., and Choudary, S. P. 2016. "Pipelines, platforms, and the new rules of strategy," *Harvard Business Review* (April), pp. 54-62.

Vance, A. 2011. "The power of the cloud," in: *Bloomberg BusinessWeek (Issue March 7-13, 2011), available at http://www.businessweek.com/magazine/content/11_11/b4219052599182.htm?chan=rss_top Stories_ssi_5 (accessed 7 Mar 2011)*. pp. 52-59.

Vascellaro, J. E. 2007. "Finding a date--on the spot," *Wall Street Journal* (6 June 2007), p. D1.

Vashistha, A., and Vashistha, A. 2006. *The offshore nation: Strategies for success in global outsourcing and offshoring*. New York: McGraw-Hill.

Vedantam, S. 2007. "Bush and counterfactual confidence," in: *The Washington Post*. Washington, DC: p. A3.

Vigna, P., and Shipman, J. 2010. "Domestic sales lag, available at http://www.wsj.com/articles/SB10001424052748704671904575194253307667086," in: *Wall Street Journal (20 April 2010)*. Washington, DC: p. B7.

Vlasic, B. 2009. "For Car Buyers, the Brand Romance Is Gone, available at http://www.nytimes.com/2009/10/21/business/21auto.html?_r=1&scp=8&sq=car%20buyers %20kiss%20loyalty%20goodbye&st=cse," *New York Times* (21 Oct 2009).

Wade, M., and Hulland, J. 2004. "Review-The resource based view and information systems research: Review, extension, and suggestions for future research," *MIS Quarterly* (28:1), pp. 107-142.

Digital Intelligence

Wagner, D. 2006. "Success factors in outsourcing service jobs: Which jobs are good candidates for global disaggregation? available at http://sloanreview.mit.edu/article/success-factors-in-outsourcing-service-jobs/," *MIT Sloan Management Review* (48:1), p. 7.

Wahlgren, E. 2001. "The Digital Age Storms the Corner Office, available at http://www.businessweek.com/technology/content/sep2001/tc2001096_253.htm," in: *BusinessWeek (6 Sep 2001)*.

Washington Post. 2008. "An $850 billion challenge, http://www.washingtonpost.com/wp-dyn/content/article/2008/12/21/AR2008122102375.html," in: *Washington Post (Dec 22, 2008)*. Washington, DC: p. A1.

Wattal, S., Langer, N., Mithas, S., Boh, W. F., and Slaughter, S. 2014. "Human Capital of IT Professionals: A Research Agenda," in: *Working paper, Temple University*.

Wattal, S., Langer, N., Mithas, S., Boh, W. F., and Slaughter, S. 2015. "Thriving with digital transformations: Redefining an agenda for research on IT human capital " in: *Working paper, Temple University*.

Weill, P. 2004. "Don't just lead, govern: How top-performing firms govern IT," *MIS Quarterly Executive* (3:1), pp. 1-17.

Weill, P., and Aral, S. 2006. "Generating Premium Returns on Your IT Investments," *MIT Sloan Management Review* (47:2), pp. 39-48.

Weill, P., and Ross, J. 2005. "A matrixed approach to designing IT governance," *MIT Sloan Management Review* (Winter), pp. 26-34.

Weill, P., and Ross, J. 2009. *IT Savvy: What top executives must know to go from pain to gain*. Boston, MA: Harvard Business School Press.

Whitaker, J., Mithas, S., and Krishnan, M. S. 2011. "Organizational learning and capabilities for onshore and offshore business process outsourcing," *Journal of Management Information Systems* (27:3), pp. 11-42.

Whitaker, J. W., New, J. R., and Ireland, R. D. 2016. "MOOCs and the online delivery of businies education: What's new? What's not? What now?," *Academy of Management Learning & Education* (15:2).

Whiting, R. 2006. "ERP gets a complete makeover, available at http://www.informationweek.com/story/showArticle.jhtml?articleID=190900779 " in: *InformationWeek (24 July 2006)*.

Whoriskey, P. 2012. "Burgeoning productivity? Some experts doubt it. ," in: *Washington Post (20 March 2012)*. Washington, DC: pp. A1, A12.

Williamson, O. E. 1975. *Markets and Hierarchies: Analysis and Antitrust Implications*. New York:

Wilson, S. 2009. "Obama's spending plans may pose political risks, http://www.washingtonpost.com/wp-dyn/content/article/2009/06/13/AR2009061302035.html?sid=ST2009061302263," in: *Washington Post (14 June 2009)*. Washington, DC: pp. A1, A14.

Winer, S. R. 2001. "A framework for customer relationship management," *California Management Review* (43:4), pp. 89-105.

Worthen, B. 2002. "Nestle's ERP Odyssey."

Worthen, B. 2012a. "Cut those costs! (But not tech.), available at http://online.wsj.com/article/SB10001424052970204573704577187212484940318.html?KEYWORDS=cut+those+costs," in: *Wall Street Journal (27 Feb 2012)*. Washington, DC: p. R5.

Worthen, B. 2012b. "H-P wants its edge back, available at http://online.wsj.com/article/SB10001424052970204789304578087041076775554.html," in: *Wall Street Journal (30 Oct 2012)*. Washington, DC: p. B1.

Worthen, B., and Sherr, I. 2012. "H-P is punished for grim outlook, available at http://online.wsj.com/article/SB10000872396390443635404578034473376159186.html," in: *Wall Street Journal (4 Oct 2012)*. Washington, DC: pp. B1, B2.

Xie, Y., and Wu, X. 2005. "Market premium, social process, and statisticism," *American Sociological Review* (70:5), pp. 865-870.

Xue, L., Mithas, S., and Ray, G. 2014. "Earnings Management and IT Investments: An Examination of IT Infrastructure Development," *Proceedings of the 34th International Conference on*

Information Systems (Dec 14-17), A. Srinivasan, B. Tan and E. Karahanna (eds.), Auckland, New Zealand: Association for Information Systems.

Xue, L., Ray, G., and Gu, B. 2011. "Environmental Uncertainty and IT Infrastructure Governance: A Curvelinear Relationship," *Information Systems Research* (22:2), pp. 389-399.

Yemen, G., Venkatesan, R., and Sriram, S. 2015. "The Times of India, 2015: Start the presses," in: *Washington Post (5 July 2015)*. Washington, DC: p. G2.

Yoffie, D. B. 2007. "EU verdict against Microsoft (9-706-503)," in: *HBS Case Collection*. Boston, MA.

Young, S., and Grant, P. 2003. "How phone firms lost to Cable," in: *Wall Street Journal (14 Mar 2003)*. Washington, DC: p. M8.

Ziobro, P. 2013. "Target fills its cart with Amazon ideas, http://online.wsj.com/news/articles/SB20001424052702304672404579184231426308394," in: *Wall Street Journal (12 Nov 2013)*. Washington, DC: p. B1.

Zuboff, S. 1988. *In the Age of the Smart Machine: The Future of Work and Power*. New York: Basic Books.

Notes

[1] Researchers have also pointed to other forms of intelligences or dimensions of human capital such as social capital and psychological capital that are no less important (Gardner 2006; Goleman 1995; Ho, Whitaker, Mithas and Roy 2012). Although digital intelligence as conceptualized in this book has rarely been articulated elsewhere, researchers have highlighted the importance of understanding digital transformation of the economy and implications for skills that will be in need (Dhar and Sundararajan 2007; Earl and Feeny 2000; National Research Council 1999).

[2] Although there are already several good books that deal with IT-related topics, this book differentiates itself in several key respects. First, unlike many good textbooks, this book is primarily written from the perspective of an informed and curious student, manager, executive, investor, or entrepreneur. There are some good trade books that cover IT management, IT-enabled transformation, and IT-enabled innovations. They cover important topics that complement or amplify some of the themes of this book. However, they do not focus as sharply on fundamental competencies that underlie what I call digital intelligence. Likewise, other books focus on how to lead change efforts, but they are silent on how to identify what type of change is needed and the role of IT in catalyzing industry transformations. Second, although I try to be brief and direct whenever possible, I provide citations to relevant scholarly research and other sources for readers who may want to explore a given topic in greater detail.

[3] This chapter draws on my work with Professor Hank Lucas (Mithas and Lucas 2010b).

[4] Chandler (2000) refers to these collective changes as "the information revolution," while Blinder (2006) suggests that these changes are "early stages of a third industrial revolution." This revolution affects everyone across the globe regardless of where a person lives and works. There are differences of opinion though on what the implications of these changes are for wages and employment prospects of workers around the world (Blinder 2006; Florida 2005; Friedman 2005; Mithas and Whitaker 2007). Certainly, with the increasing use of robots in many sectors such as Amazon.com's warehouses (Amazon acquired Kiva), milking of cows and therapy, some are concerned about prospects for human jobs and wages.

[5] Governance issues also played a role in Blockbuster's inability to counter the digital threats posed by Netflix and to react to them appropriately (Antioco 2011; Icahn 2011). Sometimes it moved too slowly as in integrating its online and offline channels but at other times it made questionable moves to end late fees prematurely that could have provided it funding for its digital initiatives. See Hardy (2011), and Chui and Fleming (2011) for P&G example. Chui and Fleming (2011) article also contains a link to the podcast of the interview with the CEO of P&G Robert McDonald in 2011, available at http://www.mckinsey.com/insights/consumer_and_retail/inside_p_and_ampgs_digital_revolution. This is not to say that digital intelligence alone is sufficient for success in a leadership role (Bustillo and Lubin 2011; Trachtenberg 2010).

[6] Here is an insider view of how Starbucks approaches its digital strategy (Brotman and Garner 2013; Jargon 2014; Murphy 2011). Digital strategy does not always mean a flashy website or app as Opower shows; the marketing versus technical framing matters and Opower's contrarian marketing framing made all the difference (Chernova 2014).

[7] Several academic studies have argued for or documented the positive effects of IT on firm performance (e.g., Aral, Brynjolfsson and Wu 2012; Aral and Weill 2007; Barua and Mukhopadhyay 2000; El Sawy and Pavlou 2008; Melville, Kraemer and Gurbaxani 2004; Mithas and Lucas 2014; Mithas, Ramasubbu and Sambamurthy 2011; Pavlou and El Sawy 2010; Piccoli and Ives 2005; Sambamurthy, Bharadwaj and Grover 2003; Tafti, Mithas and Krishnan 2013a; Tallon, Kraemer and Gurbaxani 2000; Wade and Hulland 2004). IT resources are considered intangibles because they have limited collateralizability due to their limited redeployability and uncertain liquidation values as a result of the asset-specificity of IT-related investments and systems. For example, the investments in IT services and customization of enterprise systems for a particular firm are hard to recoup if the firm is

liquidated (Kim, Mithas and Kimbrough 2012). They cannot be liquidated readily to satisfy debts, as can be done for tangible resources. Frequently, intangibles are associated with innovation and they are subject to information failures and measurement and reporting problems due to high risk, lack of full control over benefits, and absence of organized markets. They relate to discovery (e.g., R&D); organizational practices, and capabilities including alliances; and capital (customer related such as cost of customer acquisition, brands; IT, training, human resources) (Lev 2001). Lev (2001)points to their value drivers such as scalability (nonrivalry and increasing returns) and network effects; and value detractors such as partial excludability and spillovers, inherent risk (sunk costs, creative destruction) and nontradability (absence of organized markets, info asymmetry).

[8] IT has played an important role in the success of corporations such as Bank of America, American Airlines, USAA, American Hospital Supply, and Frito-Lay since at least the 1950s. See McKenney et al. (1995).

[9] IT resources encompass technological IT resources (infrastructure, business applications, hardware, software, databases, networks), human IT resources (technical IT skills, managerial IT skills), relationships with business and vendors, IT strategies, capabilities, governance processes, and ability to manage IT projects (Melville, Kraemer and Gurbaxani 2004; Mithas, Ramasubbu and Sambamurthy 2011). The importance of human capital cannot be overstated; as Alfred Marshall, a prominent economist of his time, noted in 1920: "The most valuable of all capital is that invested in human beings." Wattal and colleagues (2015) discuss how technological (cloud computing, mobile computing, consumerization of IT) and organizational (blurring boundaries between IT and non-IT workers, changes in demand for types of skills in the workplace, and changes in demographic mix of IT department) factors are reshaping the nature of the IT profession, and they call for research on skill needs and the demand-supply gap, career paths and public policy issues and related outcomes.

[10] See Boston Consulting Group (2012) and HBR (2012).

[11] I must caution readers that these figures are only estimates and sometimes there are significant differences in figures for aggregate IT spending reported by consulting companies (Montgomery 2007; Washington Post 2008; Wilson 2009).

[12] See The Economist (2009).

[13] See Mithas et al. (2012b).

[14] Part of the reason for the reallocation of expenditures may be that using IT can lead to more effective R&D and marketing. Researchers are beginning to test these conjectures empirically (Ravichandran, Han and Mithas 2012; Winer 2001).

[15] See Brynjolfsson and Saunders (2010).

[16] These fears are mostly based on anecdotal accounts (Carr 2008; Greengard 2009).

[17] The average labor productivity growth in the U.S. economy averaged only about 1.4% from 1973 to 1995. It rose to 2.6% from 1996 to 2000 and to 3.6% from 2001 to 2003. Then it dipped to 1.3% from 2004 to 2006, only to rise again to 2.4% in the 2007–2008 period (very close to 1996–2000 levels). There appears to be widespread agreement that IT has played a major role in the increased productivity evident in the 1996–2000 period. Some researchers argue that at least a part of the continued productivity growth in the 2001–2003 period can be attributed to lag effects of investments in complementary assets and business processes. See Brynjolfsson and Saunders (2010). The productivity effect of outsourcing on the U.S. economy has received much less attention than the fear of losing jobs due to outsourcing (Houseman, Kurz, Lengermann and Mandel 2010; Whoriskey 2012).

[18] Whether computers are substitutes or complements of humans have been a topic for debate for decades (Levy and Murnane 2004; Simon 1960). Assuming that computers are 100 times faster than bookkeepers in doing arithmetic but only 10 times faster than stenographers in taking dictation, employing humans in tasks in which they have a comparative or relative advantage (e.g. stenography) creates more output. This is true even though computers may have an absolute advantage in performing both bookkeeping and stenography and follows from the theory of comparative advantage, which goes back to Ricardo (Simon 1960). Autor et al. (2003) classify occupations according to their skill requirements: nonroutine manual, routine cognitive, routine manual, complex communication, and expert thinking. Their work suggests that jobs requiring expert thinking and complex communication have grown in the United States from 1969 to 1999. However, whether this pattern has held

subsequently in United States and whether a similar pattern will hold in India or China are questions that require investigation.

[19] There are numerous views of strategy and this literature continues to evolve (Bradach 1996; Brandenburger and Nalebuff 1995; Collis and Montgomery 1995; Collis and Rukstad 2008; Eisenhardt and Sull 2001; Ghemawat 2010; Grimm, Lee and Smith 2006; Hambrick and Fredrickson 2001; Porter 1996; Rivkin 2002).

[20] See Kirkland (2013).

[21] This analysis should ideally be done at the product or service level.

[22] See Hays (1999).

[23] See Hamel and Valikangas (2003).

[24] See Day and Schoemaker (2000b).

[25] An alternative way of understanding IT's strategic significance is to view IT as playing three strategic roles: automate, inform, and transform. These roles of IT can be conceptualized at industry and firm levels (Chatterjee, Richardson and Zmud 2001; Dehning, Richardson and Zmud 2003; Schein 1992; Zuboff 1988). In its "automate" role, firms use IT to replace human labor, as evident in the replacement of human travel agents by kiosks or online reservation systems. In its "inform" role, IT can provide information that enables senior managers to make better decisions and to empower employees. In its "transform" role, IT can help fundamentally change business models and market structures (e.g., music industry). These roles are not mutually exclusive—an industry or a firm can have different degrees of automate, inform, or transform roles of IT simultaneously. In general, though, some consider IT's transformation potential to be higher in more information-intensive businesses.

[26] There are other ways to conceptualize organizations such as value chain, value shops and value networks (Stabell and Fjeldstad 1998), but value chain, or what Parker, Van Alstyne and Choudary (2016) call "pipeline." Parker, Van Alstyne and Choudary contrast pipeline view with their platform view to articulate how strategy and governance concepts apply to platforms such as Google, Microsoft, Amazon, Apple, Facebook, Airbnb, Uber, eBay, SAP, Spotify, and Alibaba.

[27] The idea of ambidexterity has received significant attention in the last few years (Collins and Porras 2004; Kim and Mauborgne 2004; O'Reilly III and Tushman 2004). Also see Evans and Wurster (1997).

[28] I draw on two articles here for this rough classification (Nolan 2000; Sabherwal and Jeyaraj 2015).

[29] See Porter (1980) and Porter (1985a). Even now, some business schools have yet to recognize the significance of IT. They are yet to allocate resources for integrating IT courses into their curriculum to prepare the next generation of IT-savvy leaders. Porter and Millar's (1985) article articulates how IT can influence competitive advantage through changing industry structure; outperforming rivals through cost, differentiation, or focus; and spawning new businesses. First, IT can help change industry structure by shaping supplier power, customer power, new entrants, new substitutes, and competitive rivalry. For example, Amazon.com changed the power of buyers/customers in the book-retailing industry. Wal-Mart changed the power of its suppliers. Both Wal-Mart and Amazon.com erected entry barriers by investing in IT. ING Direct threatened bricks-and-mortar banks with its direct bank in the United States. Increased investment by all players in an industry increases rivalry (e.g., online bill paying by all banks), but IT-enabled industry consolidation helped CEMEX improve industry structure in the Mexican cement industry. Second, IT can help firms outperform rivals by informing strategic choices with respect to cost and differentiation elements and by changing competitive focus or scope. IT can also allow a firm to widen its focus vertically, geographically, or into related industries. Third, IT can spawn new businesses by helping firms come up with new products and services that were previously infeasible (remote monitoring of patients or remote processing of loans or customer orders) or by making it possible to sell information that a firm generates as part of its business. For example, Wal-Mart can sell sales information to Procter & Gamble (P&G), and credit bureaus can sell credit monitoring services.

[30] See Eisenhardt and Sull (2001).

[31] See Mithas et al. (2012).

[32] Mithas et al. (2012) used archival data from 1998 to 2003 for more than 400 global firms to test their conjectures. Among other findings, there is some evidence that as industries become more competitive (or less concentrated), the effect of IT on profitability increases. This may be because IT not enables

225

firms to satisfy customers more strongly in competitive industries leading to higher customer loyalty and lock-in, but also to appropriate some of the consumer surplus in the form of higher profits through better targeting, segmentation, and pricing power. As industry growth options increase, the effect of IT on profitability increases. This may be because firms are able to leverage IT to create a platform for future growth through new revenue and profit streams. Finally, the results show that IT has a greater effect on firm profitability in service industries than in manufacturing industries. An explanation for this finding may be that services, being more IT intensive, allow greater IT-enabled customization and personalization, thus enabling firms to retain their profitability advantage to a greater extent than in manufacturing industries. From a policy perspective, given that prior work has shown the value relevance of IT in financial markets and given that this study provides an explanation for this finding, it is time for U.S. firms listed on public stock exchanges to be required to disclose their IT investments and risks associated with them (as is already done in Australia), just as they are required to do with R&D. Doing so can lead to further transparency with respect to managerial actions and generate useful research and signals for more efficient financial markets.

[33] See Mithas et al. (2012a; 2012b). While several earlier studies by other researchers had not detected a significant effect of IT investments on profitability, we found that more recent information technologies – those deployed since 1995 -- have a significant positive impact on firm profitability. We used data from more than 400 global companies from 1998 to 2003. However, that there was significantly more variability in IT investments than in investments in R&D or advertising. Perhaps, because IT involves novel technologies, IT investments allow much more room for creativity and innovation. It may be that most businesses already know how to manage R&D and advertising to their best advantage leading to greater convergence in such investments, but there is much more variability in their abilities to manage IT which may explain higher variability in IT investments across firms. Many academic colleagues (too numerous to mention, though see the various references cited in my academic papers) have also reported related findings. Increasingly, progressive CEOs and senior executives are beginning to embrace the strategic importance of IT, across both IT-producing industries (e.g., HP) and IT-using industries (e.g., cement, steel) (Jargon 2014; Kirkland 2013; Rose 2012).

[34] Interestingly, the effect of IT on profitability was higher in more competitive industries. IT investments also had a greater effect on the profitability of companies in the service sector than on firms in the manufacturing sector. An explanation for this finding may be that services allow greater IT-enabled customization and personalization, thus allowing firms to retain their profitability advantage to a greater extent than in manufacturing industries.

[35] See Porter (2001) and Grover and Ramanlal (1999).

[36] The findings provide validation to Kulatilaka and Venkatraman (2001, p. 15)'s arguments when they note that "Cost center projects may be easy to justify and implement but can also be imitated easily by competitors." Wade and Hulland (2004) provide indirect support for these arguments by suggesting that outside-in and spanning information systems resources (IT systems typically associated with revenue-enhancing initiatives) are likely to have stronger and more enduring effects on competitive position than inside-out IT resources (IT systems typically associated with cost-saving initiatives). Advertising (see Rust and Oliver 1994) and R&D (see Raelin and Balachandra 1985) also have risks. Of course, pursuit of topline should not be for "vanity", because ultimately it is bottomline that reflects "sanity" using the colorful language of a former CEO who will remain unnamed for now. Note also that cost-focus strategies are more vulnerable than revenue-focus strategies to floor effects—that is, minimum feasible levels of IT investments. How much more can you keep cutting IT investments year after year without cutting into muscle?

[37] See Mithas (2015a) for more details on the Tata group. Tata Motors acquired JLR from Ford in June 2008 for $2.3 billion (Sood, Seth and John 2010; Spector and Bellman 2008). Ratan Tata characterized this acquisition as permanently changing the mind-set at Bombay House and noted, "We have ceased to look at ourselves as an Indian company" (Taylor III 2011, p. 88). Ford had acquired Jaguar in 1989 for $2.5 billion and Land Rover in 2000 (purchased from BMW) for $2.75 billion. It had reorganized Jaguar into the Premier Automotive Group (PAG) in 1999 with Lincoln, Mercury, and other high-end European brands such as Volvo and Aston Martin (Ford sold Aston Martin in March 2007). In 2002, Jaguar and Land Rover merged into one organization. Although the company did not disclose financial

results for each brand, some believed Jaguar to be a loss-making entity while Land Rover was viewed as a profitable brand. PAG suffered a pretax loss of approximately $5 billion in 2004–2006, with Jaguar being a major contributor. Because Jaguar Land Rover was a relatively small part of Ford (and before that BMW), it relied on many of the corporate processes that Ford followed before it was acquired by Tata Motors (CIO.com 2014; Cooter 2011).

[38] More specifically, in a research study with Ali Tafti at University of Illinois at Chicago and M.S. Krishnan of University of Michigan, we show that flexible IT systems can serve as an enabler to successful partnerships (Tafti, Mithas and Krishnan 2013a; Tafti, Mithas and Krishnan 2013b). Though strategic alliances have always been important, they are arguably more critical now than ever before. In this highly digital age, organizations rely increasingly on internet-based or computerized products and services that require the simultaneous cooperation of multiple organizations. Customer-facing applications often draw real-time information from several companies at the same time. Research and development (R&D) collaborations often require integration of data across organizational boundaries. And inventory-management systems typically link multiple companies in a supply-chain. Through strategic alliances, companies often co-develop products, jointly develop new information systems, and share technical or managerial expertise. Interestingly, managers give significant attention to cultural, marketing or product synergies in strategic alliances, information technology (IT) usually receives much less attention. This is myopic, given the significant role IT can play in determining whether a partnership will be fruitful.

[39] Our identification of these three dimensions comes from a study of 3,129 strategic alliances -- formed by 169 companies that are publicly listed in the United States -- over a seven-year period (2000-2006) (Tafti, Mithas and Krishnan 2013a; Tafti, Mithas and Krishnan 2013b). We focused on three types of strategic alliances, and examined the role of IT-enabled flexibility in formation of these alliances because not all partnerships are created equal. Some partnerships involve bilateral investments, others involve only the sharing of information. So we compared the effects of IT flexibility on several types of alliances: arm's-length, collaborative, and joint-venture alliances. In addition to examining qualitative insights in the three different types of strategic alliances and how IT flexibility can ease alliance formation, we also looked at the issue of firm performance quantitatively: We studied how flexible IT architecture enhances the effect of the alliances on company value, which we measured as the ratio of market value over book value. (This is also known as Tobin's q.)

[40] The strategy literature suggests that firms typically follow one of the two generic strategies: cost leadership or product differentiation. Of course, what a firm's strategy is subject to interpretation and also is time-specific (Colvin 2008; DeLong et al. 2005). We define IT strategic emphasis as the dominant strategic objective that the firm chooses to emphasize in its IT strategy, which can be revenue expansion, cost reduction, or a dual-emphasis in which both goals are pursued. Other studies have used other terms such as "IT strategic orientation," and "IT strategic focus," to refer to similar ideas. There are other views of IS strategy such as use of IS to support business strategy, master plan of IS function, and shared view of IS role within an organization (Chen, Mocker, Preston and Teubner 2010).

[41] Chief information officers (CIOs) also find this revenue and cost typology more useful, as reflected in comments of AstraZeneca's CIO (Hickins 2012): "The key to winning approval from executive management and boards … is to talk about IT projects in terms of the business opportunities they afford. 'Are you going to generate additional revenue or are you going to reduce the cost structure' of the organization." Recent IS research has acknowledged this need to use business-oriented metrics as IT increasingly takes on a more strategic role in corporations, and research suggests that use of business terms "helps IT personnel focus even more clearly on business value" (Mitra, Sambamurthy and Westerman 2011, p. 57). Besides, such objective metrics lend themselves for better target-setting and monitoring of progress to enable timely corrective actions that are directly tied to firm performance. See Colvin (2006). Kohli's (2007) work with UPS suggests that the company may be using IT for revenue growth as well. However, at the 2014 Frontiers in Service Conference, Romaine Seguin, President of UPS Americas Region, indicated in a question-and-answer session following her keynote presentation that the FedEx (revenue emphasis) versus UPS (cost emphasis) distinction was essentially correct, lending credence to Carter's view. There are other firms, such as Johnson & Johnson (Mithas and

Agarwal 2010) and Coca-Cola (see Levin 2013), in which CIOs have tried to emphasize revenue growth in their IT strategy.

[42] For example, UPS's Delivery Intercept Service, which has the capability to locate and intercept any package within 15 minutes, was initially deployed to improve UPS's internal processes through the use of XML, but it also enabled revenue growth over time through additional fee-based services (Kohli 2007).

[43] Rust et al. (2002) argue that the pursuit of both revenue growth and cost reduction objectives with respect to quality improvement simultaneously may hurt firm performance because of the natural tensions between these polar strategic management approaches; others have also made similar arguments (Arndt and Brady 2004; Hindo 2007; Skinner 1986; Treacy and Wiersema 1993). They show that in the short run, firms with a revenue growth emphasis in their quality strategy outperform firms with a cost reduction emphasis. In addition, firms with a primary emphasis on either revenue growth or cost reduction outperform firms that try to put equal emphasis on both (dual emphasis). Subsequently, Bardhan et al. (2006) found that U.S. manufacturing plants with a hybrid or dual cost–quality strategy had higher plant costs than those with either a high-quality or low-cost strategy, implying that dual strategies may be more costly to execute. These findings appear to be consistent with Porter's (1996) view and Rust et al.'s (2002) findings suggesting that dual advantages are rare. Further research (Rust, Moorman and van Beuningen 2016) shows that a revenue emphasis and cost emphasis are cultivated in different ways, with a revenue emphasis propagating "bottom up" and a cost emphasis propagating "top down." These results illustrate the complexities of quality management, and are generally consistent with the notion of trade-offs among different strategic emphases in the strategy literature (Porter 1980). Mittal et al. (2005) study the moderating effect of dual emphasis on the association between customer satisfaction and long-term performance and report that association between customer satisfaction and Tobin's Q positive and relatively stronger for firms that successfully achieve a dual emphasis.

[44] As I noted before, strategies that firms use can change over time (Colvin 2008; DeLong et al. 2005; Evans 2009; Treacy and Wiersema 1997). Kulatilaka and Venkatraman (2001, p. 15) note: "…the role of IT should be to pursue projects that would reduce costs and enhance revenue... the real value-added of the IT function is to simultaneously pursue and justify projects that contribute to multiple business goals in the short and long run". Even Porter (1985a, p. 18) acknowledges that firms can find dual focus strategies rewarding because "the benefits are additive--differentiation leads to premium prices at the same time that cost leadership implies lower costs". He specifically recognizes the role of IT in enabling firms to potentially pioneer "a major innovation" (p. 20) to achieve dual advantage.

[45] Prior theories in the IS literature such as the resource-based view, the accounting literature (Dehning, Pfeiffer and Richardson 2006), and the emerging literature on ambidexterity which emphasizes the power of stretch targets (Bartlett and Ghoshal 1995; Birkinshaw and Gibson 2004; Gibson and Birkinshaw 2004; Im and Rai 2008; Markides 2013; Raisch and Birkinshaw 2008) frame these arguments. We use a broader conceptualization of ambidexterity here, similar to such usage by Markides (2013) and Kude et al. (2015), as a way to frame the simultaneous pursuit of two seemingly opposing ideas.

[46] Researchers classify strategies in many ways and sometimes it is hard to neatly classify whether a particular strategy is competitive or pursued by only a functional area: exploitation versus exploration (O'Reilly III and Tushman 2004), prospector versus defender (Miles, Snow, Meyer and Coleman 1978), autonomy versus control (Tafti, Mithas and Krishnan 2007), centralization versus decentralization (Xue, Mithas and Ray 2014), standardization versus integration (Weill and Ross 2009), focused versus broad search (Leiponen and Helfat 2010), flexibility versus efficiency (Adler, Goldoftas and Levine 1999). Tafti, Mithas and Krishnan (2015; 2009) studied the implications of synchronizing IT and HR strategies. They find that (1) empowering HR practices for IT professionals positively moderate the effect of IT investment on firm productivity, suggesting a two-way complementarity relationship, and (2) that collaborative IS practices have a positive influence in the complementary relationship between IT investment and HR practices, forming a three-way complementarity relationship. Their results suggest that the business value of IT is linked to HR strategies for IT professionals. They disaggregate the HR practices further, and find that *collaborative* IS practices positively influence the complementarities between *training* HR practices and IT investment on firm performance.

[47] The notion of convergence or fusion is easy to see in case of technology firms.

[48] Governance plays an important role in achieving the tighter fit between business and IT strategies, a topic that will be discussed subsequently (InformationWeek 2012; Roberts and Sikes 2008). I have found similar instances of lack of fit between overall strategies and IT strategies in my surveys.

[49] The study uses a secondary data set comprising more than one hundred twenty companies in India (Lee, Mithas and Saldanha 2015).

[50] CIOs with additional titles are also likely to be more influential (Chabrow 2002; Colvin 2006; King 2010; Tam 2007).

[51] See McAfee et al. (2004).

[52] See Puri (2007).

[53] This section draws on my work with Ritu Agarwal and Hugh Courtney (Mithas, Agarwal and Courtney 2012).

[54] This research, conducted with Ali Tafti at the University of Illinois at Chicago and Will Mitchell at Duke University, offers some insights on what went wrong for Borders' digital strategic posture and moves (Mithas, Tafti and Mitchell 2013). Our study used data from more than 400 U.S.-based firms from 1999 to 2006. We found that digital business strategy (how much to spend on IT and the extent to which a company should use outsourcing) is not solely a matter of optimizing firm operations internally or of responding to one or two focal competitors, but it should also be responsive to the digital business competitive environment. We find that firms are better off diverging from their industry peers under higher industry turbulence, while they should converge under higher industry concentration and higher industry growth.

[55] See Rose (2012).

[56] See Ziobro (2013).

[57] See Banjo (2013).

[58] Networks and platforms are not new, one can think of energy utilities and automotive sectors providing examples of platforms (Eisenmann, Parker and Van Alstyne 2006). This section draws on several books, academic articles and business press (Edelman 2014; Eisenmann 2007a; Eisenmann 2007b; Eisenmann, Parker and Van Alstyne 2006; Gupta and Mela 2008; Hagiu 2011; Hagiu 2013; Halaburda and Oberholzer-Gee 2014; Kaplan and Norton 2003; Shapiro and Varian 1999; Yemen, Venkatesan and Sriram 2015; Yoffie 2007).

[59] In conventional businesses, indirect network effects can arise when more consumers of a particular car (say BMW) may prompt better availability of repair services on the other side.

[60] See Reed (2001). Reed makes a distinction between one-to-many (broadcast or portal), one-to-one (email or instant messaging) and many-to-many (online communities or B2B exchanges) networks and argues that the value of a network increases with network size or N linearly for broadcast, networks, using Metcalfe's Law (N squared) for one-to-one networks, and using an exponent of N (2 to the power N) for the many-to-many networks.

[61] Very few individuals can claim credit for such a wide ranging impact (Isaacson 2011), barring a few exceptions like J.R.D. Tata (Mithas 2014).

[62] Likewise, it is difficult to neatly classify Google—is it an advertising company (because of its search advertising prowess), a utilities company (it buys significant electricity), a telecommunications or phone company (it bought Motorola Mobility in 2011 but sold to Lenovo in 2014), a bank (it holds more cash than many banks), or a publishing company (Google Books, now part of Google Play)?

[63] See Crovitz (2010). The adoption rates of various communication technologies such as AM radio, the telephone, black-and-white television, FM radio, color television, CD players, cable television, cell phones, personal computers, pagers, the Internet, and satellite television show significant compression over the years (Day and Schoemaker 2000b; The Economist Blog 2012). Also see Porter and Rivkin (2000).

[64] See Agarwal and Gort (2001).

[65] According to Chandler (1977), modern large multiunit enterprises did not make an appearance in the United States before the 1840s (50 years after the ratification of the U.S. Constitution) for technological reasons. This is because of the use of traditional sources of energy based on wind and animal power before the 1840s. Landes (2005) makes a similar argument when he traces the history of technological

change and industrial development in Western Europe from the 1750s until about the 1950s. See Johnson (2010) for a chronology of key innovations between 1400 and 2000.

[66] See Bilton (2009).

[67] See Ferguson (1999, p. 65). It is hard to know what Rothschild would have thought of Internet-enabled explosion in availability of information (Crovitz 2008; Ferguson 1999).

[68] According to an article in "The Economist", AT&T exited mobile phone business in 1983 because of a pessimistic report by McKinsey.

[69] See Hagel and Singer (1999). Conventional value chains involved trade-offs among customer, employee, and infrastructure management activities, all of which have different underlying economies of scope, speed, and scale. Now, using IT, these activities can be performed by different players and companies and monitored or coordinated through market signals and prices because of reduction in transaction costs.

[70] See Chandler and Cortada (2000) and Pitroda (1993).

[71] Chandler (1977) attributes the rise of modern large multiunit enterprises in the 1840s, and later in the United States, to newer and more viable sources of energy.

[72] Day and Schoemaker (2000b) distinguish between emerging and established technologies, arguing that emerging technologies have a much greater ambiguity regarding technology (science basis and applications, architecture or standards, functions or benefits), infrastructure (value network of suppliers and channels, regulations), markets/customers (usage pattern/behavior, market knowledge), and industry (structure, rivals, rules of the game) than established technologies. They argue that emerging technologies require a different management approach for environment/industry analysis, organizational context, strategy making, resource allocation, market assessment, development process, people management, and appropriating the gains.

[73] See Day et al. (2000).

[74] See The Economist (2005).

[75] See Young and Grant (2003).

[76] See Day et al. (2000).

[77] See The Economist (2012).

[78] See Guth (2009).

[79] No wonder, then, that they often meet the fate of the fabled frog in the frying pan; there is little evidence that frogs fry to death when boiled slowly. Managers may be react to changes that are relatively radical, but they are often caught flat-footed when the change is slow and initially imperceptible.

[80] Some academics have made compelling arguments about the tautological nature of definitions or arguments that proponents of "theory" of disruptive innovations use (King and Baatartogtokh 2015; Tellis 2006); others have questioned the rigor of the underlying research that generated the initial ideas (Lepore 2014). Tellis decomposes Christensen's definition of disruptive innovations into five parts: (1) Initially underperforms established products in mainstream markets, (2) But features (e.g., cheaper, simpler, smaller, more convenient) that a few fringe and generally new customers value, (3) Less profitable, first commercialized in emerging or insignificant markets, not financially rational for incumbents to invest, (4) Performance steadily improves, until meets the needs of mainstream market, and (5) New tech displaces the old, entrant displaces the incumbent. Tellis argues that the definition of the term "disruptive" is tautological and bereft of any predictive power if it includes 4 and 5. He wonders whether Christensen's sampling is adequate and whether examples for inductive purposes to build theory are suitable for deductive purpose to test theory also (these limitations are also shared by S-curve theory of technological evolution). Tellis' article "implies" that it is hard to find support for the linear patterns of slope that Christensen shows. Tellis also questions Christensen's second premise (very little evidence for primary and secondary performance dimensions because they are hard to separate ex ante) and third premise (in practice both entrants and incumbents and large and small firms introduce new technologies) as well. King and Baatartogtokh's research finds support for the four conditions in Christensen's framework in only 9% of the cases. They question if incumbents had the capability to respond to entrants, and point to consideration of other factors such as legacy costs (e.g., in Steel industry), changing economies of scale (to explain success of Amazon.com and other players), and

simple laws of probability that favor entrants in succeeding with new business models. Christensen's latest article does not appear to fully address many of the persistent critiques (Christensen, Raynor and McDonald 2015).

[81] According to Porter (1985b), a desirable technological change has several features. First, it lowers costs or enhances differentiation and makes technological lead sustainable. Second, it shifts costs or uniqueness in favor of a firm. Third, pioneering the technology translates into first-mover advantages, in addition to those advantages inherent in the technology itself. Finally, it improves overall industry structure.

[82] Note that the word "disruptive technology" is not used here. Technologies are typically neutral—they can be sustaining and disruptive at the same time when viewed from the perspective of incumbents or entrants. Sometimes a technology can appear to be both sustaining and disruptive. Consider video-on-demand from the perspective of cable providers, they need it for their Internet or data business, but it potentially cannibalizes their own on-demand services.

[83] See Mithas (2015b) for a discussion of how Tata group used the Baldrige criteria to grow and transform itself.

[84] Christensen (1998) argues that incumbents become progressively incapable of pursuing small emerging markets partly because of the many characteristics that make them so successful at sustaining innovations.

[85] See Young and Grant (2003).

[86] See Immelt et al. (2009).

[87] According to an article in "The Economist", AT&T exited mobile phone business in 1983 because of a pessimistic report by McKinsey.

[88] See Day et al. (2000). Because digital books are more profitable than physical copies, some argue that online book publishing is not disruptive for publishers, although it may be disruptive for bricks-and-mortar retailers who may be disintermediated as happened in the music industry.

[89] See Day and Schoemaker (2000b).

[90] Day and Schoemaker (2000a) argue that established firms suffer from four traps when they face emerging technologies: delayed participation, sticking with the familiar, a reluctance to fully commit, and lack of persistence. Examples of companies such as Kodak and Barnes & Noble lend credence to these traps. For example, Kodak had a hard time imagining a film-less future even though it invented the first digital camera in 1975. Barnes & Noble exited e-reader business prematurely only to re-enter again, even though it invested in that business before Amazon.com did. They suggest four solutions to deal with these traps: widening peripheral vision, creating a learning culture, staying flexible in strategic ways, and providing organizational autonomy.

[91] See Porter and Rivkin (2000). IT is not the only lever for transformations. Elsewhere, I have discussed how a business excellence framework can be an effective method for achieving transformation and success (Mithas 2014; Mithas 2015a; Mithas 2015b). Tata group's transformation offers at least five lessons. First, leadership matters when it comes to driving transformation efforts, and top leaders matter a lot. While the TBEM and other frameworks can act as an 'internal trigger', unless the leader empowers the organisation and monitors the progress made on these opportunities for improvement, companies are unlikely to achieve success. Second, transformations need persistence, management continuity, and eschewing the pursuit of management fads. Many Tata companies have deployed TBEM and related initiatives tirelessly for many years for improved performance. Third, analytics and metrics matter; organisations suffer if they do not have metrics, but they also suffer if they focus on the wrong or narrow metrics to measure success. Fourth, frameworks like TBEM provide an operating system that ensures disciplined autonomy, providing the discipline in the form of a coherent framework and autonomy in terms of how to interpret the framework based on competitive needs. It also provides a platform for integrating various initiatives just as an operating system allows a variety of applications to be built leveraging a common platform. Strategic planning matters and it is the responsibility of senior leaders to develop inclusive but robust strategy development processes. The long-term sustainability of an organisation should be an integral part of overall planning. Formulating strategy is not enough; deployment is equally important. Finally, transformation efforts should focus the efforts of senior leaders and other managers on holistic stakeholder management (and not exclusively

on shareholder management), and 'society' as a critical stakeholder. At the Tata group, this attention to holistic management is reflected in how the group is organised, such that the majority of shareholders happen to be Tata trusts and families that have held stakes for decades. More recently, after the economy was liberalized, a focus on long-term thinking was institutionalized and emphasized through the deployment of TBEM and its integration with Brand Equity and Business Promotion (BEBP), as opposed to using a personalised approach and the charisma of leaders.

[92] See Porter (1985b).

[93] I draw on Courtney's work here (Courtney 2001; Courtney, Kirkland and Viguerie 1997).

[94] See Hagel et al. (2008). Among some examples of shaping strategies, consider Google's strategies in the telecommunications space (giving away Android or announcing high-speed Internet network in some cities), Facebook, Salesforce.com, Bill Gates in the early 1980s (Microsoft and Intel), shipping (Malcolm McLean "containerized" shipping in the 1950s and 1960s), financial services (Visa credit cards in the 1970s), and apparel (Li and Fung). Other types of shaping strategies are also possible, such as those based on mergers and acquisitions, but these are "bet-the-ranch" initiatives; they do not mobilize multiple players for risk/reward sharing in the same way. Shaping strategies require taking a shaping view, creating a shaping platform, and enabling shaping acts and assets.

[95] See Courtney et al. (1997).

[96] See Hagiu (2011).

[97] See Tiwana (2014).

[98] Adobe and Marks & Spencer are recent case studies of organizational transformation (Mari 2013; The Economist 2014). Adobe is transforming its business model using cloud strategies. It has completely abandoned disc versions of its software to move toward subscription-based pricing. Marks & Spencer, a 130 year old company, is transforming itself with its new e-commerce platform and big data strategy.

[99] See Lucchetti and Steinberg (2012).

[100] See Worthen and Sherr (2012).

[101] See Murphy (2012).

[102] See Worthen (2012b).

[103] See Banjo (2013).

[104] Although we focus on IT governance, a careful reader will realize that IT governance is closely tied to enterprise or business unit governance across a wide range of settings including academia (Frank 2012; Ginsberg 2011). Tiwana, Konsynski and Venkatraman (2013-14) propose a useful cube for conceptualizing governance involving who is governed (e.g., project, firm level), what is governed (e.g., IT artifacts such as hardware or software, contents such as data or information, or stakeholders, and how (e.g., decision rights, formal versus informal controls or architecture). Even the notions of sustaining versus disruptive innovation can be framed and conceptualized in terms of governance issues. Governance informs the metrics that organizations use to track their performance, see Meyer (2003) for an excellent discussion of metrics.

[105] I draw on academic research on IT governance here (Agarwal and Sambamurthy 2002; Grover, Henry and Thatcher 2007; Lacity, Willcocks and Feeny 1995; Mani, Barua and Whinston 2006; McFarlan and Nolan 1995; Nolan and McFarlan 2005; Ross and Beath 2002; Ross, Vitale and Beath 1999; Ross and Weill 2002; Weill 2004; Weill and Ross 2005).

[106] See Rogers and Blenko (2006).

[107] Some refer to this as "University style" approach.

[108] See Xue et al. (2011). Xue, Ray and Gu study the effect of environment uncertainty and business unrelatedness on IT infrastructure governance. Their work suggests a curvilinear relationship between environment uncertainty and IT infrastructure governance. They find that firms are more likely to decentralize IT infrastructure governance to a business unit when the business unit faces intermediate uncertainty, than when the business unit faces very low or very high uncertainty. Moreover, the relationship between environmental uncertainty and IT infrastructure governance is stronger when the headquarters and business units are in different industries than when they are in the same industry.

[109] Ultimately, governance should not be for governance sake, it has to be aligned to performance expectations of an organization (Applegate, Austin and Soule 2009; Weill and Ross 2005).

[110] See Allen (1987). One way of thinking about the role of the IT department is to realize that three types of relationship networks are important for organizing IT activities to foster collaboration among various stakeholders: visioning networks (CIO and executives), innovation networks (business and IT executives), and sourcing networks (IT executives and external partners). Agarwal and Sambamurthy (2002) propose three organizational models for the IT function depending on the primary role of IT organization based on an organization's strategy: the partner model (a catalyst for innovation), the platform model (providing the resources for global innovation), and the scalable model (using sourcing to be flexible). Because it can be difficult to distinguish clearly between these models (i.e., partner, platform, and scalable), an alternative way of thinking about the role of the IT department is to use an approach based on the notion of management accountability (Allen 1987).

[111] One can view Amazon Web Services as an example of IT as a profit center to leverage the IT assets that Amazon created initially for its other businesses. USAA provides another good example (Overby 2004).

[112] See Thurm (2015).

[113] See Lim, Han and Mithas (2013).

[114] See Banker et al. (2011).

[115] This view was also shared by two CIOs: one in the US (a cable provider) and another in India (in automotive industry).

[116] It will be hard for a CIO to report any potential concerns related to financial transactions to CEO or a board-member if CIO reports to CFO. This is not an imaginary scenario, it is based on conversation with a highly respected CIO.

[117] See McAfee (2004).

[118] See McAfee et al. (2006, p. 4).

[119] Rich-Con was a steel service center company (Margolies 1999; McAfee 2003a), I worked with a steel service center company that believed in significant investments in IT to gain competitive advantage and that company has done well over the last decade or so.

[120] See Worthen and Sherr (2012).

[121] Mithas, Tafti and Mitchell (2013) use archival data for 400 U.S.-based firms from 1999 to 2006 to examine how the competitive industry environment shapes the way that digital strategic posture (defined as a focal firm's degree of engagement in a particular class of digital business practices relative to the industry norm) influences firms' realized digital business strategy. They focus on two forms of digital strategy (general IT investment and IT outsourcing investment) to argue that three elements of the industry environment determine whether digital strategic posture has an increasingly convergent or divergent influence on digital business strategy. By divergent influence, we mean an influence that leads to spending substantially more or less on a particular strategic activity than industry norms.

[122] This logic is now finding acceptance in academic and practitioner community (Han and Mithas 2013; Worthen 2012a).

[123] From an academic perspective, there are three ways of approaching determinants and consequences of IT investments: (1) *value-creation perspective* to consider IT as a way to enhance firm performance (Mithas, Tafti, Bardhan and Goh 2012b), (2) *institutional perspective* to consider how IT investments are influenced by industry peers and norms (Mithas, Tafti and Mitchell 2013), and (3) *agency perspective* or strategic management behavior, such as earnings management (EM) (Xue, Mithas and Ray 2014). EM strategies can be of two types: *accrual-based earnings management (AEM)* and *real earnings management (REM)*. While AEM refers to the purposeful altering of reported earnings by changing the accounting methods or estimates used to present given transactions in the financial statements without altering the underlying real business transactions; REM refers to the purposeful altering of reported earnings by manipulating the timing or structuring of real business operations, investments, or transactions, which may have long-term suboptimal business consequences (e.g., heavy promotions to boost short-term unsustainable sales, overproduction to reduce costs of goods sold, and reductions of discretionary spending). Xue, Mithas and Ray (2014) examine the relationship between real earnings management (REM)—and firms' IT investment commitment (ITIC) in the context of IT infrastructure development, and how the effects of REM are influenced by three contingency factors: general corporate governance, IT decentralization, and corporate social responsibility. They find that

REM undermines firms' current commitment as well as future commitment to IT investments suggesting evidence of an agency problem in IT investment. Results also suggest that both IT decentralization and corporate social responsibility mitigate the effect of REM on firms' current commitment to IT investments, and corporate social responsibility also mitigates the effect of REM on firms' future commitment to IT investments. They did not find evidence for general corporate governance's influence on the effects of REM.

[124] There are other classification schemes worth mention. For example, Weill and Aral (2006) classify IT investments as transactional, informational, strategic, and infrastructural. Others classify IT projects in terms of "stay-in-the-race," "win-the-race," and "change-the-race" investments (Craig and Tinaikar 2006).

[125] See Jeffrey and Leliveld (2004).

[126] See Christensen et al. (2008). One can relate to examples like Borders and Blockbuster in support of this point.

[127] See Chandler (2007).

[128] Real options approach is particularly suitable for IT investments because of their modularity (Amram, Kulatilaka and Henderson 1999; Copeland and Keenan 1998; Dixit and Pindyck 1995; Dos Santos 1991; Fichman, Keil and Tiwana 2005; Leslie and Michaels 1997; Luehrman 1998). The importance of conducting pilot projects was highlighted in JCPenney's troubled attempts at transformation (Reingold, Jones and Kramer 2014).

[129] Calculating the value of an option requires information about six parameters (Leslie and Michaels 1997): S=Stock Price, X=Exercise Price, δ=dividends, r=risk free interest rate, σ uncertainty, and, t=time to expiry. Given these parameters, Option Value=$S.e^{(-\delta.t)}$ N(d1)- X.$e^{(-rt)}$ N(d2), where d1=[ln(S/X)+ (r- $\delta+\sigma^2/2$)t]/($\sigma.t^{1/2}$), d2=d1- $\sigma.t^{1/2}$, and N(d)=cumulative normal distribution function. Based on this formula, the option value can be increased by (1) increasing the present value of expected operating cash inflows to increase S, (2) reducing the present value of expected operating cash outflows to reduce exercise price X, (3) increasing the uncertainty or σ, (4) extending the opportunity's duration or t, (5) reducing the value lost by waiting to exercise or δ, and (6) increasing the risk free interest rate r. Note that you can make t, uncertainty of expected cash flows σ, and high interest rates r work in your favor under real option approach.

[130] The origin of the counterfactual view can be traced back to the 18th century, and later this approach was used by Neyman to analyze the causal effect of different crop varieties on crop yield using experimental data. Rubin (1974; 1978) extended Neyman's work to deal with the analysis of causal effects in observational studies. Holland (1986) provides an excellent introduction of the potential outcomes model for causality, which he calls *Rubin's Model*, and compares it with causal thinking in philosophy, statistics, medicine, economics, and social science.

[131] Counterfactual approaches can range from qualitative to quantitative (Mithas and Krishnan 2009; Tetlock and Belkin 1996; Vedantam 2007). In particular, use of propensity score in a comprehensive causal analysis can help to assess the treatment effect heterogeneity based on propensity score. Researchers who study the business value of IT have argued that treatment effects can be heterogeneous. For example, Lucas (1993, p. 367) notes, "A negative relationship between use and performance should not be immediately interpreted as an example of low business value from IT. It is quite possible that technology may help raise average performance by improving results for the lowest performing groups. There may be little market potential left for high performing companies and individuals." One can study heterogeneous treatment effects for CRM or ERP systems (Mithas, Almirall and Krishnan 2006; Mithas, Almirall and Krishnan 2009). Heterogeneity is even more plausible for the individual-level phenomena (Xie and Wu 2005) such as whether online investing is equally beneficial for everyone, or do IT professionals benefit equally if they acquire an MBA?

[132] This section draws on my work with M.S. Krishnan and Claes Fornell (Mithas, Krishnan and Fornell 2016). I conducted a study with M.S. Krishnan and Claes Fornell at the University of Michigan to understand the effect of aggregate IT investments on customer satisfaction. We focused on relatively large U.S. firms that are tracked by both the ACSI and *InformationWeek*; thus, our findings are likely to generalize to such very large firms in *Fortune* 500 or S&P 500–type firms. For example, the average

revenues of firms in our sample in 2006 were about $40.7 billion, which compares well with average revenues of large firms in Fortune's Global 500 firms in 2006 (the average revenues in Global 500 in 2006 were at about $42 billion). Although such firms may be only a small fraction of the overall population of U.S. firms, they contribute significantly in terms of overall economic activity, employment, and output. These firms are some of the most global in nature; approximately 48% of the revenues of S&P 500 companies in 2008 came from abroad, which helped provide significant employment opportunities to U.S. workers and helped raise profits of these firms. Our analysis of an unbalanced panel of 109 firms indicates that aggregate IT investments had a positive association with customer satisfaction; the relationship is stronger in the 1994–1996 period and for manufacturing firms than it was for the 1999–2006 period and for service firms. Further analyses indicate that the IT investments have a negative association with profits in the 1994–1996 period but a positive association in the 1999–2006 period. Although we knew that IT had a null effect on profitability before 1996 and a positive effect after 1998 from other studies that used IT data from separate sources, this study used a longitudinal panel for the 1994–2006 period to document that relationship using a consistent measure of IT investments coming from the same data set for the entire duration. Overall, our findings provide a plausible explanation for the so-called profitability paradox observed in other studies by approaching the business value of IT investments using customer satisfaction, an intangible and important leading indicator of firm performance. Our results suggest that IT applications affect perceived quality and, to a lesser extent, perceived value of a firm's offerings. Our findings linking IT to customer satisfaction, coupled with findings that link customer satisfaction with market value, stock returns, and risk provide a more complete understanding of how IT investments and IT capabilities influence firm performance. We also conducted exploratory analyses to study the effect of CRM systems on managerial assessments of improvement in customer satisfaction. This work contributes to the growing body of work that has identified other mechanisms that explain the link between IT and firm performance through various organizational capabilities such as alliance management capabilities, performance management capabilities, process integration capabilities, customer management capabilities, and process management capabilities. Our findings in this study linking IT investments with customer satisfaction complement findings in a related study that showed a strong linkage of IT-enabled information management capability with customer management capability that was shown to influence almost every measure of firm performance in panel models (e.g., customer related, financial, human resource related and organizational effectiveness related).

[133] For example, Ittner and Larcker (1998) report that one unit increase in ACSI was associated with $ 236-243 million increase in market value of equity in their sample using 1994 and 1995 data. Anderson et al. (2004) estimate that a 1% increase in ACSI in their study would lead to an increase in firm value of about $275 million for a firm with $10 billion assets as would be typical of a *BusinessWeek* 1000 firm, based on their estimate of 1% increase in ACSI to be associated with 1.016% change in Tobin's Q using 1994-1997 data. Fornell et al. (2006) report a 1% increase in ACSI to be associated with 4.5% increase in market value of equity controlling for book value of assets and liabilities using 1995-2002 data. Although the effect of customer satisfaction on market value differs across studies, the findings are generally supportive of an economically significant effect of customer satisfaction on market value. To some extent, our results showing strong link between IT and customer satisfaction explain what was characterized as the "new productivity paradox" (Anderson, Banker and Ravindran 2003), even if the word "productivity" may not have been entirely accurate here because researchers were characterizing high valuation multiples on IT related spending which ranged from 31 to 45 for 1999 to 2002 as the new paradox of too high returns on IT (Anderson, Banker and Ravindran 2003). Because IT investments also have other benefits such as revenue growth (Mithas, Tafti, Bardhan and Goh 2012b), differentiation through customer knowledge and one-to-one marketing effectiveness (Mithas, Almirall and Krishnan 2006; Mithas, Krishnan and Fornell 2005), cost reduction or productivity improvement (Brynjolfsson and Hitt 1996; Han and Mithas 2013; Rai, Patnayakuni and Patnayakuni 1997; Tambe and Hitt 2012), profitability (Mithas, Tafti, Bardhan and Goh 2012b), innovation (Kleis, Chwelos, Ramirez and Cockburn 2012; Ravichandran, Han and Mithas 2015; Saldanha, Mithas and Krishnan 2016), decrease in firm risk (Tian and Xu 2015), market value (Kohli, Devaraj and Ow 2012; Mithas and Rust 2016), and improvement in organizational capabilities (Mithas, Ramasubbu and Sambamurthy

2011; Pavlou and El Sawy 2006; Pavlou and El Sawy 2010; Rai, Patnayakuni and Seth 2006; Tafti, Mithas and Krishnan 2013a), managers should be aware of these other benefits also to make a more complete assessment of the benefits from IT systems. Recent research suggesting that high-customer-satisfaction firms not only beat the market but also do so at less risk provides further validation for why firms should consider the customer satisfaction benefits to justify and evaluate the benefits of IT (Fornell, Mithas, Morgeson and Krishnan 2006; Tuli and Bharadwaj 2009). This is not to suggest that IT will always have a positive association with customer satisfaction or that managers should maximize customer satisfaction, because there can be diminishing returns, and at some point, overinvesting in IT or customer satisfaction may not be profitable or value-adding from a shareholder perspective (Fornell, Mithas, Morgeson and Krishnan 2006). That said, in most practical situations, underinvesting in IT and customer satisfaction is more likely the norm, and managers would do well to guard against this shortcoming to avoid losing competitive advantage.

[134] I have contributed to some of this research (Fornell, Mithas and Morgeson 2009a; Fornell, Mithas and Morgeson 2009b; Fornell, Mithas, Morgeson and Krishnan 2006; Hult et al. 2016; Lariviere et al. 2016; Mithas, Krishnan and Fornell 2005).

[135] It is rare to find examples of business processes that are not outsourced to some extent these days (Engardio 2006; Lacity, Feeny and Willcocks 2003; Lacity and Fox 2008).

[136] These forces appear to have intensified due to IT (Apte, Karmarkar and Nath 2008; Apte and Mason 1995; Carmel and Agarwal 2002; Carmel and Tjia 2001; Reinhardt et al. 2006; Vashistha and Vashistha 2006).

[137] Note that while technology can enable disaggregation, humans can help to weave everything together seamlessly. I am frequently reminded of this when I teach in study abroad programs in India and China. Brian Manning, former head of CSC India once introduced himself to students by stating: "I am an American based in India heading operations of a global IT/consulting firm and report to an Indian based on of Chicago." I met another American David Briskman who was the CIO of Ranbaxy in India at that time. We met Shivaji Bose, a senior manager in TCS China, who speaks fluent Mandarin. These and many other examples demonstrate how boundary-spanners like these help to transfer knowledge across borders and weave the world together even if IT may be causing some flattening as some argue. Although immigration issues generate a lot of heat in the US, how such immigrants assimilate and fare in India or China is not fully understood.

[138] Some argue that these practices represent one aspect of globalization responsible for the movement of jobs and work away from United States and other developed economies. The other aspect of globalization—namely, the influx of workers from other countries into developed economies—has also raised heated debates. We are concerned here with movement of technology professionals across country borders. It may come as a surprise to some that although outsourcing has been used for decades, the word "outsourcing" in the context of a production process has a relatively recent origin and was first mentioned in 1979 in the *Journal of the Royal Society of Arts* in the context of the British auto industry contracting out engineering design work to Germany. In contrast, "offshoring" was mentioned as far back as 1895. Not everyone likes the use of the word "offshoring," because the word means different things depending on which "shore" you are on. Notably, the word "offshoring" was reportedly used when Manhattan workers were worried about finance jobs that began migrating across the Hudson River to New Jersey in the 1980s. See Amiti and Wei (2005).

[139] See Jones (2005) and Ghemawat (2007).

[140] This is in sharp contrast to 1960s when foreign revenues and profits were only a small fraction of the overall revenues and profits for the U.S. firms (Cooper 2008; Vigna and Shipman 2010).

[141] See Farrell (2004; 2006) and Amiti and Wei (2005; Amiti and Wei 2009).

[142] See Reinhardt et al. (2006).

[143] Outsourcing literature is replete with examples of successful transformation efforts (Gottfredson, Puryear and Phillips 2005; Linder 2004; Linder, Jarvenpaa and Davenport 2003; Rottman and Lacity 2006; Vashistha and Vashistha 2006) although such transformations can be quite risky also.

[144] This idea goes back to transaction cost economics literature that originated with the work of Ronald Coase (Gurbaxani and Whang 1991; Han, Kauffman and Nault 2011; Han and Mithas 2013).

[145] The role of standards and vendor capabilities has received significant attention in academic research (Davenport 2005; Levina and Ross 2003; Popkin and Iyengar 2007; Ramasubbu, Mithas, Krishnan and Kemerer 2008; Whitaker, Mithas and Krishnan 2011).

[146] Many of these risks can be mitigated through appropriate location and contract choices (McDougall 2006; Overby 2006; Thurm 2007).

[147] See Hamm (2005). Firms are beginning to outsource more complex services, such as medical, legal, and R&D, to their offshore business partners (Pollack 2003; Reinhardt et al. 2006). For example, DuPont offshored its legal services to Manila in a tie-up with OfficeTiger (Engardio 2006).

[148] See Murphy (2012)

[149] Target justifies such moves to create better integration between the in-store and Web experience and to avoid losing competitive advantage if vendor is to sell the same solutions to its competitors (King 2013; Nash 2015). Bharti Airtel cites reasons such as better cost efficiency and control (Philip and Sen 2014).

[150] Titan spends less than 0.5% of its revenues on IT (Narasimhan 2013).

[151] J.P. Morgan abandoned its deal with IBM for IT outsourcing when it was going through its merger process with Chase (Thurm 2007).

[152] This section is based on Han and Mithas (2013). In their sample, on average, a firm's IT costs were about 3.2% of the revenue, while a firm's non-IT operating costs were 13.8% of the revenue.

[153] See Carmel and Espinosa (2011).

[154] Mithas and Whitaker (2007) argue that firms should also think about the extent to which an activity can be codified, standardized, and modularized. Although some studies use occupation as a unit of analysis, their findings provide implications for types of activities that may be more suitable for outsourcing and offshoring (Mithas and Whitaker 2007; Wagner 2006).

[155] It is useful to understand how non-contractibility differs from asset specificity, which provides an explanation for organizational boundaries in transaction cost economics (TCE) (Malone, Yates and Benjamin 1987; Mithas, Jones and Mitchell 2008; Williamson 1975). Asset specificity refers to the degree to which investment in a particular asset has lower value in its next-best use. TCE theory argues that firms will seek to bring highly-specific investments within their boundaries in order to limit the ability of others to act opportunistically in market transactions involving such assets (Williamson 1975). By contrast, non-contractibility involves difficult-to-specify investments that a firm may need to make in the future in order to sustain a set of existing transactions or to initiate a new set of exchanges with the same partner (Bakos and Brynjolfsson 1993). Non-contractibility can be viewed as a second order construct that contains two sub-dimensions, *task-based* and *interaction-based non-contractibility*. The "task" dimension of non-contractibility (e.g., quality, technology investments, and information exchange) helps ensure high product performance standards, while the "interaction" dimension (e.g., responsiveness, trust, and flexibility) supports relationship longevity. One might expect task-based non-contractibility to overlap more directly with asset specificity because it most directly addresses performance of given products, while interaction-based non-contractibility may arise more independently of asset specificity because it most directly speaks to uncertain future transactions. The correlation between the two sub-dimensions of non-contractibility and asset specificity supports this reasoning (Mithas, Jones and Mitchell 2008): asset specificity correlates more highly with task-based non-contractibility ($r=0.69$) than with interaction-based non-contractibility ($r=0.49$).

[156] Academic research suggests that considerations involving noncontractible investments (task-based non-contractibility includes quality, supplier technological investments, and information exchange; and interaction-based non-contractibility includes responsiveness, trust, and flexibility) may be more important than asset-specific investments as argued by conventional transaction cost economics literature (Mithas, Jones and Mitchell 2008).

[157] It is possible to consider options such as cost plus fixed fee, cost plus incentive fee and fixed price incentive, depending on the particulars of a case and balance of bargaining power among parties. Here are some details on various contract types. Fixed-price or lump-sum: involve a fixed total price for a well-defined product or service. Firm-fixed price (FFP): fixed price for the well-defined product/service. Fixed price incentive (FPI): fixed price plus an incentive fee for meeting secondary project objectives. Cost-reimbursable: payment to the seller for direct and indirect costs. Cost plus

incentive fee (CPIF): the buyer pays the seller for allowable performance costs plus a predetermined fee and an incentive bonus [Example: suppose expected cost $100,000; Vendor fee = $10,000; Risk share = 80/20; Final Cost was $80,000, they save 20,000; Vendor gets = 80,000 (cost) + Fee ($10,000) + 20%(risk) of $20,000 (savings) = total of $94,000]. Cost plus fixed fee (CPFF): the buyer pays the seller for allowable performance costs plus a fixed fee payment usually based on a percentage of estimated costs [Example: Expected cost $100000, Vendor fee = $10,000, If it costs $120,000 finally, vendor gets $120,000 + $10,000, If it costs $80,000, vendor gets $80,000 + $10,000=$90,000]. Cost plus percentage of costs (CPPC): the buyer pays the seller for allowable performance costs plus a predetermined percentage based on total costs [Example: Expected cost $100000, Vendor fee = $10,000, If it costs $120,000 finally, vendor gets $120,000 + x% of ($120,000)]. Time and material contracts (T&M): hybrid of both fixed-price and cost-reimbursable (often used by consultants). Unit price contracts (UPC): buyer pays a predetermined amount per unit of service (volume discounts are common in such contracts).

[158] See Martinez-Jerez and Narayanan (2011).

[159] The "delivery" dimension of IT governance is closely tied to the "department" and "dollar" dimensions of IT governance (Han and Mithas 2013; Lacity, Willcocks and Feeny 1995).

[160] This debate is far from settled though (Bhagwati, Panagariya and Srinivasan 2004; Krugman and Wells 2006).

[161] The key here is to engage in thoughtful outsourcing and not outsourcing for its own sake and to avoid dealing with difficult issues to build strategic capabilities (Overby 2005; Overby 2006).

[162] Mudambi (2007) draws on Ensign's (2007) review and proposes what he calls "the smile of value creation" in which firms disaggregate their value chain across locations in such a way that high value-added functions such as R&D and marketing are combined with low value-added functions such as manufacturing to deliver superior customer value and profits for firms .

[163] This work can provide useful insights for understanding the role of IT and trends in inequality (Linden, Dedrick and Kraemer 2011; Linden, Kraemer and Dedrick 2009).

[164] In other words, outsourcing and offshoring create externalities and their consideration is important to assess full impact of outsourcing (Freeman 1995; Rodrik 1997).

[165] They analyzed 332 service occupations (at the detail occupation level) in the United States from the 1990 and 1999 Standard Occupational Classification (SOC) codes maintained by the U.S Labor Department, Bureau of Labor Statistics. The U.S. Labor Department, Bureau of Labor Statistics (BLS) maintains a listing of Standard Occupational Classification (SOC) codes for all U.S. occupations. The May 2004 SOC listing includes 824 detail occupation categories. Between the 1998 and 1999 reporting years, the BLS changed the SOC coding scheme and updated occupation titles. The underlying structure and nature of the occupation definitions did not change; only the coding and descriptions/terminology changed. When appropriate, new categories were added to account for emerging occupations (e.g., computer systems software engineers), and old categories were removed to account for obsolete occupations (e.g., directory assistance operators). Based on the SOC codes, the BLS conducts an Occupational Employment Statistics (OES) survey to gather employment and wage data for each U.S. occupation. Each year, the OES survey gathers data from 400,000 establishments across 400 industries. The BLS surveys 1.2 million establishments over a three-year sampling period. Until 2001, the OES survey sampled 400,000 establishments during the fourth quarter of each year. Beginning in November 2002, the OES survey sampled 200,000 establishments in November and May of each year.

[166] Codifiability is the extent to which the activities in an occupation can be described completely in a set of written instructions. Standardizability is the extent to which the activities in an occupation can be performed successfully using a set of consistent and repeatable processes. Modularizability is the extent to which the activities in an occupation can be separated into components so that the components can be performed independently by separate people and then later be integrated.

[167] Kunsoo Han at McGill University and I collaborated on a research project to gain insights into how companies can use IT outsourcing to generate substantial savings – in non-IT areas of the business (Han and Mithas 2013). While our research used data from 1999-2003, we expect these findings to remain relevant, as many companies are currently considering more intensive adoption of outsourcing, offshoring or cloud computing. This study draws on prior work that broadly investigates how firms

238

determine the degree to which they should "make" or "buy," and how such decisions impact firm performance. Among other perspectives, TCE, which focuses on transaction costs as the major determinant of vertical integration, has been used as a dominant theoretical perspective and has received substantial empirical support. Recently, scholars have augmented the TCE-based views with the resource- or capability-based view, which focuses on firms' relative advantages. For example, Jacobides and Winter argue that capabilities and transaction costs co-evolve in the determination of the vertical scope of a firm. In a related paper, Jacobides and Hitt argue that firms often engage in *tapered integration*, which occurs when firms pursue vertical integration, but at the same time, outsource a portion of their supplies or distribution to capitalize on the heterogeneous capabilities along the value chain. Similarly, firms often mix internal IT investments and IT outsourcing, to different degrees, in order to capitalize on transaction costs and tap vendors' advanced technologies and expertise at the same time. Another stream of research has examined the performance implications of vertical integration, and how outsourcing and vertical integration impact firm performance. For example, Jacobides and Billinger find that in addition to transactional alignment, firms decide on their *vertical architecture*, defined as the overall structure of a firm's value chain, to improve performance. They also find that increased permeability in the vertical architecture can lead to more effective use of resources and capabilities, which eventually provides dynamic benefits for firms. Novak and Stern examine the impact of outsourcing on performance over the product life cycle, and find that while outsourcing is associated with higher levels of initial performance, vertical integration is associated with performance improvement over the life cycle. Some studies focus on the economic impact of services outsourcing; these studies treat services outsourcing as an intermediate input in a production function, and measure its value by its contribution to output or productivity growth.

[168] One interesting observation from this study (Han and Mithas 2013)is that IT outsourcing spending and IT labor spending are positively correlated (0.54), which seems to be contrary to the widely held belief that outsourcing is associated with reduced IT labor. This seemingly counterintuitive positive relationship is consistent with arguments that firms with higher total IT expenditures are likely to make greater use of IT outsourcing. Also, in general, the higher the total IT expenditures, the greater the likelihood of higher spending on IT labor. To gain additional insights, we examined how firms in our sample changed their spending on IT outsourcing and IT labor during our sample periods. In 169 out of 559 cases (30.2%) with consecutive yearly observations, IT outsourcing and IT labor spending (as a percentage of revenue) increased simultaneously. In 152 cases (27.2%), firms decreased spending on IT outsourcing and IT labor simultaneously. In 200 cases (35.8%), the changes in IT outsourcing and IT labor spending have opposite signs. Overall, the correlation between the changes in the two variables is 0.45 ($p < 0.01$), which implies that the majority of the firms in our sample either increased or reduced spending on IT outsourcing and IT labor simultaneously.

[169] See Grove (2010).

[170] This section draws on my work with Hank Lucas (Lucas and Mithas 2011; Mithas and Lucas 2010a).

[171] See Ramasubbu et al. (2008).

[172] Several articles and studies point to the type of human capital that firms and individuals should invest in (Arthur and Rousseau 1996; Bapna et al. 2013; Garvey 2004; Ho, Whitaker, Mithas and Roy 2013; Javidan, Teagarden and Bowen 2010; Kim, Mithas, Whitaker and Roy 2014; McGee 2007; Mithas and Krishnan 2008; Mithas and Krishnan 2009; Mithas and Lucas 2010a; Mithas, Whitaker and Tafti 2013; Sullivan 2005; Wattal et al. 2014).

[173] See Mithas et al. (2012b). Firms in emerging markets such as India appear to spend much less on IT (Lee and Mithas 2014; Murphy 2008; Vallis and Murphy 2008; Vallis and Murphy 2011). For example, Tata Steel spends 0.3% of its revenue on IT in Tata Steel India, but much more in Tata Steel Europe (Srivastava, Mithas and Jha 2013), and according to an estimate, Tata Motors spends approximately 1.2% of its revenue on IT (Agarwal and Weill 2012). These lower investments in IT may not be a cause for concern if the IT spending of Indian or emerging market companies is far more productive than that of their peers.

[174] Failure is a relative term though, and sometimes perceptions are more important than the objective measures such as completion on time or within projected budget (Avison, Gregor and Wilson 2006; Brown, Chervany and Reinicke 2007; Charette 2005; CIO.com 2006; Holmes 2006; Nelson 2007).

[175] It is because of wetware and other complementary investments that switching costs for IT systems can be very high (Shapiro and Varian 1999).

[176] See Chandler and Cortada (2000).

[177] See The Economist (2008; 2011).

[178] See Brynjolfsson and Saunders (2010).

[179] Eric Raymond, the author of "The Cathedral and the Bazaar", named this law in honor of Linus Torvalds, the creator of Linux (Merrill 2012; Raymond 2000).

[180] See Damsgaard and Karlsbjerg (2010).

[181] See The Economist (2006).

[182] Some argue that Microsoft is moving to an open API and open standards approach to software, but the company appears somewhat lukewarm to open source. According to Microsoft, open API and open standards will make software much more interoperable, but it will not sacrifice supportability. Although Microsoft shares some source code with development partners, this sharing is protected by law. Examples of some software using this approach are Office 2007, SharePoint 2007, and Windows Vista.

[183] Application service provider (ASP) is another approach toward greater interoperability. Examples of ASP are Salesforce.com, Blackboard, and Sakai. Increasingly, the ASP-type model, in which users pay for services and not for ownership, is moving to the servitization of other products, such as automobiles (e.g., FlexCar, Zipcar).

[184] See Fletcher and Dan (2011).

[185] Whether big data and business analytics are a management fad or a more fundamental change is a subject of debate and academic research (Brynjolfsson and McAfee 2011; Lohr 2012; Sharma, Mithas and Kankanhalli 2014) (Gillon et al. 2012).

[186] This section draws on my work with Kirstin Gillon (ICAEW, UK), Sinan Aral (MIT Sloan School of Management), Erik Brynjolfsson (MIT Sloan School of Management), Manish Gupta (IBM), Ching-Yung Lin (IBM T. J. Watson Research Center), Jane Griffin (Deloitte), and Mark Zozulia (Deloitte Information Management Practice) (Gillon et al. 2014; Gillon et al. 2012).

[187] Although we already see significant amount of new courses and programs related to business analytics across business schools, there is a sense that often what was covered under a different label is being relabeled as "business analytics". This may change as academics and practitioners collaborate and gain a better understanding of the promise and limitations of underlying technologies and tools. Regardless of whether business analytics comes to be a "radical shift" or "incremental change", if the new energy that it has unleashed results in better curriculum, research, governance processes and ultimately decisions, those will be favorable outcomes that everyone can agree on.

[188] Reed (2001) makes a distinction between one-to-many (broadcast or portal), one-to-one (email or instant messaging) and many-to-many (online communities or B2B exchanges) networks and argues that the value of a network increases with network size or N linearly for broadcast, networks, using Metcalfe's Law (N squared) for one-to-one networks, and using an exponent of N (2 to the power N) for the many-to-many networks.

[189] See Bennett (2013). Dunbar is quoted as stating: "The figure of 150 seems to represent the maximum number of individuals with whom we can have a genuinely social relationship, the kind of relationship that goes with knowing who they are and how they relate to us...Putting it another way, it's the number of people you would not feel embarrassed about joining uninvited for a drink if you happened to bump into them in a bar."

[190] Dell market cap data for 2015 was collected from http://www.businessinsider.com/dell-reveals-losses-revenue-shrinking-2015-12. Facebook and Twitter Sales and Market Cap are based on news stories for 2011 because these firms were yet to trade at the time. Facebook data for 2011 is from USATODAY (Swartz, Martin and Krantz 2012). Twitter data for 2011 is from eMarketer (Fredricksen 2011) and Reuters (Reuters 2011).

[191] See Stone and Frier (2014).

[192] Several books discuss history of information and information technology in detail (Ceruzzi 2003; Chandler and Cortada 2000; Gleick 2011). Chandler and Cortada (2000) provide a fascinating account of the history of the Information Age in the United States beginning in the 1600s. They trace the history of Information Age dating back to 1785 with the invention of the "Crompton Mule" powered by James

Watt's steam engine. Among subsequent developments, they list the establishment of the national postal system in 1790s; the U.S. railroads in 1830s; the electric telegraph in 1840s; the telephone in 1870s; the electrical/mechanical punched-card tabulating machine (invented by Herman Hollerith), which led to formation of IBM in 1924; the founding of RCA (a joint venture of AT&T, General Electric, and Westinghouse) in the 1920s, the vacuum tube; television in 1930s; and the transistor in 1950s. Although humans have exchanged information using technologies such as fire, flashing mirrors, flags, African talking drums, pigeons, cave paintings, the abacus, or the alphabet for a long time, a precise definition of information, linking it with uncertainty, first appeared in 1948 when Claude Shannon (1948) published "A Mathematical Theory of Communication" and coined a new word—"bit."

[193] See Morris (2010).

[194] The classification of computing phases is somewhat arbitrary but informative (Mitchell 2012; Nolan 2000; Sabherwal and Jeyaraj 2015).

[195] This section draws on Mithas et al. (2016), and Andal-Ancion, Cartwright and Yip (2003).

[196] Cloud computing is touted as one of the most disruptive forces that are affecting the nature of the IT function and the skills needed by IT professionals (Bulkeley 2011; McAfee 2011; The Economist 2008; Vance 2011; Wattal et al. 2014).

[197] See Wahlgren (2001). Some attribute these failures to "managerial IT unconsciousness" (Avison, Gregor and Wilson 2006).

[198] Managing risks of IT projects has been a key concern since the early days of computing (McFarlan 1981; Tiwana and Keil 2004).

[199] See Piccoli (2007) .

[200] There is a growing interest and literature on agile methods and practices (Colby, Mithas, Orlando and Norman 2015; Foerderer, Kude, Mithas and Heinzl 2016b; Fowler and Highsmith 2001; Highsmith 2000; Kude, Schmidt, Mithas and Heinzl 2015; Liu, Kude and Mithas 2015; Liu et al. 2016; Maruping, Venkatesh and Agarwal 2009; Rigby, Sutherland and Takeuchi 2016; Rubinstein 2015; Schmidt 2016; Schmidt, Kude, Heinzl and Mithas 2014; Sutherland 2015).

[201] Among other studies, McConnell (1996) enumerates 36 classic mistakes in IT project management and groups them into four categories: people, process, product, and technology. Nelson (2007) provides a matrix of best practices to avoid classic mistakes. Brown et al. (2007) identify six implementation problems and their likely solutions: inability to identify appropriate new technology (solution: knowledge), inability to reap benefits of information to fully exploit new technology (solution: communication), getting stuck in adaptation (solution: infrastructure), slowing down and getting off track (solution: commitment), haphazard technology introduction (solution: planning), and encountering a technology roadblock (solution: planning).

[202] See Chandler (1977).

[203] SAP was among one of the first companies that tried to standardize business software solutions (Davenport 1998; Escalle and Cotteleer 1999).

[204] Business process reengineering and its linkage with enterprise systems has been an active area of research since early 1990s (Hammer 1990; Rettig 2007; Whiting 2006; Worthen 2002).

[205] I draw this section from several articles (Rettig 2007; Segars and Chatterjee 2010; Upton and Staats 2008). Narayan Ramasubbu, M.S. Krishnan and I (Ramasubbu, Mithas and Krishnan 2008) studied customer satisfaction for support services of enterprise software systems (ESS) focusing on the effect of after-sales interactions, unlike studies that focus on the effect of product and customer attributes on satisfaction with software (Kekre, Krishnan and Srinivasan 1995). We examined employee skills and customer heterogeneity, and analyzed data from 170 customer service encounters of a leading ESS vendor. We found that the technical and behavioral skills of customer support representatives play a major role in influencing overall customer satisfaction with ESS support services, and the effect of technical skills on customer satisfaction is moderated by behavioral skills. We also find that the technical skills of the support personnel are valued more by repeat customers than by new customers. From a managerial viewpoint, the results of this study have important implications for staffing and work allocation decisions to serve different types of customers effectively. For example, firms may find it beneficial to augment the behavioral skills of their customer support staff through investments in training programs. It may also be useful to deploy employees who are more technically proficient to

handle repeat customers' service calls. Finally, these findings have implications for curriculum redesign and for tailoring educational programs to IT professionals.

[206] See Rohwedder (2006).

[207] See Twiddy (2007).

[208] See Vlasic (2009).

[209] I draw on several articles and publications here (Cha 2005; Dragoon 2005; Hays 2004; Hoover 2008; Levinson 2002; McWilliams 2004; Mithas, Krishnan and Fornell 2005; Nunes and Dreze 2006; Pine, Peppers and Rogers 1995; Swift 2000).

[210] An academic study show importance of customer involvement for innovation (Saldanha, Mithas and Krishnan 2016). This study used data from more than 300 large U.S. manufacturing firms, and finds that relational information processing capability (RIPC) positively moderates the relationship between product-focused customer involvement and amount of firm innovation; and analytical information processing capability (AIPC) positively moderates the relationship between information-intensive customer involvement and amount of firm innovation. Further exploratory analysis reports a positive three-way interaction between AIPC, RIPC, and product-focused customer involvement. Taken together, the results suggest that configurations of IT-enabled capabilities alone are not enough for innovation; instead firms benefit more when specific configurations of IT-enabled capabilities are leveraged in unison with specific types of customer involvement.

[211] I draw on recent academic work here that links customer satisfaction with various facets of firm performance (Aksoy et al. 2008; Fornell, Mithas and Morgeson 2009a; Fornell, Mithas and Morgeson 2009b; Fornell, Mithas, Morgeson and Krishnan 2006; Lariviere et al. 2016; Tuli and Bharadwaj 2009). Sometimes organizations misinterpret their customer satisfaction data due to a "reverse causality effect" (Fornell, Mithas, Morgeson and Krishnan 2006). Due to this effect, customer defection or "exit" can have a positive effect on average customer satisfaction because the most dissatisfied customers vote with their feet and leave (Hirschman 1970). The remaining customers are less likely to be as discontented, and instead of benefiting from improved satisfaction, the company ends up retaining a smaller group of somewhat more satisfied customers, but often with reduced sales and profits. I have seen such situations in academic settings also where a course continued to suffer from declining enrollments as a result of what seemed like an intervention that students did not like even though the instructor seemed satisfied with almost flat student satisfaction ratings. In other cases, students, "exited" and went to other schools or simply put up with a bad situation without voicing their concerns because they were not sure if anyone will listen.

[212] Hult et al. (2016) study the extent to which managers' perceptions of the levels and drivers of their customers' satisfaction and loyalty align with that of their actual customers (along with customers' expectations, quality, value, and complaints). They used 70,000 customer surveys from the American Customer Satisfaction Index (ACSI) and 1,068 firm (manager) responses from the ACSI-measured companies, to match, on average, 250 customers and 11 senior managers for each of the 97 firms studied that had matching data.

[213] Contemporary IT systems make it possible for firms to identify their most valuable customers as well as cater to those with high price sensitivity (Anderson 2006; Brynjolfsson, Hu and Smith 2006; Levinson 2007; McWilliams 2004).

[214] IT systems play a major role in one-to-one marketing (Mithas, Almirall and Krishnan 2006; Peppers, Rogers and Dorf 1999).

[215] See Rigby and Ledingham (2004).

[216] Piccoli (2007) also suggests a framework to prioritize CRM initiatives based on upside potential and data availability.

[217] I draw here on several articles and academic research (Davenport, Harris and Kohli 2001; Johnson 2006; Mithas, Krishnan and Fornell 2005; The Economist 2002). Rigby et al. (2002) suggest avoiding four perils of CRM. The first peril is implementing CRM before a viable customer strategy is created. The CRM strategy should be based on strong segmentation analysis and building goals in each market segment. The second peril is implementing CRM systems before matching organizational changes. The firm should restructure the organization and processes first, especially customer-facing processes and their touchpoints. Incentive structures and organization structure should be modified around the

customer. The third peril is assuming that more technology is better. Technology needs to fit the context of the problem. CRM implementation is costly, and thus the options should be evaluated closely. The fourth peril is to build a relationship with all customers: build relationships only with the *right* customers, not *all* customers.

[218] This also has implications for the types of skills that are rewarded more highly by firms (Levy and Murnane 2004; Stewart 1998).

[219] A study that examined the innovation and adaptation of birds that were able to pierce tin foil with their beaks to get to the cream in new types of milk bottles with aluminum seals shows that the innovation spread faster among titmice, which frequently flock together, than among red robins, which are highly territorial birds. See Day and Schoemaker (2000b).

[220] The distinction between tacit and explicit knowledge is well-accepted in the KM literature (Leonard and Swap 2004; Nonaka 2007; Parisi, Cross and Davenport. 2006).

[221] See March and Garvin (1997) and Totty (2006).

[222] See Satariano (2015).

[223] Most of the research so far on how various approaches influence performance uses qualitative data (Dennis and Vessey 2005; Hansen, Nohria and Tierney 1999). Hansen, Nohria and Tierney (1999) find similar patterns of KM strategies in computer and health care companies. Hansen, Nohria and Tierney (1999) suggest that successful firms use one dominant strategy and the other in a supporting role. They argue that straddling or putting equal emphasis on both codification and personalization rarely works and can lead to overinvestment. A mix of implementors and innovators can be deadly, as CSC Index, a company that invented the business process reengineering (BPR) concept, discovered. However, if straddling is unwise, so is an exclusive focus on one strategy. Hansen, Nohria and Tierney (1999) recommend the 80/20 rule. Dennis and Vessey (2005) classify the knowledge needs of users on the basis of knowledge reuse goal (substitution of an expert's knowledge for that of nonexperts versus augmentation) and knowledge life span. The rate of change and the nature of degradation of knowledge determine the actual life span of knowledge. Focusing on three KM processes of knowledge creation, knowledge development, and knowledge reuse, Dennis and Vessey (2005) propose three ways of approaching them: knowledge hierarchies, knowledge markets, and knowledge communities. The knowledge hierarchy strategy works well for rapidly changing knowledge to substitute expert knowledge for the novice knowledge. The knowledge market works well when knowledge evolves slowly and the goal is to augment the knowledge of experts. The knowledge community is a hybrid of knowledge hierarchy and knowledge market and views knowledge as a communal resource. This strategy works better for moderately changing knowledge to augment the knowledge of experts.

[224] This section draws on my work with Shirish Srivastava and Bimlendra Jha (Srivastava, Mithas and Jha 2013).

[225] I draw on several articles here (Benbya and Van Alstyne 2011; Boudreau and Lakhani 2009; Coles, Lakhani and McAfee 2007; King and Lakhani 2013; MacCormack 2006; Malone, Laubacher and Dellarocas 2010; Piasno and Verganti 2008; Surowiecki 2004). Benbya and Van Alstyne (2011) provide useful tips for designing knowledge markets. For Phase 1 of market design and launch, they suggest using material and social incentives but letting price float, capturing knowledge at both ends of the "Long tail" by seeding or subsidizing, offering points for information quality, providing protected spaces to shy people, balancing competition with hoarding, and protecting strategic information. For phase 2 of market development, manage inflows for growth like a Federal Reserve and not as a central planner, manage outflows for stability, encourage cooperation and prosocial behavior, and beware of manipulation. For phase 3 of evolution, promote self-design, and use market data to help measure knowledge value. They emphasize the important role of governance in making knowledge markets effective. Some of the ideas proposed by Benbya and Van Alstyne (2011), such as those relating to seeding or creating complements, also apply to platforms sponsored by SAP and Google (Foerderer, Kude, Mithas and Heinzl 2016a; Huang, Tafti and Mithas 2012).

[226] This section is from an article with Ravi Arora of the Tata group (Mithas and Arora 2015). Tata Group is one of India's most prominent business groups; it's the largest private-sector employer in both India and the UK, and it owns brands such as Jaguar, Land Rover, and Tetley. Tata Group used innovation as part of its transformation agenda—which also included initiatives such as the Tata

business excellence model (derived from the Malcolm Baldrige Criteria developed at the US National Institute of Standards and Technology) and globalization—to transform itself from a US $5.8 billion Indian firm in 1992 to a $103 billion global corporation in 2014, with more than 65 percent of revenues coming from outside India.

[227] See Dyer et al. (2011).

[228] This quote also points to the challenges of predicting the future in a continuously changing high-technology field (Hof 2006; Mithas, Agarwal and Courtney 2012).

[229] Opportunities for IT-enabled interventions abound in almost every sector of the economy healthcare (Baumol 1985; Baumol 1993; Baumol 1996; Bohmer and Knoop 2006; Daemmrich and Pineiro 2010; Herzlinger and Millenson 2008; Reid 2009), education (Hacker and Dreifus 2010), sustainability (Boccaletti, Loffler and Oppenheim 2008), and government sector (Morgeson III and Mithas 2009; Morgeson III, Van Amburg and Mithas 2011).

[230] Despite significant advances in health care, access to affordable and quality health care continues to be an issue not only in developing economies such as India and China but even in some of the richest countries of the world such as the United States, where about 15% of the population did not have health insurance in 2009. Although access to health care may have improved after the passage of the Affordable Care Act (also known as "ObamaCare"), it is too early to declare success.

[231] Some observers point to dysfunctional governance in academic institutions and rise in non-academic and administrative staff and costs as some reasons for costs of college education continuing to go up despite IT-enabled lowering of costs in other sectors of economy (Campos 2015; Frank 2012; Ginsberg 2011). Benjamin Ginsberg (2011) notes that during 1975-2005, student enrollments in the US universities and colleges went up by 56% and a similar increase of about 50% in faculty, number of degree-granting institutions and BA degrees, the staff and administrative positions went up by 240% and 85% respectively. According to him, administrators and staffers now far exceed the number of professors, while in 1975 American colleges employed more professors (446,830) than administrators and staffers (268,952); and "most professors possess surprisingly little influence in their own school's decision-making processes..shunted to sidelines" (p.4).

Made in the USA
Middletown, DE
13 September 2016